ALSO BY NATHALIE DUPREE

New Southern Cooking
Cooking of the South

Nathalie Dupree's Matters of Taste

NATHALIE DUPREE'S

Matters of Taste

NEW YORK • Alfred A. Knopf • 1991

THIS IS A BORZOI BOOK
PUBLISHED BY ALFRED A. KNOPF, INC.

Copyright © 1990 by Nathalie Dupree

All rights reserved under International and Pan-American Copyright Conventions. Published in the United States by Alfred A. Knopf, Inc., New York, and simultaneously in Canada by Random House of Canada Limited, Toronto. Distributed by Random House, Inc., New York.

ISBN 0-394-57851-1   CIP 89-045869

Manufactured in the United States of America

Published March 16, 1990
Reprinted Twice
Fourth Printing, March 1991

To my beloved friend Dudley Clendinen with whom I have shared so many steps in the dance of life, and who understands the intertwining of food, relationships, sensuality and power and encouraged me to write about them.

CONTENTS

TABLE OF CONTENTS

Acknowledgments

Matters of Taste couldn't have been written without the help of many people. Sue Hunter, who met me daily for months to review the manuscript and recipes, was an immeasurable help. Kate Almand and Ray Overton tested, tested and retested recipes. Kay Calvert and Bobbi Sturgis cheerfully sat over the computer long hours as we changed recipes to meet the menu requirements. Cynthia Jubera, Tom Mills, Beverly Molander, Elizabeth Vaeth, and Judi Waltz proofread and read over the book many hours. Cynthia Stevens, Bobbi Sturgis, and Forsythia Chang helped me adapt recipes for the television show's criteria of timing and variety. David Dupree has always been ready to help when I need him.

Many thanks to my wonderful editor at Alfred A. Knopf, Judith Jones, who constantly encourages and supports my efforts and her assistant, Kathy Zuckerman, and Bill Kovach, Editor of *The Atlanta Journal and Constitution* who all too briefly motivated me and many others at *The Atlanta Journal and Constitution. The Atlanta Journal and Constitution*, the *Los Angeles Times* Syndicate, and *Brown's Guide to Georgia* each published some of the essays and recipes. Love and gratitude to my dear friend, mentor and former Features Editor at the *The Atlanta Journal and Constitution*, Dudley Clendinen, and to Alfred W. Brown who each inspired me to write some of these essays and reprint them here.

I've loved being invited to my friends' homes all over the world, and tasting their food. I'm grateful for the friendship, support, hospitality, recipes and ideas contributed by Kate Almand, Sharon and Bill Baker, Gwen and Jimmy Bentley, Rose Berenbaum (Bert Greene's Skyscraper Sponge Cake), Anne Berg, Brenda Brown, Faith Brunson, Jane Butel, Kay Calvert, Michael Carlton, Forsythia Chang (Parmesan Dip), Pierce and Marjorie Cline, Shirley Corriher, Pat and Lenore Conroy (Spinach Tortellini Salad), Evelyn Cook, Robert Coram and Jeannine Adams (Zucchini Soup and One Pot Lamb), Marion Cunningham, Celeste Dupree, David Dupree, Merle Ellis, Alma Freedman, Anne Galbraith, Bruce Galphin, Kay Goldstein (Zucchini Stuffed Tomatoes), Cliff Graubart and Cynthia Stevens (Grilled or Roasted Beef Tenderloin), Charles Gandy, Bert Greene, Leila Hansell, Mary Hataway (Gravlax), Sue Hunter (Make-Ahead Green Salad), Cynthia Jubera, Rick Cramer, Mary Lee, A. Lee McGowan, Elliott Mackle (Key West Paella and Mango Ice

Cream), John Markham (Szechwan Noodles), James and Linda Meyer, Marie Meyer (Country Cherry Tomatoes), Col. Walter G. Meyer, Lloyd Montgomery, Vickie Mooney, Marie and Steve Nygren (Shrimp and Watercress Salad), Audrey Odegard, Ray Overton (Oatmeal Spice Cookies), Russ Parsons, Ted Pedas, Toula Polygalaktos, John Papageorge (Greek Salad), Glenn Powell and Elise Griffin (Oreo Cheescake Pie), Susan Puett (Sierra Grill Gravlax), Barbara Robinson, Betty Rosbottom (Christmas Cheesecake), Pat Royalty, Merijoy Rucker (Honey Whole Wheat Rolls), Barbara St. Amand (Grape Delight), Carmen Sanders, Phillip Schultz (Smoked Brisket with Dinah's Barbecue Sauce), Deni and Russ Seibert, Anne Rivers Siddons, Donna Siebert and Mrs. Alfredo Ricci (Roman Chicken and Mama Ricci's Potatoes), my friend Roberta Salma and her mother-in-law, Fatima Saada (Palestinian-style Olives), Charles Carden Snow (Mint Julep Meat Loaf), Jean Sparks (Fried Chicken), Margaret Ann Sparks, Bobbi Sturgis (Party Antipasto, Wild Rice and Orange Salad, Cold Curried Tomato Soup, Pepper Stripe Salad, and Steamers for a Crowd), Martha Summerour, Judy Tabb, Pierre Henri Thiault (Ham and Cheese *Gougère*), Jean Thwaite, Flora Undercofler, Bill Urick (Garlic Bread), Jerry and Diane Uslaner, Jean Van den Berg (A Different Spaghetti and Herbed Tomatoes), Julius, LuLen and Savannah Walker, and, finally Stuart Woods (Rich Herbed Dressing).

The writing community of Atlanta allowed me to test recipes on them at authographing parties, for our mutual pleasure, and, last but not least the television crew and Georgia Public Televison, the Georgia Department of Agriculture, Commissioner Irwin, Lisa Ray, and Lannie Williams deserve much credit for all their efforts on my behalf.

INTRODUCTION

The twenty-seven menus gathered here are the menus I am doing on my new television series *Nathalie Dupree's Matters of Taste*. They are designed specifically for the home cook and reflect the comfortable, unpressured kind of recipes that people are looking for today. I find as I travel around the country that, like me, most of you want to do your shopping ahead and buy everything in one supermarket rather than go chasing around. You want company meals that can be prepared ahead and, except for the occasional splurge, you don't want to spend too much or indulge in *too many* calories. At the same time, you want your food to be special, to express your caring, and you want to be able to offer a variety of dishes drawn from the many different cultures that make up this melting pot cuisine of ours. I think that you will find the recipes in this book fill the bill on all of these scores. Fortunately today our markets do have a variety of ethnic ingredients, and I have worked out carefully what can be done in advance so you are not overwhelmed when company comes and also are not constantly jumping up from the table and leaving your guests. Even for family meals there are times on a rainy Sunday when you might want to make a soup, a stew, a loaf of fresh bread ahead and freeze them.

Teaching people how to feed themselves and others is a joy to me and it has enriched my life. I've felt it was my mission since I taught my first class in Social Circle, Georgia in 1972. The recipes here have all been tested by me as well as by the students I've been teaching at Rich's Cooking School. Teaching on television is an extension of my teaching and what I demonstrate on camera incorporates the comments and questions of my students. They have helped me to formulate the tips and variations that follow the recipes in this book. Because it was written before the new show was actually filmed, I have had to anticipate the kinds of remarks and suggestions that I make ad lib on camera.

Television has brought me in touch with a lot of people across the country who often respond by telling me their stories about food experiences. It has confirmed my long-held belief that food is intertwined with life—with its laughter and tears, with the good times and the bad times, with love and power and control. When friends and family get together over tea in front of a fire or over a splendid, well-planned meal, they share much more than the food together. With such thoughts in mind I started writing a column for *The Atlanta Journal and Constitution,* and when I came to put this book together, I realized how many of the themes I explored and stories I told in those columns connected with the menus I was devising for the new show. So I have included a selection of those columns here, matching them to menus. And I hope that as you cook the food, the stories will be meaningful to you and make you realize how important food is to all of us on many levels.

Note: The order of the menus here does not necessarily reflect the order of the new television series.

Nathalie Dupree's Matters of Taste

✕ 1 ✕

SUMMER DINNER
PARTY

Heroine's Feast

In the way that foods have of becoming fashionable, pigeon is now in vogue. Sometimes it is called squab, which is really a baby pigeon.

My first experience in cooking pigeons was with my Uncle Ray. As my mother liked to remind us, Uncle Ray was only an uncle by marriage. The implication was that *he* did things that our family would not do. One of them was to catch pigeons on the railroad trestle. He had done this since he was a small boy, bringing them home to his mother for supper. As a grown man, he relished the memory of his mother's squabs and wanted his wife—my Aunt Marion—to bring back for him the magic of his mother's cooking by cooking the pigeons he brought home. My Aunt Marion was not the best of cooks although she made a wonderful Kool-Aid punch full of fresh fruit, and a great sliced ham sandwich. But she did not like cooking those pigeons.

Each summer when we went to visit my grandmother and aunt, we would go out with Uncle Ray to catch the squabs. My sister and I would be roused from our beds early in the morning to pile into the car, the sleep barely washed from our eyes. We would drive out a ways to the country. We wore what girls wore in those days—cotton pants, a halter, and a cotton long-sleeve shirt.

Ray's railroad trestle (our abiding name for it, although it belonged, clearly, to the railroad company) was over a big body of

1

water, perhaps a rushing stream, and stretched a considerable distance. It was wooden, with gravel and stones between the tracks. Uncle Ray would park the old car at the bottom of a very steep embankment, which we would then climb up with nothing to hold on to except scrubby grass and dirt and an occasional scrawny tree.

Each of us would carry shoe boxes under our arms with holes punched by a screwdriver, in which we would place our prey. We would also bring some tape to hold the lid down as we slipped and slid down the hill with our quarry.

Once on top of the trestle, we would walk the tracks looking for the birds. They had to be exactly the right size to suit Ray, who knew just what he wanted. Whenever he had settled for large pigeons he had been disappointed. We were looking for little pigeons he could take home, fatten up and clean out for a few days, and then get my aunt to kill in some unspeakable manner and to roast them. We liked the idea of garnering the squabs, bringing them home to my Aunt Marion, and having them to play with for some days. We liked neither the killing nor the eating of them.

Neither did Aunt Marion, who found keeping the squabs on the side porch a dirty, nasty process, and who muttered constantly about the fact that pigeons were filthy birds—as anyone could tell by going down to the Capitol and seeing the mess they made.

Goodness knows what Ray fed them to fatten them up and clean out their systems. Chicken feed? Certainly some worms, as he made us dig them up.

The last time my Aunt Marion let us go squab hunting was when a train came over the tracks. One thing Uncle Ray had always neglected to tell Aunt Marion was that there were a lot of KEEP OFF signs on Uncle Ray's trestle. There was no room on the trestle for anything but a train. What railings there were were not suitable for hanging on to. So, when the train came, there was general confusion. Fortunately, we had heard the sound of the train from a distance.

This time we were in the middle of the narrow trestle, and there was no room for anything but the train. We had filled our boxes with some plump little birds, and were sitting with our feet dangling over the side, looking at the water, basking in the sun, when suddenly we heard the sound of the train. There was no whistle. Maybe trains don't whistle on bridges that are supposed to be empty. But we heard the chugging and looked up to see it heading right for us. We grabbed our boxes, leaving behind our shirts, running all the while to the end of the trestle.

Uncle Ray was a coward to boot. Running ahead of us, he yelled back to us to hurry. We were running as hard as we could, unthinkingly clutching those shoe boxes. At the end of the trestle, which he reached way before we did, he found an insecure perch on the side of the steep hill and grabbed for us. By then the conductor had spotted us, and the train was whistling loud and clear. But, of course, the train couldn't stop, and we had the good sense to know that seeing us and stopping the train were two different things.

We made it. We got some cuts and scratches as we scrambled down the hill with our boxes wedged under our arms. I had slipped on the gravel and had some fragments embedded in my arm. We washed in the stream as best we could, but it didn't clean us up much. We had lost our shirts as well as tearing our pants. When we got home, we were all scolded, including Uncle Ray.

Before we left that summer, we ate those birds. In spite of my Aunt's grumbling that we could have all been killed, Uncle Ray persisted in feeding them and, finally, "putting them to rest." Aunt Marion browned them and set them in a pan in the oven and finished them off. They were delicious, fat, moist. For some reason I didn't mind eating those squabs. Maybe because by then I had embellished the story of my near-death so that in my mind it was a heroine's feast.

⎨ M E N U ⎬

SUMMER DINNER PARTY

Jeannine's Zucchini Soup

Grilled Squab *or* **Lemon Roasted Cornish Hen** *(p. 192)*

Baked Onions

Steamed Garlic Vegetables

Jean Van den Berg's Herbed Tomatoes

Roman Lemon Rice

Brown Sugar and Prune-Nut Cake
and/or **Barbara St. Amand's Grape Delight**

SERVES 6 TO 8

LOGISTICS

The cake may be made earlier in the day, a day ahead, or frozen. The zucchini soup may be made a day or two in advance, as may the tomatoes. The onions may be made a day or two ahead and served cold. To serve hot, reheat cooked onions or start the onions on the hot grill or in the oven 1 hour and 15 minutes before serving. The vegetables may be made ahead and reheated as directed. Add the squabs to the grill 1/2 hour before serving, then start the rice. Or, the rice may be made ahead and reheated in the microwave. Serve the soup, removing squabs and onions from the grill when done, and serve with the rice and tomatoes. The sauce for the grapes may be made several days ahead and kept refrigerated. The entire grape dish may be made early in the day and served chilled or assembled at the last minute. Serve alone or with the cake.

ℰ RECIPES ℰ

JEANNINE'S ZUCCHINI SOUP
Serves 6 to 8

4 tablespoons butter
4 zucchini, thinly sliced
1 small green pepper,
   thinly sliced
3 medium onions,
   thinly sliced
2 garlic cloves, chopped
1 small white potato,
   peeled and thinly
   sliced
salt
white pepper
4 sprigs fresh thyme
   (optional)
8 cups chicken stock
1 cup light cream
Garnish:
1/2 cup (or more)
   minced parsley
fresh chives

Heat the butter in a heavy pan. Add the zucchini, green pepper, onions, and garlic and sauté over low heat for 10 minutes, stirring often, until the vegetables are soft, but not browned. Add the potato, salt and pepper, thyme, and chicken stock, stirring well. Raise the heat, cover the pot, and bring the soup to the boil. Immediately lower heat, partially uncover the pot, and simmer for about 30 minutes, or until vegetables are very tender. By now the thyme leaves will have fallen away from the stalks. Remove the woody stalks, leaving the leaves in the soup.

Let the soup cool and then ladle it into a food processor and purée. Chill for at least 12 hours. Before serving, add as much of the cream as you like and season to taste. Garnish each serving with minced parsley and a few chives. May be made a day or two in advance.

GRILLED SQUAB
Serves 6 to 8

6 to 8 squabs (each 12 to
  15 ounces)
8 to 10 tablespoons
  butter or olive oil
salt
freshly ground pepper

Split the squabs in half. Brush them with butter or oil, and then sprinkle with salt and pepper. Place them on a hot grill or under a broiler, skin side toward the heat. Turn when brown. Cook until they register 170°F when an instant thermometer is inserted into the breast (not touching the bone), about 1/2 hour depending on the heat of the coals.

Comment: Squabs are now farm-raised and can be found in grocery stores as well as mail ordered.

BAKED ONIONS
Serves 6 to 8

6 to 8 medium onions,
  peeled
8 to 10 tablespoons
  butter or oil
salt
freshly ground pepper

Preheat oven to 400°F. Arrange the onions in a greased baking dish, dot with butter or oil, and bake until nearly charred, tinged with black and brown, for 45 minutes to 1 hour and 15 minutes, adding more butter or oil as necessary to keep moist. Salt and pepper. Serve hot or chilled.

Variation
Cut the onions in half or quarters to speed cooking and increase brownness. Place halves, drizzled with oil, cut side down on hot grill or under a broiler. Turn once until lightly charred. May be made a day or two in advance and served cold.

Variation
Top with herbed browned bread crumbs.

Variation
Use 1-1/2 pounds peeled shallots rather than onions, and reduce cooking time.

Variation
Drizzle quartered onion with olive oil. Bake until brown. Top with goat cheese or herb cheese and sun-dried tomatoes and return to oven for a few minutes. Serve with Baked Garlic Cloves (p. 234).

Continued

Variation
Microwave until soft, then heat in 450°F oven or under broiler until tinged with black and brown.

Tip: Use butter if serving hot, oil if cold.

STEAMED GARLIC VEGETABLES
Serves 6 to 8

1 head broccoli
24 baby carrots, scraped
24 button mushroom
    caps, cleaned
2 unpeeled zucchini,
    cut into 2-inch × 1/2-
    inch sticks
1/2 to 2 cups garlic
    pepper oil (see tip
    below)
5 tablespoons red wine
    vinegar
1/4 cup fresh parsley,
    chopped
1/4 cup fresh thyme or
    oregano, chopped
salt
freshly ground pepper

Separate the florets of the broccoli from the stalks. Remove the tough ends. Peel and slice the stalks into 1/4-inch coins. Cook each vegetable separately on a rack over boiling water, steaming them until they are crisp-cooked, then remove them to a large bowl. While they are still warm, toss them with some of the garlic pepper oil, then the vinegar, parsley, and thyme. Taste for seasoning, adding salt and pepper as desired. Add more oil as you think necessary. May be made ahead and then tossed over high heat in a large frying pan with some of the oil until heated through, or served cold.

Variation
Instead of the broccoli, use 1 cauliflower, separated into florets, as Bill Rice did in *Feasts of Wine and Food.*

Variation
Follow your microwave directions and microwave the vegetables rather than steam them.

Tip: To make garlic pepper oil, combine 2 cups olive oil, 6 garlic cloves, chopped, and 1 teaspoon hot pepper flakes in a jar. Let sit overnight. Keep, refrigerated and covered, indefinitely.

Comment: Garlic pepper oil is a great "secret weapon" whenever a recipe needs zipping up. It may also be purchased in the imported foods section of many grocery stores.

JEAN VAN DEN BERG'S HERBED TOMATOES
Serves 6 to 8

2-1/2 pounds cherry
   tomatoes, halved
1 cup olive oil
1/3 cup red wine
   vinegar
1/3 cup parsley,
   chopped
3 garlic cloves, chopped
3 tablespoons fresh
   basil, chopped
salt
freshly ground pepper
sugar (optional)

Put the tomatoes in a glass bowl. Mix together the oil, vinegar, parsley, garlic, basil, and salt and pepper to taste. Drizzle over the tomatoes. Cover and refrigerate. Marinate several hours, if possible, or longer, basting occasionally. May be fixed a day or two in advance and will keep a week or so.

Variation
Try substituting fresh oregano or cilantro for the basil.

Variation
Serve on red lettuce, Bibb lettuce, or spinach leaves.

Variation
Serve over cucumber slices.

Variation
Snip scallion or green onion greens on top.

Tip: 1 pint of cherry tomatoes equals 3/4 pound.

Tip: For a special occasion, peel the tomatoes before halving by pouring boiling water over them, then plunge them into cold water. The skins will slip off easily.

Tip: The skin softens the longer the tomatoes marinate.

Tip: If a salad is too oily, add a little salt. When all the salt you wish has been added, add sugar to balance.

ROMAN LEMON RICE
Serves 6 to 8

4 to 5 cups chicken
   stock
4 tablespoons butter or
   olive oil
1/2 medium onion,
   chopped
2 garlic cloves, chopped
1-1/2 cups long grain
   white rice, preferably
   Arborio or
   Valenciano or
   American-style
   converted rice
peel of 3 large lemons,
   grated
juice of 3 large lemons
1/2 cup heavy cream
1/2 cup imported
   Parmesan cheese,
   grated
salt
freshly ground pepper
Garnish:
2 tablespoons lemon
   balm, chopped
   (optional)

Bring the chicken stock to the boil in a pot. Heat the butter or oil in a large frying pan, add the onion and garlic and cook until soft. Add the rice to the pan and continue cooking, stirring with a wooden spoon, about 2 minutes, until the grains are all well coated. Add 2 tablespoons of the lemon peel and the hot chicken stock, 1/2 cup at a time, stirring frequently and letting the liquid be nearly absorbed before adding more stock. Continue stirring frequently and adding stock for about 18 minutes, when the stock will be nearly all absorbed. Add the lemon juice and cook briefly until absorbed. Pour in the cream and boil until nearly absorbed. With a fork, stir in the Parmesan and more lemon peel to flavor. Season to taste with salt and pepper. Cover and leave 5 minutes or until ready to serve. Stir again with a fork and turn into a hot serving dish. Garnish with optional lemon balm. May be made ahead and reheated carefully in the microwave. May be frozen and reheated with a little loss of quality.

Variation
Omit the lemon, add 1/2 cup sliced mushrooms to the butter. Substitute white wine for some of the stock.

Tip: Reheats well in the microwave.

Tip: Always fork rice—a spoon makes it mushy.

Comment: This recipe may be made with a long grain rice or converted rice quite satisfactorily. If either kind is all that is available, use it. The rice will be a bit mushy but still quite tasty. But if you can find Arborio or Valenciano in your grocery store, by all means use it.

BROWN SUGAR AND PRUNE-NUT CAKE

Makes 1 (10-inch) tube pan cake

1/2 pound butter,
  softened
1/2 cup shortening
2 cups brown sugar,
  firmly packed
1 cup sugar
5 large eggs
3 cups all-purpose flour
1/2 teaspoon baking
  powder
1/2 teaspoon salt
1 cup milk
1 tablespoon vanilla
1 cup pecans or walnuts,
  chopped
1 cup prunes, chopped
confectioners' sugar

Preheat oven to 325°F. Beat the butter and shortening until light. Mix the sugars together on a piece of wax paper and add them gradually to the mixture, beating well. Add the eggs, one by one, beating after each addition.

Sift together the flour, baking powder, and salt on a piece of wax paper. Add to the base mixture alternately with the milk, beginning and ending with the flour mixture. Stir in the vanilla, prunes, and nuts.

Grease and flour a 10-inch tube pan. Cut a circle of wax paper to fit the bottom, grease, and flour. Pour the batter in. Bake for 1-1/2 hours or until a toothpick inserted in the center comes out clean. Cool in the pan 10 minutes; remove from pan and cool completely on a wire rack. Remove wax paper circle. Sprinkle with confectioners' sugar. May be made earlier in the day, a day ahead, or frozen.

BARBARA ST. AMAND'S GRAPE DELIGHT

Serves 4

2 cups plain or low-fat
  yogurt
2 teaspoons orange juice
2 cups fresh or 2 (8-3/4-
  ounce) cans seedless
  grapes, drained and
  chilled
Garnish:
2 teaspoons orange peel,
  zested

Combine yogurt and juice. Into each of 4 glasses, spoon 1/4 cup of the yogurt mixture; top with 1/4 cup grapes and then another 1/4 cup mixture. Top with orange peel.

Variation
Shave chocolate curls over each dessert.

Continued

Variation
Substitute sour cream for yogurt.

Variation
If calorie conscious but the sauce is too tart for your taste when made with low-fat yogurt, add nonsugar sweetener to taste.

✄ 2 ✄

AN INFORMAL
SPAGHETTI PARTY

Spaghetti

Spaghetti is one of those dishes that is timeless, will never be dated, and always is a pleasure to anticipate. When I was a girl, spaghetti was the first thing you wanted to learn to cook. It was a bride's first meal, to be served to neighbors and friends with garlic bread. It was what your mother made in the fall, simmering the sauce for hours on the back of the stove.

The pasta invariably came in long packages in long dry pieces, which were plunged into large pots—sometimes two or three—of boiling water. Only we didn't call it pasta then, we called it spaghetti or noodles. No one I knew ever had fresh noodles, but we loved our spaghetti. And we were always careful to cook it so that it was ready the minute that supper went on the table, not a minute before.

As families grew, they purchased tall pots that were called spaghetti pots, which, when the rage of gourmet cooking swept the country, were then retitled stockpots.

The spaghetti sauces were as good then as they are now, although limited in variety as each family only had one sauce, combining the best of ingredients and letting their flavors blend for a long time. We knew that spaghetti was supposed to be Italian, but to us it was all-American, with a defined position in the weekly calendar, starting in September and ending in May. Most homes had it once each week on a rotating cycle—every Thursday for instance. It couldn't be Wednesday because that would interfere with going to church Wednesday night. Since my mother worked, at our house it would be Saturday or Sunday, days when she had time to let the sauce cook all day.

One recent September Saturday, I yearned for a thick, rich spaghetti sauce made from scratch; I wanted to luxuriate in the promise of crisp fall weather, to fill my home with its aroma. I had an abundance of fresh, lush, nearly overripe tomatoes, ready to burst with juiciness, purloined from a friend's garden. Although so many of my favorite spaghetti recipes called for canned tomatoes, or Italian plum tomatoes, I used what was in the house and made up my recipe as I went along, relying partly on a base recipe taught me as a young girl by my "second mother," Jean Van den Berg. I've remade it many times since, with canned tomatoes, and it is nearly as good.

What a convenience to know how to reheat the pasta and the sauce and to do it properly. And, God bless the microwave, in which the sauce, if you've frozen it, may be defrosted and reheated and the pasta reheated as well.

ᘓ M E N U ᘒ

AN INFORMAL SPAGHETTI PARTY

Bill Urick's Garlic Bread
Party Antipasto or *Greek Salad (p. 202)*
A Different Spaghetti
Everybody's Favorite Chocolate Cake or *Chocolate Kiss Cookies*

SERVES 8 TO 10

LOGISTICS

Almost everything cooked in this menu may be made ahead and reheated. The cake or the cookies may be made ahead a day, or frozen and defrosted the day of serving. The spaghetti sauce may be made several days in advance, or frozen and defrosted. The spaghetti may be cooked ahead, drained, and placed in cold water or a plastic bag, ready to reheat. The vinaigrette for the antipasto or Greek salad may be made ahead and the Brussels sprouts, artichoke hearts, and mushrooms marinated overnight. The rest of the ingredients may be prepared and refrigerated, ready to be dressed before serving. The bread may be prepared and wrapped in foil earlier in the day. After tossing the antipasto, preheat the oven, then heat the bread 15 to 20 minutes before serving. Reheat the spaghetti—with sauce in the microwave, or in boiling water, or after tossing with the sauce over a low burner. Dress antipasto or salad.

ᑫ R E C I P E S ᑫ

BILL URICK'S GARLIC BREAD
Makes 1 loaf

1 loaf Italian or French
   bread
2 to 3 garlic cloves,
   crushed or finely
   chopped with salt
5 tablespoons olive oil
   or butter, at room
   temperature
8 tablespoons imported
   Parmesan cheese,
   grated (optional)

Preheat oven to 400°F. Make thick slices 7/8 way down the loaf. Mix together the garlic, oil, and optional Parmesan, and with a brush, coat each slice. Wrap the loaf in foil and place in oven for 15 to 20 minutes until heated through.

Alternate
Garlic Baguettes

Substitute 4 short French baguettes for the bread. Split in half lengthwise. Spread garlic mixture on each half. Place on greased cookie sheet and bake uncovered for 15 minutes.

PARTY ANTIPASTO
Serves 8 to 10

1 tablespoon chopped
   basil, preferably fresh
   or 1 teaspoon dried
1 tablespoon chopped
   oregano, preferably
   fresh or 1 teaspoon
   dried
1 double recipe
   Vinaigrette (p. 140)
1 pound fresh Brussels
   sprouts
1 (16-ounce) can
   artichoke hearts,
   drained and hearts
   halved
1 pound fresh
   mushrooms, cleaned
1 (16-ounce) can hearts
   of palm, cut into 1/2-
   inch pieces (optional)
3/4 pound cherry
   tomatoes
1 pound dried
   pepperoni or salami,
   peeled and cubed
1 pound Swiss or other
   hard cheese, cubed
1 (5-3/4-ounce) jar
   green Spanish olives,
   drained
1 (16-ounce) can jumbo
   black olives, drained
1 (12-ounce) jar hot
   peppers such as
   pepperoncini,
   drained (optional)

Add the basil and oregano to the vinaigrette and pour equal amounts into 2 bowls. Cut an X into the bottom of each Brussels sprout and place in a large pot of boiling water. Cook sprouts until barely tender, drain, and run under cold water. Drain again. Put them in one of the bowls of vinaigrette, cover, and marinate overnight. Mix the artichoke hearts and mushrooms together in the other bowl of vinaigrette and marinate overnight.

Up to 1/2 hour before serving, combine the optional hearts of palm, cherry tomatoes, pepperoni or salami, cheese, olives, optional hot peppers, and marinated vegetables with the vinaigrette in a large serving dish. Toss well.

Tip: One 10-ounce package frozen baby Brussels sprouts may be substituted for the fresh Brussels sprouts. Just defrost and drain them, further cooking is not necessary.

Tip: Cherry tomatoes vary in size. If too large, cut in half.

Serving tip: Frequently this kind of antipasto is used as a vegetable or salad on a buffet table rather than a first course in the traditional Italian method.

A DIFFERENT SPAGHETTI

Serves 8 to 10

4 tablespoons olive oil
2 onions, chopped
4 garlic cloves, chopped
3 pounds fresh or
   canned red Italian
   plum tomatoes
1 cup tomato juice
   (optional)
1 tablespoon fennel
   seeds
5 tablespoons combined
   fresh herbs—basil,
   thyme, oregano and/
   or rosemary,
   chopped, or 2-1/2
   tablespoons dry
1-1/2 pounds
   homemade hot and
   sweet sausage
   or 3/4 pounds each
   hot Italian and sweet
   sausage, whole if
   links or in 1/2-inch
   patties
1/2 cup red wine
   vinegar
2 tablespoons tomato
   paste
1 tablespoon sugar
salt
1/8 teaspoon cayenne or red pepper (optional)
freshly ground pepper
2 (7-ounce) packages spaghetti
1 cup imported Parmesan cheese, grated

Heat the olive oil in a heavy saucepan. Add the onions and garlic and cook until soft. Cut up the tomatoes roughly and add to the pot. Add half of the juice from the cans, along with the fennel seeds and 2 tablespoons of the herbs. Cover and simmer for 2 hours.

Fry the sausage in a separate pan, drain off fat, cut into slices or break into pieces and add to the sauce. Taste the sauce and add the remainder of the juice, vinegar, tomato paste, sugar, salt and peppers as necessary to have a rich flavor. Move lid to half cover, and simmer over very low heat for 1/2 hour, stirring occasionally, so that the sauce does not scorch on the bottom of the pan. The sauce may be frozen or refrigerated for several days at this point.

Cook spaghetti in boiling water 9 to 10 minutes. Drain well. Taste sauce, add the remaining fresh herbs, sauce the spaghetti with some of the sauce, passing the rest. Serve with the grated Parmesan. Leftovers may be mixed together and refrigerated or frozen to be reheated later.

Tip: To reheat noodles, place in a colander over a pot of simmering water, toss in oil briefly, or reheat in microwave.

Tip: I make a double batch of the sauce and freeze it in pint containers. One pint serves 2 to 3 handily.

Variation
Try a mixture of 2 or 3 pastas—such as 1/3 multicolored rotini, 1/3 shells, and 1/3 vermicelli—to dress up this meal for company.

CHOCOLATE KISS COOKIES
Makes about 3 dozen 2-1/2-inch cookies

2-1/2 cups all-purpose
　　flour
1 teaspoon baking soda
1 teaspoon salt
1/4 teaspoon cinnamon
1 cup butter, softened
1 cup brown sugar,
　　packed
1 cup sugar
2 eggs
2 teaspoons vanilla
1 teaspoon almond
　　extract
2 cups (16 ounces)
　　chocolate kisses
1-1/2 cups chopped
　　pecans, walnuts, or
　　almonds

Preheat oven to 375°F. Combine the flour, baking soda, salt, and cinnamon; set aside. Beat butter and sugars until light. Beat in the eggs, vanilla, and almond extract. Blend in flour mixture. Chop 1 cup of the kisses. Stir in the chopped kisses and chopped nuts. Add 1 cup whole kisses. Drop heaping tablespoonfuls of the mixture onto an ungreased baking sheet 2 inches apart. Bake in hot oven 8 to 10 minutes. Cool on wire rack. These freeze well, too!

Variation
For chewy cookies, decrease temperature to 325°F and bake 10 to 13 minutes.

Variation
Use 1/2 cup grated coconut and 1 cup chopped macadamia nuts in place of the 1-1/2 cups chopped pecans, walnuts, or almonds. Bake as directed.

EVERYBODY'S FAVORITE CHOCOLATE CAKE

Makes 1 cake

Rich Chocolate Cream Frosting

1 pound semisweet
   chocolate, chopped
   or grated
2 cups heavy whipping
   cream
1 teaspoon vanilla

Cake Batter

2 cups all-purpose flour
2 cups sugar
1/2 cup unsweetened
   cocoa powder
1 teaspoon baking soda
1/2 teaspoon salt
3/4 cup vegetable oil
1/2 cup buttermilk or
   sour milk
2 eggs
2 teaspoons vanilla
1 cup boiling water
Garnish:
raspberries

To make frosting, melt the chocolate with the cream in a saucepan over medium-low heat, stirring constantly with wire whisk. Cool the mixture in the refrigerator about an hour. Stir in the vanilla. Beat at highest speed just until mixture becomes thick and fluffy, about 1 to 2 minutes. Store in refrigerator.

Preheat oven to 350°F. Grease three 8-inch or two 9-inch round pans or a 13 × 9 × 2-inch pan. Line the bottom of the pans with wax paper cut to fit. Grease and flour the paper.

Combine the flour, sugar, cocoa powder, baking soda, and salt in a large mixing bowl. Add the oil, milk, eggs, and vanilla. Beat 2 minutes at medium speed. Stir in the boiling water until blended. The batter will be thin.

Pour the batter evenly into the prepared pans. Bake 30 to 35 minutes or until a toothpick inserted near the center comes out clean. Cool in the pans on wire racks 5 minutes. Remove the cakes from the pans and finish cooling them on wire racks. Spread Rich Chocolate Cream Frosting between the layers and on the outside of the cake. Garnish with raspberries.

Tip: To make sour milk, add 1-1/2 teaspoons lemon juice to 1/2 cup milk.
Tip: Chop or grate chocolate in food processor.
Tip: The cake may be frozen, frosted or unfrosted.

✕ 3 ✕

A DINNER
OF LUSTY FLAVORS

Mussels Bring Back Memories
of Early Days as Chef

Tonight, as I scrub mussels for dinner, removing their beards, and carefully lifting them from the water so the sand is left in the sink, I remember the time when I became chef of C'an Poleta, a small country restaurant between Alcudia and Polensa, in Majorca, Spain. I had more courage than knowledge.

Having just received my Advanced Certificate from the London Cordon Bleu, I had never worked in a restaurant before, and didn't really know what I didn't know. In fact, many years before, I had been convinced by my mother and friends that ladies didn't work in restaurants, and so I had given up the idea.

Then, one night, I asked the owner of a restaurant in Palma, where we were living for a few months, if I could hang around in the kitchen and observe for a few nights. She agreed, and, in the way that life has, the next day I was offered a job in the country, an hour from Palma, at what was reputed to be the best restaurant on the island. The French chef had quit because there were no women for him to date there, and the owners were desperate enough to hire an inexperienced young woman as chef.

The deal was that all dinners were to be by reservation only, so the kitchen could accommodate my pace, which was bound to be slower than the French chef's. But, as happens in so many restaurants, the desire for exclusivity, good food, and service was over-come by greed, and the maitre d' took all comers, reservations or no. Mussels were on the menu the first night.

When I was attending cooking school in England, I had scrubbed and cooked up many a batch of mussels for crowds of friends, so I felt confident. Of course, those mussels had come from the market. *These* mussels had come directly from the ocean, but I felt they were the same.

I hadn't reckoned on the Majorcan yellow jackets and hornets. I had assumed the windows of the kitchen were screened—after all, it's been hot there every summer for centuries. I was wrong. There were no screens anywhere. But there were venomous flying insects. And they liked me. They liked me a lot. Seven bites in ten minutes worth, just before we started serving.

With tears streaming down my cheeks from the bites, from frustration, from the fear of being the chef of a restaurant, I put the mussels on to cook. First I had put them in a big sink in the middle of the kitchen, covered them with ocean water, and scattered over them an oatmeal-type product, to feed and plump them up before serving. The little Spanish maids who were my helpers had scrubbed them, removing their beards, and put them in the pan back in the sink in clean ocean water. Still crying, I added salt and pepper to the water. When their shiny black shells opened to show the sensuous flesh of the mussels inside, I sent them to the table where the proud owners sat, awaiting their first meal by their new chef.

Moments later the two ladies who owned the restaurant stormed into the kitchen. It didn't take long to find out the source of their wrath! Unthinkingly, I had added salt to the water, then sent the mussels to the table without tasting their broth. The broth was so salty, the owners said, a spoon would have stood up in it. (I personally think they were exaggerating. Still, it *was* salty enough to be nearly inedible.) I began crying in earnest now. My first job in a kitchen, and I had blown it! Partly due to the flying creatures, partly because I had forgotten all the things I'd ever learned—most impor-tantly, to taste, taste, taste.

The owners left the kitchen. After all, they couldn't fire me in the middle of the meal. And so we started a rocky relationship, which lasted until the season ended and our contract was up. They never did fire me, and I didn't quit. And I never again salted mussels until I was quite sure the broth needed flavoring! But I don't think they ever hired a novice cook again.

ͼ M E N U ͽ

A DINNER OF LUSTY FLAVORS

Pasta with Oil and Garlic
Mussels
Rouille Sauce (optional) or Aioli (optional)
Stir-fried Red Bell Peppers and Snow Peas
Caesar Salad (p. 267)
Beginner's Quick Peasant Bread or Toasted French Bread
Chocolate Roll

SERVES 4

LOGISTICS

See recipe for Mussels (p. 23) to determine quantity. All of this menu may be prepared in advance; also, the menu may be served in many ways—some people prefer mussels or salad first (I prefer the pasta as a starter). The red bell peppers and snow peas may be made a day in advance, covered, and refrigerated until serving time. The rouille sauce and aioli may be made a day ahead, covered, and refrigerated. The chocolate roll may be made ahead and filled several hours or a day in advance, or, if necessary, frozen filled. The peasant bread may be made earlier in the day or it can be made ahead and frozen; or a crisp store-bought French bread may be substituted. If serving the rouille, the peasant bread or French bread may be sliced and toasted early in the day. Store-bought pasta may be used or the pasta dough may be made ahead several hours, or several days in advance and dried or frozen; or it may be cooked several hours ahead, drained, and placed in cold water or a plastic bag, ready to reheat by tossing in the sauce, or reheating in the microwave. The cooked bell peppers and peas should be placed in a large frying pan ready to be reheated. The mussels may be made an hour in advance and reheated, or if done at the last minute, started when serving the pasta. Preheat the oven to 300°F, then add the bread to warm through 15 minutes before serving. Reheat the mussels and scatter them on top of the pasta; reheat the peppers and peas, toss the salad, and serve with the mussels.

↻ R E C I P E S ↺

ALL-PURPOSE PASTA

Serves 4 to 6

2-1/4 cups bread flour
3 extra large eggs
1 tablespoon olive oil
1 teaspoon salt
1 to 3 tablespoons water

In a bowl, mix together the flour, eggs, olive oil, and salt until you have a loose dough. Turn and knead by hand or place ingredients in a food processor and process, adding water as necessary to keep the dough smooth, moist, and pliable, but not sticky. Total kneading time will be a little more than 1 minute. Cover with plastic wrap and let rest 30 minutes.

Feed the dough through a pasta machine at the widest opening. Repeat, continuing to pass the dough through, stretching it until it is 1/32 of an inch thick, or as thick as you want it. The traditional machine has a linguine cutter as well as a fettucine cutter, or the dough may be cut by hand. To prevent sticking, let the cut strips of dough dry on a rack or a floured surface for 15 to 30 minutes before cooking. The cut pasta may also be wrapped in plastic wrap and refrigerated up to 24 hours or frozen to be cooked later.

To cook, drop the fresh pasta into a large pot of rapidly boiling water for a very brief time, 2 to 3 minutes if very thin. The thinner and fresher the pasta, the shorter the cooking time. However, dried pasta can take up to 10 minutes in boiling water; check the package directions. Taste to test doneness, or pull a piece of pasta from the water and throw it against the wall. If it sticks to the wall, it is not done. If it drops off, it is ready to serve! When cooked it will be slightly resistant to the bite. Drain and serve with any of your favorite pasta sauces, with mussels, or with butter and grated Parmesan.

Continued

Variation
Add 1 tablespoon hot peppers, finely chopped, to the pasta dough.

Variation
1/4 package thawed and chopped frozen spinach or turnip greens may be added to the flour before proceeding with the dough recipe.

PASTA WITH OIL AND GARLIC
Serves 4 to 6

8 ounces fresh thinly cut
or dried spaghetti,
linguine, or thin
vermicelli

Sauce
1/4 to 1/2 cup olive oil
6 to 8 garlic cloves,
  finely chopped or
  thinly sliced
1 cup chicken stock or
  broth, preferably
  homemade
1/2 cup fresh parsley,
  chopped
2 teaspoons fresh lemon
  juice
salt
freshly ground pepper

Bring a large pot of water to the boil. Add the pasta, stirring. Bring back to the boil and boil until the pasta is tender but still firm in the center, 6 to 8 minutes or according to package directions. Drain and run under cold water to stop the cooking. If making in advance, place in a pan of cold water or in a tightly sealed plastic bag.

To make the sauce, heat enough oil to coat the bottom of a large frying pan. Add the garlic and cook over low heat until the garlic turns golden. Do not brown. Add the stock and bring to the boil. Boil until the liquid is reduced by half. Set aside.

When ready to eat, bring the liquid back to the boil. Add the well-drained pasta and toss with wooden forks or a pasta spoon until heated through. Add the parsley, lemon juice, salt and pepper, and more oil if needed.

Variation
Add 1/4 to 1/2 teaspoon red pepper flakes or crushed hot red pepper to the garlic before adding the broth.

Variation
Add 1/2 cup freshly grated imported Parmesan cheese. Pass 1/2 cup more.

Variation
Substitute butter for the olive oil.

MUSSELS
Serves 6*

10 dozen mussels,
  cleaned and
  scrubbed*
2 cups white wine or dry
  white grape juice (see
  tip below)
1 onion, chopped
6 tablespoons mixed
  chopped fresh basil
  and parsley
salt
freshly ground pepper

Place the mussels in a large, heavy pot with the wine or grape juice and the onion. Cover and cook over medium-high heat until the shells just open, approximately 5 to 8 minutes. Remove cover. Add the basil and parsley. Taste for seasoning and add salt and pepper as needed. Can be made an hour or so in advance. Reheat, stirring, until at the boil, about 2 minutes. Serve with juices, by themselves, or over cooked pasta.

Variation
Place 4 cups marinara sauce in the pot instead of the wine, onion, and herbs, and cook as directed.

Variation
Serve with a rouille sauce and toasted French bread. Spread some of the rouille on the bread, and pass the rest, to be spooned into the broth.

Variation
Serve with Pico de Gallo (p. 86); substitute cilantro for the basil and parsley.

Tip: Mussels will stay fresh on ice or in the refrigerator several days but may lose their plumpness. Wrap in newspaper to store.

Tip: There are several dry nonalcoholic wines now on the market, which are dry white grape juices.

Comment: Mussels can vary considerably in saltiness and grittiness, depending on their source. Some grocery stores clean their mussels before sale; others sell them as muddy as you can imagine. To clean, place in a pan or sink with lukewarm water. Using a stiff brush, scrub each shell. If you are serving them in the shell, you may need to scrape the

---

Mussels are equally suitable for a starter or a main course, depending on the rest of the meal. Three pounds of mussels in their shells yield 30 to 40 small mussels, enough for 4 to 6 starter or "shared main course" servings. Nine pounds yield 10 dozen, enough for 6 main course servings when no pasta is served.

barnacles off of them, using a knife. With your hands, pull off the beard, if there is one. (The beard is aptly named. If you don't see anything that looks like a beard, there isn't one!) Scoop the cleaned mussels out of the sink, being careful not to tip the mussels out, thereby pouring the gritty water back over the mussels. Do not store them in tap water. They will stay alive a week or so if wrapped in newspaper and kept in the refrigerator, although the longer you keep them the more the flesh will shrink (as they will not have had anything to eat).

Comment: If you are concerned about your broth being sandy, strain it through cheesecloth or through paper towels. Add some more fresh herbs to the strained broth and reheat.

Purchasing tip: The smaller the mussel shells, the more tender and flavorful the mussels are.

Leftover tip: Any leftover juices may be strained, cooled, and frozen. Defrosted, the juices are a good substitute for fish stock when fish stock is not available. The leftover mussels are good cold in a salad.

ROUILLE SAUCE
Makes 2-1/2 to 3 cups

1/3 cup fresh bread crumbs
8 garlic cloves, chopped
1/2 cup broth from the mussels or fish stock
1/2 teaspoon paprika
1/4 teaspoon cayenne pepper
1/2 teaspoon salt
1 egg yolk
3/4 cup olive oil

Purée together the bread crumbs and garlic in a food processor or blender. Add the fish stock, paprika, cayenne, salt, and egg yolk. Purée until smooth. Add the oil slowly, as you would in a mayonnaise or aioli, and process again until smooth. Refrigerate, covered, until needed.

Tip: Add 1/4 cup cooked, mashed potatoes to add thickening to this spicy mayonnaise when not serving on pasta. If no cooked potatoes are on hand, cook a small potato in the microwave or boiling water, peel, and mash it. Don't substitute dehydrated mashed potatoes.

Tip: To serve, pass separately or spread on slices of toasted French or peasant bread.

AIOLI
Makes 2 cups

2 egg yolks
salt
freshly ground pepper
3 tablespoons fresh
   lemon juice
8 garlic cloves, chopped
1-1/3 to 1-1/2 cups
   olive oil
1 small fresh hot red
   pepper, finely
   chopped, or cayenne
   pepper to taste

In a small bowl or a food processor, whisk the egg yolks with a pinch of salt, the pepper, and 1 tablespoon of the lemon juice until thick. Add the garlic. Gradually whisk in the oil, drop by drop at first, until the mixture thickens. Continue whisking, adding the oil in a slow, thin stream until the sauce is thick. Season with the remaining 2 tablespoons lemon juice, add salt and the red peppers to taste.

Tip: Can be made a day in advance if tightly sealed in the refrigerator.

STIR-FRIED RED BELL PEPPERS AND SNOW PEAS
Serves 4

1-1/2 tablespoons olive
   oil
1 red bell pepper,
   seeded and julienned
   (cut into fine strips)
1/2 pound snow peas,
   tipped, tailed, and
   julienned
salt
freshly ground pepper

Heat the oil in a large skillet or wok. Add the pepper and snow peas and sauté 2 or 3 minutes. Season with salt and pepper to taste.

Variation
Add 1 garlic clove, finely chopped, or 1 tablespoon ginger, finely chopped, with the other ingredients.

Variation
Use 1/2 sesame oil and 1/2 olive or vegetable oil to sauté.

Tip: Not all snow peas have tough strings, but be sure to test each one. To "tail," pull the string down if you find one, and remove it.
Tip: Can be made a day in advance, covered, and refrigerated.

BEGINNER'S QUICK PEASANT BREAD
Makes 4 loaves

2 packages active dry
  yeast
1 tablespoon sugar
2 cups water (105°–115°F)
2 teaspoons salt
5 to 6 cups bread flour
cornmeal
1 egg yolk mixed with a
  dash of water
poppy, caraway, or
  sesame seeds

In a large bowl or in a food processor, dissolve the yeast and sugar in the warm water. Add the salt, then enough of the flour, 1/2 cup at a time, to make a soft dough. For this rough, peasant-type bread, knead just enough to mix the flour and liquid (usually less than 1 minute in the food processor, a couple of minutes by hand). Shape into a ball and place, turning to coat, in an oiled bowl or oiled plastic bag. Cover the bowl with plastic wrap and let rise in a warm place until doubled. Punch down; then turn out dough on a floured board and shape into 4 long, thin loaves. Place on a baking sheet heavily sprinkled with cornmeal. Slash the tops of the loaves in 2 or 3 places with a sharp knife and brush tops with egg yolk mixture before sprinkling with poppy, caraway, or sesame seeds.

Place loaves on the middle rack in a cold oven. Turn on oven, set at 400°F, and place a large pan of boiling water on the bottom of the oven. Bake for 25 to 30 minutes until crusty and loaves sound "hollow." Cool on a rack. Although this bread is adequate frozen and reheated, it is really at its best the day it is made.

Tip: Dough may also be shaped on an oiled surface if too much flour has been incorporated.

Tip: This is a fast bread to make as it requires little kneading and does not rise in the traditional manner after being shaped. Instead, it goes into a cold oven, and rises while the oven is preheating.

CHOCOLATE ROLL

Serves 6

6 ounces semisweet
   chocolate bits
3 to 4 tablespoons water
5 egg yolks
1 cup sugar
1/2 cup chopped
   pecans or walnuts
   (optional)
5 egg whites
confectioners' sugar

Filling

1-1/2 cups heavy
   whipping cream,
   whipped with sugar
   and rum flavoring
1/4 cup confectioners'
   sugar

Oil a 15-1/2 × 10-1/2-inch jellyroll pan. Line with wax paper extending slightly over the sides of the pan. Oil the paper.

Preheat oven to 350°F. Melt the chocolate with the water in a heavy saucepan over low heat or in the microwave. With an electric mixer, beat the egg yolks and sugar until thick and lemon-colored. Stir the melted, but not hot, chocolate into the egg-yolk mixture. Fold in the nuts if desired. Beat the egg whites until stiff, but not dry. Add the nuts to the base mixture. Mix a large spoonful of egg whites with the chocolate mixture to soften; then fold in the remaining whites as lightly as possible.

Spread the mixture evenly in the prepared pan and bake in the hot oven for 20 to 25 minutes. Remove from oven and cool to room temperature. Cover with a lightweight dish towel that is only slightly damp. (This prevents crusting of the top.) Refrigerate overnight or up to 3 days. The cake freezes well at this point, but needs to be defrosted to room temperature before rolling and filling.

To serve, remove the cloth and flip cake out onto a large piece of wax paper that has been dusted with confectioners' sugar. Carefully strip off all paper from the top of the cake. You may trim away any burned or rough edges. Spread cake with 1-1/2 cups whipped cream to which sugar and any desired flavoring have been added. Roll up like a jelly roll. Cracks are fine! Sprinkle generously with confectioners' sugar, slice, and serve. This freezes fine, but if frozen, defrost in refrigerator or serve partially frozen.

Continued

Variation
Serve with chocolate sauce.

Tip: The log may be rolled lengthwise or horizontally. A horizontal roll serves more people, but they get a smaller portion. I've served ten "in a tight spot," but I've also seen two grown men finish off one by themselves.

Tip: This recipe doubles well. If you double the recipe, be sure to stagger the two pans in the oven; otherwise the bottom of the one on the lower rack will burn and the top of the higher one will burn.

Tip: If it breaks, crumble up and serve in a glass bowl!

❧ 4 ❧

THE FAMILY BREAKFAST

A Special Family Breakfast

They'd been divorced nearly forty years when he telephoned their daughter, asking her to help him see his former wife together with the rest of their children. His second wife and her second husband were now dead and each of the parents was alone.

Surprisingly, the mother agreed to the meeting, "for the sake of the children." Her rancor at having been left with three demanding children had cooled in the slow oven of time and now it rarely flared, only sizzled.

He had suggested they have breakfast—his favorite meal—at his local diner. He is now 82 and rises before dawn, finishing eating before the sun is up. On those rare occasions when he waits until seven or eight in the morning, it is a grave concession to the rest of the world's rhythm.

The mother, now 75, still works three days a week, for the church library. In her heart of hearts, she thinks the world would be a better place if everyone slept a bit later (at least until dawn), ate breakfast after sunrise, and came gently into the world each morning, only after reading and praying.

The daughter knew that diner only too well, for that is where she had met her father many times at barbaric hours of the morning, for grits and eggs and bacon. They serve cheap margarine, and the waitresses parcel out the sugar and Sweet and Low packets from their apron pockets only upon request. There's always a crowd there, always a din, with salesmen calling to each other across the red vinyl booths.

What kind of meal, what kind of place, should it be for all the family to meet, 40 years later? Surely a place where they wouldn't have to shout. Because if they started to shout, only to be heard, maybe it would continue, their voices rising distinct over the cacophony, spiraling above them all with the stifled angers of bygone years.

No, it had to be a place where the atmosphere would temper those feelings if that pot was uncovered. It had to be at an hour when the crowds were sparse, when the world had already moved into its daily rhythm. The place had to serve butter, the bread had to be warm.

The children, grown, terrified of the event, had to be able to leave without bolting, if the pain became too great. But, what if they all left? Who would pay the check in the swirl of emotions?

It was agreed. They would all get together at a small elegant hotel at nine in the morning. They met in the gilded lobby, and proceeded to the dining room, where, mercifully, they were greeted expeditiously and seated in the rear of the room.

He ordered the same breakfast he always had nearly every day of his life. The mother was swept up by the occasion, the splendor of the room, the length of the menu. She vacillated, unsure of what would be the best, wanting to remember the best. The children ordered the safest items. No crumbled croissants for them.

Breakfast came. The bread was hot, the butter was real. It melted easily. It was terrifying to them all to find they were civilized, polite, that they liked each other.

"Do you miss your husband?" he asked. "Yes," she said, "he was good to me. And we had the church." She paused, then asked shyly, "Do you miss your wife?"

"Yes," he answered, "although she wasn't herself for a long time. Your husband wasn't either, was he?" "No," she said, "he didn't know me for some time."

They looked at each other from lowered eyes. The children faded, shadowed, and didn't know the people their parents had become in just a few moments. He said to her at last, "I see you still drink too much coffee." She said, "Yes" and laughed, a small, delicate bell-like laugh her children had never heard before. It even surprised her. As she raised her hand to cover her mouth, her napkin fell to the carpet. "I only drink one cup a day," he said, and stooped to retrieve her napkin. "You still have the most beautiful legs of any woman I have known," he remarked, wiping the drops of his single cup of coffee from his smile. "I've always liked your mustache," she returned, watching as his napkin left the mouth she used to know. Everyone started talking at once, sharing memories, laughing and teasing, the pot of emotions now bubbling like a good soup.

They took pictures. He called the waiter over. He was always more comfortable with strangers than intimates. "This is my family," he said. "These are my children. This is their mother. And this is the first time we've all been together in forty years." The waiter smiled politely and took more pictures for them.

"You did a good job with the children," the father said. Turning to the children, she said, "God helped me. They are my jewels."

They called for the check, and he said, "Next time, let's go to my favorite diner. A bit earlier. I can't afford this expensive restaurant again." She smiled and nodded her head as he took her arm and walked her to the car, the children only moments behind them, dazed with the wonder of it all. They were a family. Maybe they always had been.

The daughter decided she would try to have them all to her home next, for another, special family breakfast.

⟨ᵍ M E N U ⟩

A SPECIAL FAMILY BREAKFAST

Poached Eggs with Red Pepper or Lemon Hollandaise Sauce

Crepes

Maple Glazed Ham Steak

Baked Cheese Grits Casserole

Nut Bran Muffins with Caramel and/or Everybody's Favorite Blueberry Muffins

Fresh Peaches with Raspberry Purée and Nuts

Baked Bananas or Baked Stuffed Apples and Pears

SERVES 4 TO 6

LOGISTICS

Some of this menu may be made in advance. The grits casserole and the crepes may be made ahead several days and refrigerated, or frozen for several months, defrosted, and reheated. The eggs may be poached the night before, then kept refrigerated in a bowl of water, and reheated. The muffins may be made ahead a day, or well ahead and frozen. For a winter breakfast, the apples and pears may be cooked the day ahead and reheated, or served cold. As a summer alternate, the raspberries and peaches may be done a day ahead. The peppers may be roasted and peeled and kept tightly sealed. The hollandaise may be made an hour ahead of time and kept in a *bain marie* or water bath (see p. 75). The oven should be preheated to 350°F so that 30 minutes ahead of serving time the defrosted grits may be reheated. Fifteen minutes later add the foil-wrapped muffins; pears and apples can be reheated. Put the ham under the broiler (a double oven would be helpful!) and place the foil-wrapped crepes and the bananas in the oven shortly before serving. Place the eggs in a slotted spoon or strainer and reheat in the boiling water about 1 minute before serving. Remember, eggs are cheap, and you should always cook more ahead of time than you might need, in case one breaks.

❝ R E C I P E S ❞

POACHED EGGS
Serves 4 to 6

6 to 8 eggs
1/4 cup white vinegar

Grease the bottom of a large pot or frying pan or use a nonstick pan. Add water twice the depth of an egg and heat with the vinegar. Break an egg into a small bowl. When the water comes to a boil, swirl it into a vortex with a spoon. Drop the egg into the well formed in the center of the pot. The swirling water should surround the egg. Reduce the heat. Simmer 3 to 4 minutes or let stand off the heat for 8 minutes. By this time the white should be firm and the yolk soft. Remove with a skimmer and drain well. Trim off any

streamers of egg. If not using the egg immediately, plunge it at once into cold water. Store
in this way up to 24 hours. Repeat the process
for each egg. To reheat the eggs, place into
simmering water for 1 minute. Drain and
serve with sauce.

Comment: Eggs are inexpensive enough that I recommend
poaching more eggs than needed to guarantee perfect eggs
for serving. If an egg yolk breaks, leave the egg in the water to
cook. When cooked through, remove and refrigerate. Use for
egg salad or another purpose.

LEMON HOLLANDAISE SAUCE

Makes 1 cup

4 egg yolks
juice of 1 lemon
1 tablespoon water
boiling water
8 tablespoons (1/4
   pound or 1/2 cup)
   butter, cut in small
   pieces
salt
1/8 teaspoon red
   cayenne pepper

Place the egg yolks, 2 tablespoons of the
lemon juice, and the 1 tablespoon of water in a
heavy nonmetal bowl, and set it in a frying pan
that has 1 inch of boiling water in the bottom
(called a *bain marie*). Whisk the yolk mixture
steadily. The water may be boiling as long as
the mixture in the bowl is 160° to 180°F. Do
not let the water evaporate. Whisk for 5 minutes or until thick. Slowly add the butter, piece
by piece, whisking after each addition. Season
with salt and pepper to taste. If the sauce
doesn't thicken, turn up the heat, but be sure
the temperature of the sauce remains below
180°F. The hollandaise may be made up to
one hour ahead of time and kept in the *bain
marie*.

Variation

For Red Pepper Hollandaise, just before serving, add to the hollandaise 1
red bell pepper, roasted, peeled, chopped and drained of juices.

Variation

For herbed hollandaise, add 1 tablespoon fresh chopped dill, thyme, or
tarragon.

Variation

For a ginger hollandaise, add 1 tablespoon chopped fresh ginger.

Continued

Variation
For mustard hollandaise, add 2 to 3 tablespoons Dijon mustard.

Variation
Place 1/2 cup dry white wine in a small saucepan and boil until reduced to 1 to 2 tablespoons liquid. Substitute for the lemon juice. Proceed with other variations if desired.

Tip: To bring back a separated hollandaise, first add 1 to 2 tablespoons of cold water. It may be separating because there is not enough liquid. If it still does not come back, place a small portion of the curdled mixture and 2 tablespoons water or lemon juice in a new heavy pan. Whisk until smooth, then add the curdled mixture. You may also start with a fresh egg, whisk until thick, then add the curdled mixture.

Tip: If the eggs for a hollandaise go over 180°F, you will have scrambled eggs. Try straining it. If still scrambled, call it a scrambled egg sauce, or start over.

Tip: Hold the hollandaise by keeping it in the hot water, off the heat.

CREPES

Makes 2 cups batter

Crepe Batter

1 cup milk
1 cup flour
1 egg
1 egg yolk
1/2 teaspoon salt

To make the crepes, whisk together milk, flour, egg, egg yolk, and salt. Let sit 1 hour. Thin with additional milk if necessary. Heat a small, nonstick skillet. Pour a small ladle-full of batter into pan, swirling to cover bottom. When lightly brown, about 1 minute, turn over; let slightly brown, 30 to 45 seconds. Turn out on a rack to cool. Repeat with remaining batter until it is gone. May be refrigerated or frozen, tightly wrapped. Defrost, serve at room temperature or reheat briefly in oven, filled or unfilled.

Variation
Lemon Crepes: *Filling:* 1 cup sugar, 1/2 cup butter, 8 to 10 tablespoons lemon rind, and 2 teaspoons lemon juice. To make the filling, mix sugar, butter, lemon rind, and lemon juice in a bowl. Place 1 tablespoon filling on each crepe and roll up. (This amount of filling should fill about 20 crepes.) Preheat oven to 350°F. Bake in oven for 15 minutes. This can be made up weeks in advance and frozen. Thaw before baking.

MAPLE GLAZED HAM STEAK
Serves 6

1 (3-pound) precooked
   ham steak, 1-1/2 to 2
   inches thick
1/2 cup maple syrup

Place the steak, lightly brushed with the syrup, on a pan 3 inches under the heat of a hot broiler or place directly on the grill. Broil or grill 3 to 4 minutes. Turn and cook second side. Brush with syrup during broiling. Tip the pan juices, if any, into a pan with the remainder of the maple syrup. Bring to the boil and boil 1 minute. Serve the ham with the syrup.

Variation
Brush with 4 to 5 tablespoons soy sauce and 1/2 to 1 tablespoon fresh ginger.

Variation
Substitute 1/2 cup barbecue sauce for the maple syrup.

Variation
Brush with 1/4 cup honey mixed with 1/2 cup Dijon mustard.

Variation
You may substitute 3 (1-pound) precooked ham steaks, 1/2 inch thick. Broil or grill for 2 minutes on each side.

BAKED CHEESE GRITS CASSEROLE
Serves 4 to 6

4 cups water
1 cup grits
2 eggs
1-1/2 teaspoons salt
1 to 2 garlic cloves,
   crushed
1 teaspoon paprika
dash of Tabasco
2/3 pound sharp
   cheese, grated
1/3 cup butter

Preheat oven to 350°F. Butter a 1-1/2-quart casserole. Bring the water to the boil in a large saucepan, stir in the grits, and continue to stir until they are completely mixed. Cook, stirring, until thickened. Whisk the eggs slightly, then stir a small amount of grits into the eggs to warm them. Beat egg mixture into the grits off the heat. Add the salt, garlic, paprika, Tabasco, cheese, and butter, mixing well. Pour the grits mixture into the buttered casserole. Bake for 25 to 45 minutes, depending on the depth of the dish. May be cooked in advance and reheated. Freezes well.

Continued

Variation

For Elizabeth Vaeth's "Oh So Fine Grits Casserole," add 1-1/2 cups cooked and drained chopped turnip greens or spinach, 2 teaspoons tarragon, and a hot pepper or two, chopped. She substitutes Provolone and goat cheese or herb cheese for the sharp cheese. Serves 6 to 8.

Tip: Different grits—instant vs. stone ground—vary radically in cooking time (from 5 minutes to 45). Follow package directions.

Tip: This is very portable.

Tip: This recipe doubles easily.

NUT BRAN MUFFINS WITH CARAMEL
Makes 12 muffins

1/2 cup whole bran cereal

2/3 cup milk

1/2 cup brown sugar, preferably dark

2 tablespoons corn syrup

5 tablespoons (1/3 cup) melted butter

1/3 cup almonds, sliced *or* 1/3 cup walnuts or pecans, chopped

1/3 cup raisins

2 tablespoons molasses

1 egg

1-1/2 cups self-rising flour (see Tip, page 37)

Preheat oven to 400°F. Grease 12 muffin cups. Combine bran cereal and milk and let stand about 5 minutes. In a small saucepan, combine 1/4 cup of the dark brown sugar, 2 teaspoons of the corn syrup, and 2 tablespoons of the butter. Place over low heat for 1 to 2 minutes or until sugar is melted but still thick. Divide this evenly into prepared muffin cups, then sprinkle nuts evenly over the mixture. Add the remaining 1/4 cup dark brown sugar, the raisins, the rest of the melted butter, corn syrup, molasses, and egg to the bran cereal and mix thoroughly. Stir in the flour until just moistened. The batter will be lumpy; do not overmix. Fill muffin cups 2/3 to 3/4 full. Bake on center rack 15 minutes. Remove the pan from oven and invert on a rack immediately. Allow to cool 5 minutes before removing pan. May be made ahead and frozen.

Tip: If brown sugar is too hard, use the microwave to soften it. Place 1/2 cup water in a 1-cup measuring cup, and microwave on high until boiling. Place the brown sugar in a microwave-proof container near the water and heat, uncovered, until soft (about 1-1/2 to 3 minutes for 1/2 pound brown sugar).

EVERYBODY'S FAVORITE BLUEBERRY MUFFINS
Makes 12 muffins

Danish Crumb Topping

2 tablespoons self-rising
   flour
2 tablespoons sugar
1 tablespoon butter,
   softened

Muffins

1 cup blueberries
2 cups self-rising flour
1/3 cup sugar
3/4 cup milk
1 egg
1/4 cup butter, melted

Preheat oven to 400°F. Grease muffin tins or line with paper baking cups. For the topping, mix the 2 tablespoons flour and sugar with the softened butter until crumbly. Set aside.

To make the muffins, rinse, drain, and thoroughly dry blueberries on paper towels. Combine flour and sugar. Lightly toss dried blueberries in 1/4 cup of the flour-sugar mixture. Whisk milk, egg, and melted butter together until blended and add to flour-sugar mixture; stir briefly. Carefully fold in floured blueberries. Stir only until the ingredients are moistened. The batter will be lumpy; do not overmix or berries will bleed. Fill muffin cups 2/3 to 3/4 full. Sprinkle with Danish Crumb Topping. Bake on center rack about 15 to 18 minutes until golden brown.

Variation
For Streusel Topping, substitute 2 tablespoons brown sugar for the 2 tablespoons of sugar.

> *Comment:* You may use fresh or frozen blueberries. Obviously, fresh are better, but the frozen do pass muster. The muffins freeze well.

Tip: To make self-rising flour, combine 1 cup all-purpose flour with 1 teaspoon baking powder, 1/4 teaspoon salt, and 1/4 teaspoon baking soda.

FRESH PEACHES WITH RASPBERRY PURÉE AND NUTS

Serves 4 to 6

1 (12-ounce) box frozen
   raspberries
1 to 2 tablespoons
   granulated sugar
1 to 2 tablespoons
   orange juice
1 tablespoon lemon
   juice
1 quart fresh peaches,
   peeled and sliced
8 tablespoons
   confectioners' sugar
1 teaspoon pecans or
   walnuts, chopped

Drain raspberries of their liquid, then purée in a blender. Stir in the granulated sugar and the orange and lemon juices. Keep cool. Just before eating, make layers of peaches, pouring purée over each layer. Sprinkle confectioners' sugar and chopped nuts on top.

Variation
Pour 2 tablespoons orange liqueur over the layered peaches and confectioners' sugar.

BAKED BANANAS

Serves 4

4 bananas, peeled and
   split
2 tablespoons butter
2 tablespoons brown
   sugar
4 tablespoons chopped
   walnuts or pecans

Preheat oven to 350°F. Place each of the bananas in a square of buttered aluminum foil. Top with dots of butter. Sprinkle with brown sugar and nuts. Fold foil over to make a packet. Place the packets on a baking sheet. Bake until bananas begin to soften, about 5 to 8 minutes. Remove, unwrap, and serve warm on a platter.

Variation
Butter an oven-to-table dish, add the bananas, dot with butter, sugar, and nuts. Cover dish. Bake 5 to 8 minutes. Serve in baking dish.

BAKED STUFFED APPLES AND PEARS

Serves 6

3 apples, preferably
  Granny Smith or
  Golden Delicious
3 pears, preferably
  Bartlett
1/2 cup raisins
4 tablespoons chopped
  walnuts or pecans
2 tablespoons
  granulated sugar
1 tablespoon lemon
  juice
1-1/2 cups cider

Cut off the top third of the apples and set aside. Core the apples, leaving the bottoms intact, and set aside. Peel the pears, leaving the stem on. Core the blossom end of the pears (the bottom). Mix together the raisins, nuts, sugar, and lemon juice. Fill the cavities of the apples and pears with the fruit-nut mixture. Place upright in a deep baking dish. Cover the apples with their tops. Pour the cider around the upright fruit, about halfway up the sides of the fruit. Cover and bake at 350°F for 1/2 to 3/4 hour or until fruit pierces easily with a fork. If some of the fruits are done sooner, remove and set aside until the rest are done. May be served hot or cold. If serving hot, when ready to serve, sprinkle with brown sugar and put under broiler 2 to 3 minutes to brown.

Variation
Serve with cream.

Variation
Poach in a sugar syrup of 1/3 cup sugar, 1/2 cup water, and zest of 1 lemon. Make a sugar syrup by placing the sugar, water, and lemon zest in a heavy saucepan. Heat, without boiling, until the sugar dissolves. Bring to the boil and boil 2 minutes. Remove from heat.

Tip: Pack the fruit mixture into the pears to prevent the mixture from falling out. Place in pan. Remove cooked pears with a flat metal spatula to prevent fruit from falling out.

Variation
Use all apples or all pears instead of mixing them.

Comment: Try to purchase apples and pears of the same size.

⚘ 5 ⚘

A HAPPY FAMILY MENU

Grannie Kate's Biscuits

It was a hot night, and the sun was setting later and later each day. Worrying about her grandmother, the small child couldn't sleep. She was staring at the ceiling, when her mother came in to tuck her in. Since she normally fell to sleep when her head hit the pillow, her mother asked if anything was wrong. "No," Jamie replied. "Are you sure?" her mother asked again. "Well," the tot replied, knowing somehow she wasn't concerned about her grandmother's mortality as much as her own self-interest, "I was just wondering—who's going to make biscuits for us when Grannie Kate dies?"

At a young age, the child had hit upon something most of us only learn late in life. There are certain foods that will linger in our memories and hearts long after the people who made them are gone. And it's important to learn from them how to make their treasures so they will live on.

Grannie Kate, still in robust good health, is the best biscuit maker I know. Her biscuits are tender, light, a bit smaller than the average, just large enough to hold sautéed pork tenderloin or a sausage without crumbling until the very end when the juices break it up. Whenever Kate Almand is around, everyone else is tempted to take a backseat and let her make the biscuits. Although I frequently tell people she was born with a biscuit bowl in her hands, she's only been making them since she was a small child herself. One of thirteen children, she was told by her dad one day, when her mom was gone, to make the biscuits. She tried, and made a mess. The next day he had her make them again, and told her how, and she's been making them ever since.

Biscuits are quite cheap to make—just flour, baking powder, salt, and shortening in most cases, with a bit of milk or buttermilk. But it's like learning to hit a golf or a tennis ball; the chances are you aren't going to be happy until you practice a bit, and study the basics.

First, the right ingredients help. Kate uses a southern soft winter wheat flour, White Lily, because it is low in protein, and that contributes to the fluffy lightness of the biscuit. She also likes Crisco better than any other shortening. She prefers sweet milk (the southern term for homogenized milk) to buttermilk, but she can make a biscuit out of any flour and shortening because she has the technique down pat.

She doesn't measure her flour. This probably goes back to the days when she bought it in huge sacks and used those sacks to make her daughter dresses. The flour, in an opened flour sack then, was as susceptible to change as it is today. In a dry season, it will absorb water differently than in a rainy one.

When possible, she uses a biscuit bowl, larger in circumference than it is deep. She places a large quantity of flour in it, makes a well in the center, then cuts in shortening and milk in a soft motion that kneads the flour briefly as the liquid is mixed in. She winds up with a very soft dough, which she turns and coats in flour, leaving it nearly wet in the middle, but dry enough to handle on the outside. She pulls off a piece of the dough, dips the wet portion in the flour, and rolls it lightly in her floured hand. She places it on a baking sheet, keeping all the biscuits close together, so they will stay tender. When finished, she sifts any leftover flour back into a container, ready for the next day's use.

Too much kneading will make a tough biscuit. Too little will not give you as nice a rise. Too much shortening makes a crumbly dough, too little robs it of tenderness. I've stopped Grannie Kate in the midst of tossing in the flour and she let me measure her proportions so that I could give you a guide to go by until you become confident enough to wing it yourself.

⟨ MENU ⟩

A HAPPY FAMILY MENU

Basic Biscuits
Cabbage Apple Slaw
Happy Family Stew or Curried Beef and Vegetable Stew
Beets with Lemon and Olive Oil
Butter Toffee Cookies or Ray Overton's Oatmeal Spice Cookies

SERVES 4 TO 6

LOGISTICS

Slaw may be made a day ahead or earlier in the day, as may the beets. The stews are best made a day ahead, or well ahead then frozen, defrosted, and reheated. The cookies may be made ahead and kept in an airtight container or frozen. The vegetables may be made several hours ahead and reheated after the biscuits are in the oven. The biscuits should be made as close to serving as possible.

⟨ RECIPES ⟩

BASIC BISCUITS
Makes 12 to 18 biscuits

2-1/2 cups all-purpose
    flour
1 tablespoon baking
    powder
1/2 teaspoon salt
3/4 cup shortening
1 cup milk or buttermilk

Preheat oven to 450° to 500°F. Sift 2 cups of the flour with the baking powder and salt into a bowl. Cut in the shortening with a pastry blender or fork, or work in with your fingers. Add the milk to make a soft dough, mixing just until the dough holds together. Flour your hands. Pull off a piece of dough the size of a biscuit and dip the wet edge into the extra flour. Then roll or pat into a biscuit shape. Place the biscuits, slightly touching, on a lightly greased baking sheet. Bake until golden brown, 8 to 10 minutes.

Variation

Try adding 1 tablespoon black or red pepper when you want a peppery biscuit.

Variation

Some people prefer "sweet" (homogenized) milk, others like buttermilk. For a cheese biscuit, add 1/2 cup Cheddar cheese; for an herbal biscuit, add 1 tablespoon of your favorite fresh herbs such as chopped basil or thyme.

Tip: You may substitute self-rising flour for the flour (omitting baking powder and salt).

Tip: Keep on hand as a refrigerator dough. Combine only the flour, baking powder, salt, and shortening and store in a covered container in the refrigerator. Remove a portion, add enough milk or buttermilk to make a soft dough. Shape the biscuits. Bake as directed.

CABBAGE APPLE SLAW

Makes 8 cups

1 small head cabbage, or
   1/2 large head,
   (about 1-1/2 pounds)
   grated in food
   processor or with
   hand grater
1 Granny Smith or
   Golden Delicious
   apple, cored and cut in chunks
1 small carrot, peeled and grated
1 cup mayonnaise, sour cream, or yogurt
juice of 1 lemon (optional)
salt
freshly ground pepper
Garnish:
1 apple, unpeeled, sliced

Toss together the cabbage, apple, carrot, and mayonnaise, sour cream, or yogurt. Taste for seasoning and add lemon juice, salt, and pepper as needed. Refrigerate until serving time. May be made a day ahead or earlier in the day. Garnish with apple slices when ready to serve.

Variation

Substitute red cabbage for all or half the cabbage.

HAPPY FAMILY STEW

Serves 4 to 6

1/4 to 1/3 cup oil
3 pounds boneless beef
   chuck, sirloin tip, or
   round, cut into 2-inch
   cubes
2 onions, chopped
2 garlic cloves, chopped
4 cups canned plum
   tomatoes, with juice,
   chopped
1-1/2 cups canned beef
   stock
1 cup mild green chilies,
   drained and chopped
1 tablespoon fresh
   oregano, chopped, or
   1 teaspoon dried
2 teaspoons ground
   cumin
3 tablespoons
   Worcestershire sauce
salt
freshly ground pepper
3 cups cooked rice (see
   Boiled Rice, p. 110)

Heat enough of the oil to cover the bottom of a heavy pan until the oil is sizzling. Dry the meat well and add enough to the pan to brown without crowding. Brown on high heat, turn when brown on one side, brown the second, and continue until all sides of the meat are completely brown. Remove and set aside. Repeat with the rest of the meat. Reduce the heat, add the onions and garlic to the pan and cook over low heat until soft. Return the meat with its juice to the pan, add the tomatoes with their juice, the stock, chilies, oregano, cumin, and Worcestershire sauce, and bring the liquid to the boil. Reduce heat and simmer, partially covered, for 2 to 3 hours or until the meat is tender. Remove meat and cut into bite-sized pieces. Season with salt and pepper. May be made a day or two ahead or frozen. Reheats well. Serve over rice.

Tip: You only need to flour beef before browning when you want to thicken a stew, or to get color from the flour. In this case it's not necessary.

Tip: The stew meat sold in grocery stores is frequently cut too small to make a nice stew. Meat is better for browning when cut in 2-inch pieces, as it shrinks. You can always retrieve the pieces from the stew and cut them smaller after the stew is finished.

Tip: This recipe doubles easily. I usually double it, freezing half for another time. It reheats well in the microwave as well as on the stove top.

CURRIED BEEF AND VEGETABLE STEW
Serves 6

1/4 cup oil
2 pounds beef chuck or
  round roast, cut in
  2-inch chunks
1 tablespoon curry
  powder
2 garlic cloves, chopped
1-1/4 cups beef stock
1/4 cup vinegar
3 carrots, cut in 2-inch
  pieces
3 stalks celery, cut in
  2-inch pieces
3 potatoes, peeled and
  cut in large chunks
3 onions, chopped
salt
freshly ground pepper

Heat the oil in a Dutch oven to sizzling. Add the beef to the oil and brown on one side without crowding the pan, then turn to brown the next side, continuing until all brown. Do in batches if necessary. Remove meat and set aside. Stir in the curry powder and garlic. Add the stock and vinegar. Bring to the boil, cleaning the pan by stirring sides and bottom to get the goodness. Return the meat, reduce the heat, and simmer 3/4 hour, covered. Add the carrots, celery, potatoes, and onions. Cover and cook until vegetables are cooked but not mushy, about 45 minutes to 1 hour. Skim the fat. Bring back to the boil and boil until slightly thickened. Add salt and pepper to taste. May be made one or two days in advance and reheated.

Variation
Substitute chili powder or creole seasoning for the curry.

Variation
Substitute canned tomatoes and a dash of Worcestershire for the stock.

Variation
Substitute 3 cups red wine for half the stock and all the vinegar.

Variation
Add 1 to 2 tablespoons chopped thyme and marjoram.

Tip: Check the pan to be sure the liquid has not evaporated while cooking the meat. Add more stock, or even water, if it has!

Tip: The meat may be sliced after the stew is done and before reheating.

Tip: Try to make it a day ahead as it gets the kitchen (as well as your hair!) greasy.

BEETS WITH LEMON AND OLIVE OIL

Serves 4 to 6

4 to 6 medium beets,
  trimmed of greens
2 to 3 tablespoons
  butter or olive oil
juice of 1/3 to 1/2
  lemon
salt
freshly ground pepper

Bring a large quantity of water to the boil. Add the beets, reduce heat, and simmer 30 to 45 minutes until done. Drain. Slip off the skin to peel. Quarter the beets. When ready to serve, melt the butter or olive oil in a large pan, add the beets, and toss until heated through. Add lemon juice and season with salt and pepper. May be made a day ahead or earlier in the day.

Variation

Toss 3 tablespoons chopped fresh parsley or thyme in with the cooked beets or 1 slice fresh ginger, chopped.

Variation

Grate or slice the cooked beets.

Variation

Cool, serve grated or sliced, in a vinaigrette with herbs.

Variation

Toss with 3 to 5 tablespoons oriental sesame seed oil, 2 tablespoons ginger, and 2 tablespoons fresh lemon balm or lemon thyme.

Tip: Many people cut off the greens of young beets. Treat them as you would any other green. (See p. 210.)

BUTTER TOFFEE COOKIES

Makes about 4 dozen cookies

3 cups all-purpose flour
1 teaspoon baking soda
1/2 teaspoon salt
1/2 pound butter,
  softened
1 cup sugar
1 cup brown sugar,
  packed
2 eggs
1 teaspoon vanilla
6 (1-1/8 ounces each) bars chocolate-coated English toffee, crushed

Preheat oven to 350°F. Combine the flour, baking soda, and salt; set aside. Beat the butter and sugars until light. Beat in the eggs and vanilla. Stir in the flour mixture just until blended. Add crushed toffee. Drop by level tablespoonfuls onto an ungreased baking sheet. Bake 10 to 12 minutes. Cool on a wire rack.

RAY OVERTON'S OATMEAL SPICE COOKIES

Makes 3-1/2 dozen 2-1/2-inch cookies

1/2 pound (1 cup)
  butter
1 cup brown sugar, packed
3/4 cup sugar
1 egg
1 teaspoon vanilla
1/2 teaspoon almond
  extract
1-1/2 cups all-purpose
  flour
1 teaspoon baking soda
1 teaspoon salt
1 teaspoon cinnamon
1 teaspoon nutmeg
1/2 teaspoon ground
  cloves
1/2 teaspoon ground
  ginger
3 cups quick-rolled oats
1 cup chopped pecans
1 cup raisins

Preheat oven to 375°F. Beat the butter and sugars together until light. Beat in egg and flavorings. Sift together flour, baking soda, salt, cinnamon, nutmeg, cloves and ginger. Add to butter mixture, stirring just until blended. Batter will be stiff. Add oats, pecans, and raisins, stirring thoroughly to mix. Drop by tablespoonfuls onto a lightly greased cookie sheet. Bake 8 to 10 minutes or until edges of cookies are a golden brown. Remove from oven. Let cool 1 minute on the cookie sheet. Then remove cookies to baking rack until completely cool. May be made ahead and kept in an airtight container or frozen.

Variation
Omit pecans and raisins. Add 1 cup dried apple bits and 1 cup chopped walnuts. Proceed as above.

Variation
Omit pecans and raisins. Add 1 tablespoon grated orange zest, 1 cup coconut, and 1 cup slivered almonds. Proceed as above.

Variation
Use chopped dates or prunes in place of raisins.

⚘ 6 ⚘

A CELEBRATION
DINNER FOR EIGHT

NARCS *and the Lamb Well Done*

From the open door came the smell of garlic, herbs, and tomatoes, underlined by the sweet musky smell of lamb. Robert Coram was in the doorway of his home, wooden spoon in hand, ready to celebrate completion of his book, *NARCS* (New American Library), a fast-paced story that is to the drug war what Tom Clancy is to submarines. Robert is married to Jeannine Addams, and it is amazing that the passion and violence of *NARCS* can come from the pen of such a genial host and husband.

I'd been invited to dinner along with Cliff Graubart of the Old New York Book Store (who had read an early galley), a couple of Drug Enforcement Agency agents who had helped with the book, and some other friends.

My role was simple. In the fashion of Atlanta authors, Bob had named some of his characters after his friends. There is usually no resemblance between the character named and the friend whose name has been garnered. When he had told me he was borrowing my last name for the only woman in the book, my only requests were that she be skinny and sexy. (Well, what would *you* ask for if it was *your* name?)

As Robert was slowly stirring his pot of lamb, I was in the living room having my own anxieties. While we ate the hot cheese hors d'oeuvres he had served, I was concerned that the lamb would be too well done.

Going to other people's homes is a mixed blessing for me. I love seeing what they cook, peeking into the intimacies of their kitchens. But I'm terrified that if I don't like the food, my gracious hosts will know. In this case, I was worried because I was sure I wouldn't like well-done lamb, and Robert had been cooking it for hours.

As the evening developed, the DEA agents, who are married to each other, told enough tales to fill another novel. The food wouldn't have mattered. After our salad we peered into the oven at the lamb. Robert had been checking on it frequently, generously pouring more liquid into the pot whenever it seemed dry. I hoped something that smelled that good would taste as good. Finally, he brought the lamb surrounded by potatoes, onions, and carrots to the table. The tomatoes, bay leaves, marjoram, thyme, and rosemary had boiled down and thickened enough to coat the meat he was slicing.

My fears were unfounded! I should have had more faith in my old friend. This braised lamb in tomatoes was moist, tender, and flavorful.

MENU

A CELEBRATION DINNER FOR EIGHT

Cheese Boxes

One Pot Lamb

Wild Rice and Orange Salad

Brussels Sprouts

Corn Bread

Spanish Flan

SERVES 8

LOGISTICS

The cheese boxes may be made ahead. Half of them may be reheated when guests arrive, the rest saved for another time. (A small toaster oven can be used for reheating.) The flan should be made one or two days in advance and refrigerated, covered in its dish. The lamb may be made one or two days in advance and reheated 15 minutes in a heavy pan on top of the stove, 20 minutes in a 350°F oven, or in the microwave. The ingredients for the salad may be prepared earlier in the day and put together just before guests arrive or just before serving. The corn bread may be made a few hours ahead and reheated 5 to 10 minutes in a hot oven, or in the microwave, or it may be started just before guests arrive, if the cook has time to watch it. Invert the flan and turn out of its dish just before serving. The Brussels sprouts may be made earlier in the day and reheated 5 minutes before serving.

ꙅ RECIPES ꙅ

CHEESE BOXES

Makes 5 cups cheese spread or 140 boxes

1/2 pound sharp
    Cheddar cheese,
    grated
3 cups mayonnaise
1 small onion, chopped
2 tablespoons Durkee's
    Famous Sandwich
    and Salad Sauce
    (optional)
2 teaspoons Dijon
    mustard
1 tablespoon
    Worcestershire sauce
salt
freshly ground pepper
2 loaves thin-sliced
    bread

In a food processor or blender, purée the cheese, mayonnaise, onion, optional Durkee's sauce, mustard, and Worcestershire sauce. Season with salt and pepper. Trim the crusts from the bread. Spread 2 slices of the bread with some of the cheese mixture, place one atop the other, then cut into 4 squares. Repeat until the desired number of "2-story boxes" are formed. Ice the sides of the boxes lightly with the cheese mixture. May be made ahead to this point and refrigerated or frozen. Toast at 400°F 5 to 8 minutes, immediately before serving.

Tip: If Durkee's is not available, add 1 teaspoon more Dijon.

ONE POT LAMB

Serves 8 to 10 (makes 6-1/2 quarts)

1 five-pound leg of
   lamb, bone in
12 garlic cloves, peeled
   and cut in slivers
8 onions, peeled and
   quartered
8 carrots, peeled and
   quartered
6 bay leaves, crumpled
3 tablespoons thyme,
   chopped
3 tablespoons marjoram
   or oregano, chopped
2 tablespoons rosemary,
   crushed
5 pounds boiling
   potatoes, peeled and
   cut in 2-inch pieces
2 cans (28 ounces each)
   Italian plum
   tomatoes, chopped,
   reserving juice
1/4 cup lemon juice
salt
freshly ground pepper

Preheat oven to 425°F. Remove the fell (the outer papery-like skin on the leg of lamb) and as much of the fat as possible. Make a number of incisions in the flesh of the lamb. Insert the slivers of garlic. Season with salt and pepper. Spread 1/2 of the onions, 1/2 of the carrots, the bay leaves, and 1/2 of the thyme, marjoram, and rosemary on the bottom of a roaster or large pan. Place the lamb on top and roast in the oven, uncovered, for 1 hour. Remove the pan from the oven and pour in the tomatoes, the lemon juice, and enough water to cover. Place the pan on the stove over low heat, and bring the liquid to the boil. Cover the pan and return it to the oven, then reduce the heat to 350°F. Cook, turning from time to time, adding water if necessary, until the meat is tender enough to fall off the bone, about 2 hours more. May be made ahead several days to this point

One hour before serving, add the remaining onions and carrots, and the potatoes, making sure they are covered with the liquid. Cover and continue cooking until vegetables are nearly done, about 1/2 hour. Remove the lamb from the pan and add the rest of the herbs. Boil down the juices and the vegetables, about 15 minutes, until the sauce is thick enough to serve, like a nice soup. Add salt and pepper to taste.

Meanwhile, slice the lamb. Serve with the vegetables and sauce around the meat in a big bowl. This dish freezes and reheats fine with the lamb sliced.

Variation

The lamb may be simmered on top of the stove in a very heavy casserole 2 hours, rather than returning to the oven to cook.

Continued

Variation

I have used a whole, 12-pound leg of lamb, with 1 pound more potatoes and 8 more carrots, leaving the rest of the ingredients the same—and this fed nearly 20 people.

Variation

Use only 1 can of the tomatoes and add 1 bottle of dry white wine. Omit the water. Add more wine if necessary.

Tip: The cooking pan makes a big difference as to how much wine is needed to cover the meat.

Tip: This dish is even better made a day ahead.

> **Comment:** Legs of lamb vary incredibly in size. The average Australian leg is 4 to 6 pounds. The average New Zealand leg is 5 to 7 pounds. The average American leg is 10 to 12 pounds. You may have to use half an American leg of lamb for this recipe. Cook it the same amount of time.

WILD RICE AND ORANGE SALAD

Serves 8 to 10

1-1/2 cups wild rice
4 cups boiling water
1/2 pound fresh
   spinach, washed and
   stemmed
3 green onions or
   scallions, sliced with
   green tops
1 small red onion, thinly
   sliced
4 oranges, peeled and
   sectioned, with their
   juice
1 double recipe
   Vinaigrette, page 140
salt
freshly ground pepper

To prepare the wild rice, place it in a sieve and wash under cold running water for 2 minutes. In a heavy saucepan bring 4 cups of water to the boil. Add the rice. Cover, place over low heat, and simmer until the rice is cracked and puffy, about 50 to 55 minutes. Drain the rice and chill. To make a chiffonade garnish, place 4 to 5 spinach leaves on top of each other, roll up cigar-style, and slice thinly. Repeat with 4 to 5 more leaves and set aside.

Marinate the rest of the spinach leaves in a bowl with the orange juice. Place the chilled rice in a bowl. Add the sliced green onions, red onion, orange sections, and vinaigrette, and toss gently. Taste for seasoning and add salt and pepper as necessary. Refrigerate until ready to serve.

To serve, place the marinated spinach leaves on a salad plate, top with the wild rice mixture, and sprinkle with a few strands of the spinach chiffonade.

Tip: Making a chiffonade with its curly strands is a surefire way to get everyone to consume a bed of greens.

Tip: Ingredients can be prepared earlier in the day and put together just before the guests arrive.

Tip: 6 ounces of wild rice = 1 cup uncooked wild rice and makes 3-1/2 to 4 cups cooked.

Tip: Cooked wild rice refrigerates, covered, for up to ten days, and freezes very well. If using in a recipe that calls for it to be reheated, add a little hot water and reheat in a heavy saucepan or in the microwave.

BRUSSELS SPROUTS

Serves 8

2 pounds Brussels sprouts, stalk removed, trimmed
2 to 4 tablespoons butter
salt
freshly ground pepper

Cut a small cross in the root (bottom) of each sprout and trim off any damaged or tough outer leaves. Bring a large quantity of water to the boil, add the sprouts, and boil 5 to 7 minutes. Drain and rinse under cold water. Set aside until serving time. When ready to serve, melt the butter in a frying pan, add the sprouts, and season with salt and pepper. Toss quickly over high heat until coated with butter and heated through.

Variation
Add cooked chestnuts or water chestnuts, pecan or walnut halves to the butter prior to reheating sprouts.

Variation
Toss with 1 pound sliced or quartered mushrooms that have been sautéed in some of the butter.

Variation for two
1/2 pound Brussels sprouts, 1 to 2 tablespoons butter, salt, freshly ground pepper.

Tip: The cross in the root of the vegetable allows the stem to be cooked without overcooking the leaves.

Variation
Coat in a garlic cream sauce.

CORN BREAD

Serves 8 (makes 1 skillet of corn bread)

1 cup cornmeal
1/2 teaspoon salt
1/2 teaspoon baking
  soda
1 cup milk or buttermilk
1 egg
2 teaspoons oil or
  shortening

Preheat oven to 450°F. In a medium bowl, whisk together the cornmeal, salt, and baking soda. In another bowl, whisk together the milk or buttermilk and egg. Add the milk mixture to the cornmeal and whisk until combined.

Heat the oil in an 8-inch skillet by placing it in the oven for 5 minutes. Pour the batter evenly into the hot pan. Bake 25 to 30 minutes until set. Let cool briefly. Invert the pan onto a wire rack. Serve warm or at room temperature.

Tip: Cornmeal mix may be substituted for the cornmeal, salt, and soda.

Tip: Heating the skillet before pouring in the batter keeps the corn bread from sticking and gives it a nice crust.

Variations

Try snappy corn bread by adding 1 to 2 tablespoons of finely chopped rosemary and 1 tablespoon chopped red pepper to the buttermilk. What a difference! Substitute olive oil for the oil or shortening. For a lighter corn bread, add 1/2 cup self-rising flour to 1 cup of cornmeal.

Tip: May be made ahead a few hours, and reheated or even frozen, but it is best freshly made.

SPANISH FLAN

Serves 8 to 10

1 cup sugar
1/4 cup water
2-2/3 cups milk
1 strip lemon peel
8 eggs
1/2 cup sugar
2-1/2 teaspoons vanilla

Preheat oven to 325°F. Melt the sugar in the water in a small heavy pan over low heat, brushing the sides of the pan with a wet brush. Don't boil. When dissolved, turn up heat, and boil until the liquid turns golden caramel. Meanwhile warm a 1-quart ovenproof soufflé dish in the oven. Remove and pour the caramel into the soufflé dish, using oven mitts to hold the hot dish, turning to coat the bottom and lower sides of the soufflé dish with the caramel. Add the milk to the original caramel pan with the lemon peel and heat until small bubbles form around the side. Mix together the eggs and sugar. Pour the milk into the egg mixture, stirring constantly. Strain. Add the vanilla. Pour, carefully, so it doesn't foam into the prepared soufflé dish.

Place a kitchen towel in the bottom of a roasting pan with sides. Put the soufflé dish on the towel in the middle of the pan. Carefully pour enough boiling water into the pan to come halfway up the sides of the soufflé dish. Place the pan in the center of the oven and cook approximately 1 to 1-1/2 hours or until custard is set. Do not let the water boil, as the boiling will overcook the custard and make holes in it: if necessary, add cold water to the pan. Remove the pan from the oven; remove the soufflé dish from the pan. Cool slightly. Cover and refrigerate.

When dish has chilled completely, run a knife around edge, then shake the dish or pull the custard lightly away from the sides with your knife. Place a shallow serving plate on top, then invert the dish so that the custard unmolds. The caramel will form a topping and sauce. Serve chilled.

Tip: This is a stiff flan. If a looser one is desired, try 3 whole eggs and 5 egg yolks.

Tip: If the custard clings to the dish and will not unmold, let sit at room temperature for a few minutes until the caramel softens.

⊀ 7 ⊁

MENU FOR TWO

Love Bloomed

She always wondered if they would have fallen in love if she hadn't brought the cold soup. It had been an unusually hot day when she was leaving the house, and it had come to her that he would like the soup. The sun beat down on the flat roof above his office in the sleepy Georgia town. It would be cool and soothing for him, in contrast to the energy that radiated from him.

So she packed the soup in a plastic container and put it inside a nondescript paper bag. An afterthought, really. She figured he wouldn't have eaten lunch. Even if he had, what would it matter, it was only a bowl of soup.

It changed her life, that bowl of soup. She had served it the night before and it had been good. As she climbed the dusty staircase, the container opened a crack, and a few drops fell out on her red sundress. She flicked them off with her hand, smudging the file folder she was bringing him to review.

He never commented about the spots on the file or on her dress when he recalled that day. She remembered how hot she had been, her shoulders nearly glistening, the cotton dress clinging to her back. She had opened her slightly soiled sack on his desk, first covering the desk with a paper towel from the tiny bathroom near his office. From his office window she could see the town's main street—a dog walking across the road, her own car with the windows rolled down (she wished the car had been air-conditioned). She could hear music from the offices below.

56

She hadn't known she would remember it forever, the way he looked at her—as if she was beautiful—when she opened the sack. She smiled at him, telling him she had something for him. He held the plastic bowl as though it were crystal, cupping it with his hands and drawing it to his lips. If she had known she was going to fall in love with him that moment, she would have brought him a spoon.

"See what she brought me," he exalted to his coworker, "a bowl of cold soup!" The other man didn't know the soup was mystical. "Ah, yes," he replied, "I've had it before. I liked it." He gave a small nod, and a tiny smile, wondering at the tension before him over a bowl of soup in the middle of the day. "Like it?" her new love protested, "like it? It's marvelous! I've never had anything as marvelous before. This is remarkable!"

A small, hard, untrusting part of her, deep inside, was touched, and opened to him. After he ate the soup, they worked together, she on one side of his desk, he on the other. The sun filtered through to her work in a golden beam, moving around the room as they worked. He taught her so much that the small, hard part of her soul became plump and tender, like a raisin soaked in wine. Without a touch or a word of love, they had each given the other a new world. She never made the soup again without thinking of him.

Later in the summer she served him a meal she thought he would love—including the soup.

᧒ M E N U ᧒

MENU FOR TWO

Cold Curried Tomato Soup
Baby Crown Roast of Lamb with Coriander
New Potatoes with Summer Savory
Snow Peas
Glazed Carrots
Refrigerator Rolls (variation of Food Processor Rolls, p. 280)
Truffle Filled Pastries
Small Pound Cake with Poached Figs or Berries

LOGISTICS

To adapt the recipes to only 2 servings, see variations on the bottom of each recipe. The pound cake, truffles, rolls, soup, and figs may be made several days in advance (or the rolls and pound cake may be frozen). Alternately, the dough for the rolls may be made in advance and the rolls baked earlier in the day. The crown roast may be prebaked a day in advance, reheating it for 15 minutes at 450°F, or if cooking it entirely, place it in the oven about 1/2 hour before serving the soup. The potatoes should be reheated in the butter. The vegetables may be cooked early in the day and reheated, or cooked at the last minute. Preheat oven and reheat rolls for 15 minutes. Slice and serve the cake with figs or berries and, if desired, yogurt, whipped cream, or sour cream.

Any remaining soup will last up to three days.

ᏩR E C I P E S ℚ

COLD CURRIED TOMATO SOUP
Serves 4

1 cup plain yogurt
2 cups tomato juice
3 tablespoons onion, finely chopped
1 tablespoon fresh lemon juice
1 tablespoon red wine vinegar
1/8 teaspoon hot sauce
1-1/2 to 2 tablespoons curry powder
salt
freshly ground pepper
1/4 cup fresh chives, finely chopped

Whisk together the yogurt, tomato juice, onion, lemon juice, vinegar, hot sauce, and curry powder and mix well. Refrigerate until well chilled. Taste and add salt and pepper as necessary. To serve, pour into a serving dish and sprinkle with chives. May be kept 3 to 4 days, covered in refrigerator.

Variation
Add 1 cup finely chopped cooked shrimp or crabmeat.

Variation

Doubles easily to serve 8. *For two:* Use whole recipe and save the rest for another day, or mix 1/2 cup plain yogurt, 1 cup tomato juice, 1-1/2 tablespoons chopped onion, 1-1/2 teaspoons lemon juice, 1-1/2 teaspoons red wine vinegar, a dash of hot sauce, and 1 to 2 teaspoons chives.

BABY CROWN ROAST OF LAMB WITH CORIANDER

Serves 2

1 (3-pound) rack of
   lamb, trimmed, fat
   and fell removed
2 garlic cloves, crushed
2 tablespoons coriander
   seeds, crushed
1/2 cup white wine,
   mixed with 1
   tablespoon water

Sauce

2 tablespoons red
   currant jelly
2 tablespoons Dijon
   mustard
2 tablespoons Madeira,
   dry sherry, or lemon
   juice

Allow 1 to 1-1/2 pounds per person.

The bones of the rack need to be "frenched" in order to provide the spokes of the crown. To do this, start at the end of the bone farthest from the backbone and cut out the web of fat, flesh, and skin between each rib, ending above the fleshy part of the meat. Mix together the garlic and coriander seeds and rub over the meat. Turn the rack into a circle, or crown, with the scraped bones curved outward. Join the ends by sewing the flesh together with a trussing needle. Place a tight ball of aluminum foil in the center to keep the meat from shrinking.

Preheat oven to 350°F. Place the crown in a shallow roasting pan, surrounded by wine and water, and cook about 40 minutes until 140°F when tested with an instant meat thermometer for medium rare, or less for rare. Remove foil and let roast rest while preparing the sauce.

To make the sauce, remove any excess fat from the pan. Add about 1-1/2 tablespoons each of the red currant jelly, mustard, and wine or juice. Bring to the boil. Taste, then add more of whatever ingredient is needed, according to your taste. Pour the sauce onto a warm serving platter, place lamb on top with string removed, and arrange the vegetables in the center.

Tip: When purchasing, try to have the butcher remove the backbone, or cut with his saw slightly between each of the vertebrae. If the butcher has not done so, cut between each vertebrae slightly, using a cleaver and hammer.

Tip: Trim only the *excess* fat. Don't take all of it off, because the fat keeps it moist while roasting. Many of us consider lamb-fat delicious, besides!

Variation

Although you won't have the spectacular presentation, you may roast a rack of lamb without turning it into a crown for this dish.

> *Comment:* A crown roast is traditionally made from 2 racks of lamb, joined together. This single crown is a pretty dish for two and only requires 1 rack of lamb.

NEW POTATOES WITH SUMMER SAVORY

Serves 2 to 4

1 pound new potatoes, scraped
2 to 4 tablespoons butter
3 tablespoons summer savory, chopped (optional)
freshly ground pepper (optional)

Bring a large quantity of water to the boil, add the scrubbed potatoes, and bring back to the boil. Boil 15 to 20 minutes or until tender. Drain, return the potatoes to the pan with the butter over low heat for a minute, rolling them, to dry off and coat with butter. Add the summer savory and pepper and shake the pan to coat the potatoes with herbs and butter. Serve right away.

Tip: The best way to serve new potatoes straight from the garden is to cook them as described above and serve them right away; however, if you bought potatoes from the store, there is no reason why you can't boil them ahead, place them in the pan with the butter off the heat, and set aside. When ready to eat, place the pan over the heat and reheat the potatoes as you heat the butter. They rarely need salt.

Variation

I treat new potatoes like a green vegetable, plunging them into boiling water. Larger, more starchy potatoes do better going into cold water, peeled, and coming to the boil. They take a bit longer.

Variation

Place cooked, peeled potatoes in a pan with 4 tablespoons butter and 1/8 cup sugar. Heat the potatoes in the butter until brown.

Variation
Undercook the potatoes slightly, then put the drained potatoes into a skillet of hot bacon or sausage drippings. Brown until crusty and serve. Good with a mixed grill.

Variation
Substitute parsley, marjoram, thyme, or another chopped fresh herb.

Tip: 10 to 12 new (2 to 3-inch) potatoes make a pound.

> *Comment:* If you have never grown your own potatoes, you cannot imagine the difference between a freshly dug potato and one that has been stored. That's what I mean by a new potato. They don't need or want peeling, just scrub them and cook them. My favorites are marble-sized, but I enjoy them up to 2 or even 3 inches. You may trim down larger peeled potatoes to new potato size if you want the look, when new potatoes are out of season.

SNOW PEAS
Serves 4 to 6

1-1/2 pounds snow peas
4 to 6 tablespoons
   butter or oil
1 to 2 tablespoons
   ginger, freshly
   chopped
salt
freshly ground pepper

Defrost peas if frozen. Tip and string the fresh peas if necessary. Heat the butter or oil in a pan and add the peas and ginger. Sauté until done—no more than several minutes. Season with salt and freshly ground pepper to taste.

> *Comment:* Fresh or frozen, these add crunch, color, and zip to a meal. (You eat the whole thing.)

Variation
Stir-fry with shrimp.

Variation
Add to sautéed mushrooms.

Variation for two
1/2 pound snow peas, 1 to 2 tablespoons butter or oil, dash of ginger, salt and pepper to taste.

GLAZED CARROTS

Serves 6 to 8

2 pounds carrots, peeled
4 tablespoons butter
1 to 2 teaspoons sugar

Peel and slice large carrots. Scrub baby ones. Place in a heavy saucepan and add water to cover. Bring to the boil, reduce heat, cover, and simmer until nearly tender. Remove cover, stir in the butter and sugar, bring back to the boil, and boil steadily until glazed, being careful not to burn.

Variation
Add 2 tablespoons chopped fresh ginger, chopped parsley, chopped chervil, or chopped cilantro as a garnish.

Variation for two
1/2 pound carrots, 1 to 2 tablespoons butter, dash of sugar.

TRUFFLE FILLED PASTRIES

Makes 20

1/2 cup butter
1/4 cup confectioners'
  sugar
1/4 teaspoon vanilla
1 cup all-purpose flour,
  sifted
4 ounces skinned
  hazelnuts, almonds,
  or pecans, finely
  ground
4 ounces semisweet
  chocolate, finely
  chopped
1 egg white
Garnish:
cocoa or ground
  chocolate

Using a food processor or an electric mixer, beat the butter with the sugar until smooth. Add the vanilla. Mix in the flour, then remove the dough and divide into 20 pieces. Wrap and chill.

Preheat oven to 350°F. Mix together the nuts, chocolate, and egg white. Using a rounded tablespoon, roll the mixture into 20 balls. Flatten and press each of the chilled pastry pieces completely around a ball of filling, rolling it in your palms to get the pastry evenly around the ball. Place the pastry balls on an ungreased baking sheet 1 inch apart. Chill briefly.

Bake 15 to 20 minutes in middle of preheated oven until very light brown. Cool briefly, until you can handle pastry without having it crumble, then move to a wire rack to cool, or serve right away. May be served hot or cold. They freeze well. Reheat on a baking sheet in a 350°F oven for a few minutes until warm to the touch. Dust with sieved chocolate or cocoa just before serving.

Tip: To skin hazelnuts, spread them on a tray and place them in a 400°F oven. Roast until the skin is brown and will slip off from the nut. Place a handful of nuts on a tea towel or good quality paper towel and rub to remove the skin.

SMALL POUND CAKE WITH POACHED FIGS OR BERRIES
Makes 1 small cake

6 tablespoons butter
3/4 cup sugar
2 large eggs
1 cup flour
1/4 teaspoon baking
   soda
1/2 teaspoon vanilla
1/2 teaspoon lemon
   flavoring
Garnish:
1 cup cream, whipped,
   or yogurt, drained
1 cup berries
   (blueberries,
   blackberries, or
   raspberries)
   or Poached Figs
   (p. 64)

Preheat oven to 350°F. Beat the butter and the sugar until light. Add the eggs, one by one, beating until incorporated. Mix together the flour and baking soda and blend in; then add the vanilla and lemon flavorings, beating well. Grease and flour a $7\text{-}1/2 \times 3\text{-}3/4 \times 2\text{-}1/4$-inch pan. Cut a piece of wax paper to fit bottom of pan, place in pan, and grease and flour the wax paper. Spread the batter into the pan. Bake on middle rack of oven for 45 minutes. Let the pan cool on a wire rack for 10 minutes. Use a knife to loosen the cake around the edges, turn out, and remove paper. Slice and place on pretty plates. Garnish with fruit and serve with cream or yogurt. Freezes well.

Variation
This is wonderful sliced and toasted.

Variation
Doubles easily for a larger pan.

Tip: To beat, use the beater attachment of a large mixer or beat by hand. The whisk attachment creates too much air. Do not overbeat.

POACHED FIGS WITH ORANGE AND GINGER

Serves 2

4 dried figs
1/2 cup orange juice
1/2 cup water
1 slice fresh ginger root,
    the size of a quarter

Rinse and drain figs. Combine the orange juice and water in a small saucepan. Add the figs and ginger root, bring to a boil, reduce heat, cover, and simmer for 30 minutes. When figs are plump, remove from the pan and slice into quarters. Bring to a boil and reduce the liquid in pan by half. Strain liquid to remove orange pulp and ginger root. Put the quartered figs back into the fig syrup. Serve warm, at room temperature, or chilled, in the syrup by themselves, or with pound cake and sour cream.

Variation
Use a cinnamon stick in place of ginger. Proceed as above.

Variation
Add 1 teaspoon dry sherry to chilled syrup. Refrigerate overnight.

Tip: Poached figs will keep very well chilled in their syrup in the refrigerator ready for a quick breakfast or afternoon snack.

Tip: For every four figs increase basic recipe by 1/4 cup juice and 1/4 cup water. (The ginger root does not need to be increased.)

≯ 8 ≮

FOOD FOR A REMEMBRANCE OF LIFE

Food for Funerals

Only recently have I experienced empty places at the tables of my life. I find that when I eat certain foods that remind me acutely of someone I cared for, that person is with me again, and death's power is diluted. Food is such an integral part of friendship that when death occurs, there is a longing to use food as a final present, something to bond the living to those gone.

My friend Bert Greene left without saying good-by to many of his friends. A giant of a man, he was vain only about his looks, and he hadn't wanted many of us to come to the hospital to see him, unshaven. In August, the "Thanksgiving friends" (those friends who were always invited as family at Thanksgiving even if they couldn't attend), gathered once again at Bert's Long Island home. Phillip Schultz, his longtime companion, hosted a small garden party there, to celebrate Bert's life.

The brisket was still warm when I arrived late the night before. Phillip had marinated and smoked it that day for many a long, slow, lonely hour. I sliced off a bit of the tender, flavorful piece of meat, eating it out of hand, standing over the burnished wood kitchen table. My goodness, it was wonderful. Phillip snitched it away,

65

exclaiming it needed Dinah's sauce. How could it be any better, I wondered? Besides, the brisket was for tomorrow's lunch, and Dinah is one of the cats!

Early the next morning, Phillip was up, making the sauce. Dinah is mostly fur surrounding a tiny frame that is more Jell-O than bones. She's not overly affectionate, but wants a great deal of attention, which is manifested in her indecision. You know the kind, always hanging at the door wanting out when she's in and in when she's out. Once, because of this distraction, some onions had burned. Phillip went ahead and made the sauce anyway, and the result was marvelous, thanks to Dinah's diversions. Hence the name, whenever nearly burned onions are used by me in a sauce.

We ate all day, people arriving at different hours, some going to the beach for a while, some sitting around and talking, some playing croquet, all the while tasting the foods brought in cars or, like Elizabeth Schneider's cake, on the bus from the city. Arthur Schwartz made a punch full of boozy fruit, Rose Beranbaum brought Bert's sponge cake from her new book, *The Cake Bible*. I lost, badly, at croquet, grilling the chicken in between swats of the mallet. And so the long day went.

When we were all assembled, the heat was cooling down in the back of the garden where a hole had been dug. Bert's ashes were mixed together with his sister Myra's, who had passed on a year earlier. Together again, they were planted under a star magnolia. Arthur read from a borrowed Jewish prayer book. Sue Huffman read from the Bible, still others spoke from their hearts. Some just sat on the grass, choked up with their grief, and cried.

After we had said good-by in our own ways, we filled up our plates and sat in a circle outside near the kitchen and talked about Bert, how we met him, what he meant to us—long stories that made us laugh, others that exemplified how he gave to friends and fans when the temptation was to be churlish. We remembered the good he enabled us to pass on, his enthusiasm for life. When the late summer sun went down over the star magnolia, we parted. I ate the last of the brisket before I went to sleep, full of gratitude that Bert goes on, as he did before I met him, in his books, his recipes, and in the laughter of his friends.

ᎶMENU℘

FOOD FOR A REMEMBRANCE OF LIFE

Onion and Herb Focaccia

Phillip Schultz's Fancy Country Fair Smoked Brisket

Dinah's Sweet Barbecue Sauce

Tart Barbecue Sauce

Make-Ahead Green Beans

Sautéed Mushrooms

Orange, Spinach, Avocado, and Jerusalem Artichoke Salad

Bert Greene's Skyscraper Sponge Cake

SERVES 6

LOGISTICS

One friend says she thinks of her mother's death whenever she sees a ham. Several days after the funeral, a few of the family were still there, sorting out affairs. A cousin went in to get a snack from the refrigerator, and came out to where everyone was sitting, blurting out, "There are more hams than people." Rather than ham, then, a nice roasted rare beef tenderloin or brisket is a welcome change. It is helpful when some food that has been brought can be frozen—there may be an abundance of food the day of the funeral, but out-of-town family and friends may need to be there for several days, and it is a blessed relief to have something to pull out of the freezer.

If food is taken on a platter or dish that needs to be returned, the appropriate name, address, and telephone number should be taped on the bottom, able to be read even after it goes through the dishwasher. Disposable dishes and platters sound like a better idea, but when remembering a deceased friend's love of china and crystal, sometimes it seems a defamation to put something on the table that would jar his or her sensibilities. Consider buying garage-sale platters and plates and using them to place your portable meals on upon arrival. (Never pack portable food on ceramic, glass, or china until arrival.)

Nearly all of this menu may be made in advance. The onion and herb focaccia may be made earlier that day, or several days in advance, and frozen. Reheat 10 minutes in a hot oven or serve at room temperature. The brisket may be made one or two days in advance, wrapped well, and either served at room temperature or reheated in foil with barbecue sauce at 350°F for 10 to 15 minutes, with the additional sauce served in side dishes. The vegetables may be made the night before or several hours in advance, and reheated in a large frying pan 5 to 10 minutes before serving. The salad ingredients, washed and sliced, may be placed in plastic bags several hours in advance, or if a large platter can be refrigerated, all of the salad may be assembled, with the exception of the vinaigrette and the avocado, which should be prepared at serving time.

The skyscraper sponge cake may be done in advance, kept fresh or frozen. (There are two other versions of this dessert—one in Bert Greene's *Honest American Fare* and one in Rose Beranbaum's *The Cake Bible*.)

ᓂ R E C I P E S ᓂ

ONION AND HERB FOCACCIA

Makes 1 large bread or 2 small breads

3-1/2 cups bread flour
3/4 teaspoon salt
1 package dry active yeast
1 cup water, at 115°F
1 tablespoon sugar
5 tablespoons olive oil

Preheat oven to 400°F. Combine 2 cups of the flour and the salt in a mixing bowl or food processor. Add the yeast to the water along with the sugar and dissolve. Add the olive oil. Pour the liquid mixture into the dry ingredients. Knead in enough additional flour to make a soft dough. Continue to knead until elastic and smooth.

Divide the dough in half, and roll each half to 1/8 inch thick, making a 10-inch-diameter circle or a square. Spread some olive oil on 2 baking sheets. Place the dough on the baking sheets; prick the surface evenly with a fork. Press small indents into the surface of the dough with your finger or the end of a wooden spoon. Meanwhile, to prepare the

Topping

1/2 cup olive oil
4 onions, sliced
3 garlic cloves, chopped
1/4 cup red wine
   vinegar
1 to 2 tablespoons
   rosemary, crumbled
1/2 cup imported
   Parmesan cheese,
   grated
1 teaspoon coarse salt
Garnish:
fresh rosemary sprigs

topping, heat the olive oil, then add the onions and garlic, and cook until soft. Remove from heat, and add the vinegar, rosemary, Parmesan, and salt to taste. Spread the mixture over the dough. Place in the oven and bake for 20 minutes or until golden brown. Move to a rack to cool briefly. Cut into squares or wedges. Serve warm. You may freeze and later reheat for 10 minutes in a hot oven or serve at room temperature.

Tip: The dough shouldn't rise for this recipe. If it does, however, it will simply result in a product more like a pizza than a crisp flat bread.

PHILLIP SCHULTZ'S FANCY COUNTRY FAIR SMOKED BRISKET

Serves 4 to 6

1 (4-pound) untrimmed
   beef brisket
1 cup red wine vinegar
1 cup water
1 onion, sliced
2 garlic cloves, chopped
1/2 cup parsley,
   chopped
2 bay leaves, crumbled
1 teaspoon fresh or
   dried thyme,
   chopped
2 teaspoons fresh or
   dried rosemary,
   chopped
2 teaspoons fresh or
   dried basil, chopped
1 tablespoon brown sugar
1 recipe Dinah's Sweet Barbecue Sauce (p. 70)

Place the brisket in an enamel-lined or nonaluminum pan. To make the marinade, combine the vinegar, water, onion, garlic cloves, parsley, bay leaves, thyme, rosemary, basil, and brown sugar in a bowl. Pour the marinade over the brisket and marinate it in the refrigerator up to 2 days, turning occasionally. Remove 2 hours before cooking.

Preheat a water smoker, or a charcoal or gas grill for indirect cooking. Put the water pan in place and add the marinade from the meat. Add water to fill the pan. Place the brisket on the highest food grid. Cover and smoker-cook, keeping the temperature between 190° and 250°F, until the meat is tender enough to cut with a fork, about 6 to 7 hours. Add more preheated coals to the fire

Continued

pan and more liquid to the water pan as required. Serve sliced on the bias or "pulled" (shredded) with barbecue sauce. May be made one or two days in advance, wrapped well and served at room temperature, or reheated in foil with sauce.

Variation

Move uncovered meat and marinade in pan to rack. Cover with foil and cook over indirect heat 5 hours, replenishing coals as needed. Open foil at one end to allow smoke to permeate and cook 1 to 2 hours more, until tender.

Variation

Place with the marinade in the oven. Cover tightly with foil. Bake at 250°F for 5 hours, then move in the pan to a hot charcoal grill and cook over indirect heat 1 to 2 more hours until tender.

Tip: To prepare gas or charcoal grill or kettle for indirect cooking: position the charcoal rack as far as possible to the outer edge of the lower grill, leaving a large area in the center for a drip pan. Place an equal number of briquettes on left and right sides of lower grill—*see your grill guide*—but usually 30 briquettes for the first hour, with 9 more to be added to each side every hour. Light charcoal. Leave cover off until coals have light coat of gray ash. Place drip pan in center of lower grill. Place meat on cooking grill directly above or in a roast holder inside the drip pan and centered on cooking grill. Cover. Proceed as with smoker.

Tip: A drip pan should be larger than the meat so all of the drippings from the meat will be collected in the pan.

DINAH'S SWEET BARBECUE SAUCE

Makes 4 cups

2 tablespoons butter
2 medium onions, sliced
5 garlic cloves, chopped
2 cups chili sauce
1/2 cup dark corn syrup
1 chicken bouillon
   cube, crumbled
1/2 cup red wine
   vinegar

Melt the butter in a heavy skillet, add the onions and garlic, and cook about 10 minutes, or until the onions are a burnished brown. Transfer to a food processor or blender. Process until smooth. Put the purée in a medium saucepan. Stir in the chili sauce, corn syrup, bouillon, vinegar, soy sauce, lemon juice, and Worcestershire. Add herbs and pepper to taste. Bring to the boil, stirring, then reduce

4 tablespoons soy sauce
juice of 2 lemons
1/4 cup Worcestershire
   sauce
3 tablespoons fresh
   herbs
freshly ground pepper

heat. Simmer uncovered for 30 minutes.
Doubles easily. Freezes well.

Variation
For a chunkier sauce, do not process onion/garlic mixture.

TART BARBECUE SAUCE
Makes 6 cups

4 to 6 tablespoons
   Garlic Pepper Oil
   (see tip below)
1 to 2 slices ginger,
   chopped, to make 2
   tablespoons
2 onions, chopped
4 tablespoons chili
   powder
4 garlic cloves, chopped
2 (12-ounce) cans beer*
1 cup tomato juice
1/2 cup Worcestershire
   sauce
juice of 1 lemon or lime
3 tablespoons paprika
5 tablespoons Dijon
   mustard
2 tablespoons chopped
   basil, thyme, or
   parsley
salt
freshly ground pepper

Heat the garlic pepper oil in a saucepan, add the ginger, onions, chili powder, and garlic, and cook until soft. Add the beer, tomato juice, Worcestershire sauce, lemon juice, paprika, mustard, and herbs. Bring to the boil and then simmer briefly. Season to taste with salt and pepper. Will keep several days in the refrigerator.

Tip: Use the recipe for Garlic Pepper Oil (p. 6) or buy chili oil at Mexican or Indian shops.

*Nonalcoholic beer works fine in this recipe.

MAKE-AHEAD GREEN BEANS
Serves 4 to 6

2 pounds green beans,
    tipped and tailed
4 tablespoons butter
salt
freshly ground pepper

Drop the beans into a pot full of boiling water, and after it returns to the boil, cook 5 to 7 minutes until the beans are no longer raw but still crisp. Drain and run under cold water to refresh and set the color. Set aside. The beans may be made ahead a day and refrigerated, or frozen at this point for defrosting and reheating later. When ready to serve, heat the butter to sizzling in a large frying pan. Add the beans and toss until heated through. Season with salt and pepper to taste.

Variation
Quarter 1 pound of button mushrooms or slice large mushrooms. Melt 4 tablespoons butter in a frying pan and sauté the mushrooms along with 3 or 4 chopped shallots or scallions, if you like, for 1 to 2 minutes. Add the green beans to the mushrooms and reheat. A few tablespoons of fresh chopped herbs, such as savory, if available, will finish off the dish nicely.

Variation
Sauté 1 small chopped onion and 1/2 chopped large green pepper in olive oil and lime juice until soft. Add the beans and toss over heat.

Variation
Top with room temperature Pico de Gallo (p. 83) or warm Tomato Sauce (p. 284).

Variation
Top with about 1/2 cup slivered or sliced almonds or pecan halves, tossed in butter until toasted.

Comment: There are many varieties of green beans, from the small French green beans to the large pole beans of the South. Styles of cooking vary radically too. The French like to cook their beans only a short time and American Southerners are partial to long cooking. My favorite string beans are "half-runners," about the size of my little finger. They need little, if any, stringing, and I snap or cut off the ends, which my mother always called "tipping and tailing." I normally pre-cook a large quantity at a time, freezing what I don't need for use later.

Comment: How much to make is dependent on how many other dishes you are serving. Since this recipe reheats well and freezes well, you may wish to double the recipe in any case.

SAUTÉED MUSHROOMS
Serves 4 to 6

1 pound button,
   shiitake, or
   chanterelle
   mushrooms, cleaned
5 tablespoons butter
juice of 1 lemon
   (optional)
cayenne pepper
   (optional)

Slice the mushrooms if large or quarter if small. Heat the butter in a skillet, add the mushrooms, and sauté gently until tender. If desired, stir in lemon juice and cayenne pepper, and boil briefly. May be made a day in advance, refrigerated, and reheated in a frying pan, but may turn browner. They freeze satisfactorily, but become watery and browner.

Variation
Add 2 chopped garlic cloves to the butter.

Variation
Add 1 chopped onion to the butter. Cook over low heat 5 minutes before adding the mushrooms.

Variation
Add 4 tablespoons chopped fresh thyme or marjoram.

Variation
Add 2 tablespoons chopped ginger.

Tip: To clean mushrooms, brush with a special mushroom brush or a small clean nail brush; wipe with a wet paper towel dipped in salt, or place in a plastic bag (that seals tightly!), add 2 tablespoons flour, fill with water, shake madly. Pour into a colander and dry. Never soak mushrooms to clean them. They are a sponge and will absorb the water!

Tip: Sautéed mushrooms will keep in the refrigerator for a couple of days.

ORANGE, SPINACH, AVOCADO, AND JERUSALEM ARTICHOKE SALAD

Serves 6 to 8

1 pound flat spinach
    leaves, stems removed
1 small red onion, sliced
1/6 (1 wedge) red
    cabbage, sliced
3 ounces Jerusalem
    artichokes, peeled
    and grated or
    julienned
5 small seedless oranges,
    peeled and sliced
1 large avocado, firm
    but ripe, peeled, split
    vertically, and pitted
2 teaspoons lemon juice
1 double recipe
    Vinaigrette (p. 140)

Wash the spinach leaves and dry. Line a large salad or glass bowl with the leaves. Tear the remaining leaves into bite-sized pieces and place on top. Arrange the onion, cabbage, and Jerusalem artichokes on top of the spinach leaves. Top with oranges. The salad may be made ahead to this point. When ready to serve, slice the avocado, sprinkle with lemon juice, and arrange over the top. Drizzle vinaigrette over the salad.

Tip: There are now many varieties of spinach on the market. The two I see most frequently are quite different. One is curly and thick, the other flat. Since you want the spinach to lay flat in this recipe, use the flat kind.

Tip: Jerusalem artichokes are a root vegetable that may be eaten raw or cooked. Raw, they have a texture similar to water chestnuts. Cooked they have a texture similar to potatoes with a flavor reminiscent of globe artichokes.

Tip: If possible choose the less knobby artichokes. Peel the artichokes with a knife or peeler, working around the knobs.

Tip: 3 ounces peeled Jerusalem artichokes amounts to one very large one or six small ones.

BERT GREENE'S SKYSCRAPER SPONGE CAKE

Makes one 10-inch tube pan

5 large eggs, divided
1-1/4 cups granulated
   sugar plus 2
   tablespoons
peel of 1 lemon, finely
   grated
1-1/2 teaspoons vanilla
1 cup cake flour or all-
   purpose soft wheat
   flour, sifted
2 tablespoons orange
   juice
4 additional egg whites
To decorate:
1 package mini-
   chocolate chips
   (optional)

Preheat oven to 350°F. Place an un-greased tube pan in the middle of the pre-heated oven for five minutes. (If the sides or bottom of the pan are greased or non–stick, the cake will slide out and collapse when in-verted.) Beat the egg yolks in a *bain marie* of hot water, gradually adding the 1-1/4 cups of sugar to the yolks. Add the lemon peel and vanilla, and continue to beat over the water until the mixture doubles in volume.

Fold the cake flour and orange juice into the beaten egg mixture. Beat the egg whites until stiff; fold a portion into the batter to lighten. Fold the lightened batter back into the whites until just mixed. Pour the batter into the hot pan (to about half full). Sprinkle the remaining 2 tablespoons of sugar over the top and bake about 35 to 40 minutes until golden and firm to the touch.

Invert pan and let cool 1 hour. When cool, run a sharp knife or spatula around the edges of the cake to unmold before turning out onto a plate. Keeps 3 days at room temperature, nearly a week refrigerated. Freezes well. Serve at room temperature.

Place 1 package mini-chocolate chips in a good quality zip-close plastic bag. Place in very hot tap water until melted. Snip off one corner and use as a piping bag. Drizzle on top of cake to decorate.

Tip: Beating egg yolks over a water bath—called a *bain marie* in French, *bano mario* in Spanish—enables them to give more volume without cooking them. A *bain marie* may be as simple as a pan of water into which the bowl fits, or it may be a specially constructed piece such as one fitting over the bottom of an electric mixer bowl. If no *bain marie* is available, rinse the bowl with hot water and wrap the sides with a hot towel. The hot pan helps

Continued

prevent the cake from collapsing during baking. Water in a water bath should ideally be about 150°F and not come up higher than the level of the batter in the bowl.

Tip: Using a copper bowl and a wire whip to beat egg whites will give you a third again as much volume, and is a preferred technique for volume and lightness.

Serving variation
Serve with berries and cream. Pipe melted chocolate over the cake.

⚜ 9 ⚜

A PARTY TO TALK ABOUT

The Difficult Dinner Guests

If you have the single most important ingredient of a dinner party—the right guests—nothing can go wrong, because they will laugh through the worst of disasters, from fallen soufflés to burnt dessert, and somehow it won't matter to you, either. But the wrong dinner list will make even the perfect menu a miserable experience.

A city can be like any small town in that, unfortunately, not everyone likes each other. There are times when your guest list might not coincide with your ideas of an easy, happy dinner party. Maybe one person had been married and acrimoniously divorced from another's sister. Or the guest of honor had turned down a grant proposal request by one of the other guests. Or, perhaps, one guest has just fired the other. And yet you must have these people to dinner.

It is easier to have them in your home than in a restaurant, because you can control the situation. The first thing to do is to study the guest list and make a seating plan. Even for a casual or semiformal dinner party, place-cards are a help in an awkward situation.

If you have only two people who are at odds with each other, you have a good chance of making it through a dinner party of six or more. If there are more feuds than that, try to add convivial, easygoing people to the guest list. It is easier to deal with a difficult situation when there is a crowd present.

Seating guests at two or more tables allows difficult individuals to be separated. A very long table accomplishes the same thing—space between the feuders—but many people don't have room enough for that. Round tables, seating six, can be rented from party houses and draped with fine linen or decorative sheets. Have a person at the other table upon whom you can rely to troubleshoot for you and to keep the conversation going smoothly.

When issuing invitations, mention who else you are inviting so they can anticipate awkward situations. If the person you're inviting chooses to decline, you have done the right thing by asking, and everyone can be happy.

Review the menu. If possible, remove anything from the menu that will require personal attention or that has the potential for disaster. Keep it simple and try to make it fun.

Once my friend Alma Freedman had a gothic novel birthday party for me. She asked everyone to write two pages of a gothic novel about me. The centerpiece table arrangement was made up of gothic paperback novels and cutouts of book-cover characters. The menu items were named after Victorian titles. When the "novel" was read aloud, each person reading his or her portion in sequential nonsense, there were gales of laughter. No one had the time or inclination to fuss.

It doesn't take money and formality to make a dinner party a success—what it takes is your caring enough for your guests for them to have a happy time. There are several choices of menu themes that will set the tone for the occasion, and ensure as delightful an evening as possible. The ultraformal menu will usually tame the worst situations, but it also augurs a fairly tedious evening and entails a good deal more expense because it requires a staff and mountains of china and silver.

The right theme, however, can turn the party around. Once my friend and editor at the *The Atlanta Journal and Constitution*, Dudley Clendinen, had an office party. I volunteered to prepare the main course. We felt we needed beef for the traditionalists but wanted to add some zip for the adventurers. And, since we didn't know each other, we wanted something to keep the conversation going. We decided on a buffet-style serve-yourself approach. We all served ourselves, wrapping the beef in the tortillas or pancakes, if we wished, with a choice of the various condiments—or if cautious, just choosing one or two. It was great fun, easy to serve, and a great catalyst for the evening.

ᏇMENUᏇ

A PARTY TO TALK ABOUT

Colorful Company Soup or A Taste of Summer Soup

Charcoal Rib Eye or Beef Fajitas with Tortillas or Chinese Pancakes

Guacamole

Scallion Brushes

Hoisin Sauce (store-bought)

Pico de Gallo

Lime and Cilantro Salsa

Marco Polo Sauce or Italian Basil or Pesto Sauce

Chocolate and Nut Snowball

SERVES 10

LOGISTICS

When a meal is potentially stressful, the last thing you need is to be rushing around at the last minute. Everything on this menu may be made in advance. The soup may be made a day or two in advance, reheated 5 minutes before serving. The meat may be grilled or roasted up to a day in advance, but preferably sliced the day of the party. It may be reheated in the microwave or wrapped in foil in a 350°F oven for 10 minutes, or it may be left at room temperature (with the shredded spinach around it) for several hours, covered, then unwrapped and served at room temperature. The green onions or scallions may be cut into brushes a day ahead and refrigerated. The mushrooms may be sautéed a day ahead and reheated for a few minutes before serving. The guacamole may be made a few hours ahead. Wrap the tortillas or pancakes in foil and reheat in a hot oven 5 minutes, or place in a steamer. Make the snowball in advance and freeze. Defrost the snowball and decorate several hours before the guests arrive.

The pestos, salsa, and pico de gallo may be made in advance several days, and refrigerated until 1/2 hour before serving. For the sauces, make at least 1 double recipe of a spicy sauce (Marco Polo or pico de gallo) and 1 double of a nonspicy (guacamole or Italian pesto) or make *all* the sauces, as I do, which is the most fun, and label them for your guests. Definitely make everyone stand up and fix their own tortillas or Chinese pancakes to get them moving.

Be sure to make a checklist of all the condiments for the main course so you won't forget anything in the refrigerator.

RECIPES

COLORFUL COMPANY SOUP
Serves 10 to 12

4 pounds tomatoes,
   peeled, and seeded
   or 4 pounds canned
   plum tomatoes and
   their juice, chopped
2 onions, sliced
2 carrots, peeled and
   sliced
peel of 1 orange,
   shredded finely
8 cups chicken stock
2 bay leaves
6 parsley stalks
2 to 3 teaspoons ground
   cumin seed
6 tablespoons butter
8 tablespoons flour
juice of 2 oranges
2 tablespoons sugar
salt
freshly ground pepper
1 cup whipping cream
1 to 2 tablespoons fresh cilantro, chopped (optional)

Combine the tomatoes, onions, carrots, 1/2 of the orange peel, and the stock in a large pot. Tie together the bay leaves and parsley and add, along with 1 teaspoon of the cumin seed. Cover and simmer 1/2 hour. Remove the bay leaves and parsley. Strain and purée the solids with a little liquid, in a food processor or blender until smooth. Melt the butter in a clean pan, and stir in the flour. Pour on the liquid, stirring until it boils. Blanch the remaining orange peel in a small pan of boiling water for 30 seconds, drain, and set aside. The orange peel should be curly shreds. You may make the soup ahead to this point, reheating just before you serve. Add 1/2 of the orange juice to the soup, check the seasoning, add sugar, the rest of the cumin if desired, salt, and pepper. Add more juice as needed. Stir in the cream and garnish with orange shreds and chopped cilantro. Taste again. May be made ahead several days. Reheat without boiling.

Variation

Omit cumin and cilantro. Serve without, or substitute 1 tablespoon chopped fresh basil.

A TASTE OF SUMMER SOUP

Serves 10 to 12

6 tablespoons olive oil
1 large leek, white part
   only, chopped
1 onion, chopped
1 large potato, peeled
   and cut in 1/4-inch
   cubes
2 medium carrots,
   peeled and chopped
8 cups chicken or turkey
   stock
1 zucchini, cut in 1/4-
   inch cubes
1/2 pound green beans,
   snapped and cut in
   1/2-inch pieces
4 garlic cloves, chopped
6 ripe tomatoes, peeled
   and seeded
   or 1 (12-ounce) can plum tomatoes with their juice
1 cup chopped fresh basil
1/2 pound okra, stem end removed, cut in 1/2-inch slices
salt
freshly ground pepper

Heat 3 tablespoons of the olive oil in a large pot. Add the leek and onion and sauté over low heat 5 minutes until onion is soft. Add the potato, carrots, and stock and bring to the boil. Add the zucchini and beans. Bring back to the boil, reduce heat, cover, and simmer for 20 to 30 minutes, until the potato and carrots are tender but not mushy.

Meanwhile, heat the rest of the oil in another pan, add the garlic, and cook until soft over low heat without burning. Purée along with the tomatoes and basil in a blender or food processor, then stir into the hot soup base. Add the okra and simmer 2 to 3 minutes, uncovered. Salt and pepper to taste. May be frozen or made ahead several days. Reheats easily.

CHARCOAL RIB EYE WITH TORTILLAS OR CHINESE PANCAKES

Serves 10

1 (6-pound) rib eye roast
2 cups hoisin sauce
4 to 6 tablespoons
  butter
1 pound mushrooms,
  sliced
20 green onions or
  scallions
1 cup Dijon mustard
2 pounds shredded
  spinach
1 cup cilantro leaves
1 recipe Pico de Gallo
  (p. 86)
1 recipe Marco Polo
  Sauce (p. 87) and/or
1 recipe Italian Basil or
  Pesto Sauce (p. 88)
20 flour tortillas

Rub the meat with 1 cup of the hoisin sauce and let marinate 1 hour or more. Meanwhile, melt 4 tablespoons of the butter, add the mushrooms, and sauté. Add more butter if necessary. Set aside, refrigerating if necessary until needed. Cut the green onions into brushes and place in cold water to form (p. 86). Remove meat from marinade, reserving marinade. Place meat, fat side down, on a hot charcoal grill. Brown the fatty side quickly. Turn and brown the other. Place the meat in a large roasting pan and put the pan on the grill. Cover the grill; cook 45 minutes to 1 hour until roast registers 140°F for rare meat. For well-done meat, cook about 1-1/2 to 2 hours. Remove from the heat and let the meat rest 10 minutes. (May be cooked ahead several days.) A few hours before serving, cut into finger-sized strips and heap on a platter. Add the reserved marinade to the meat juices in the pan, bring to the boil, and transfer to a bowl. Reheat the mushrooms and then place in separate bowl. Place the mustard in yet another bowl. Surround the meat with some of the shredded spinach, green onions, and cilantro. Place the rest of the spinach, cilantro, onion brushes, the remaining cup of hoisin sauce, and the pico de gallo and other sauces in separate bowls. Wrap tortillas or pancakes in foil and reheat in oven or steamer. Let your guests assemble their own tortillas from the bowls, choosing their own fillings.

Variation
If you prefer, you may roast the meat in a hot oven, after searing on top of the stove.

Tip: The technique of browning the meat then placing it on a pan on the grill is to keep the juices. You may place the meat directly on the grill if you prefer, but your sauce will lack the flavor of the juices.

BEEF FAJITAS
Serves 10

4 pounds beef skirt or
   bottom round, sliced
   1/4 inch thick
juice of 2 limes or
   lemons
8 garlic cloves, finely
   minced
20 flour or corn tortillas
Garnish:
Pico de Gallo (p. 86)
Guacamole (p. 85)
sour cream
fresh cilantro

The word *fajitas* is derived from "faja" and "ita" in Spanish and means something like "sweet little belt." The skirt steak is located along the inner rib of the beef forequarter short plate. It is also called the "inside belt" or "inside" or "outside" "skirt steak." The inside steak is more flavorful and tender. Marinating increases tenderness. Now fajitas are made from all sorts of meats, seafood, and vegetables, and the word is usually used to describe a shape of meat.

Pound the beef slices to 1/4-inch thickness for tenderizing. Place the lime or lemon juice and garlic in a shallow bowl. Press each beef slice into the mixture and let sit for at least 30 minutes before grilling, broiling, or pan broiling. Heat the grill, lay the steak on the rack, and cook 2 to 3 minutes on each side. Remove and slice into strips 2 inches wide and about 4 to 6 inches long. Wrap tortillas in foil and reheat in oven or steamer. Place beef on warm tortillas or let guests fill their own tortillas. Serve with pico de gallo, guacamole, sour cream, and cilantro.

Variation
Make fajitas from chicken breasts, shelled shrimp, or stir-fried vegetables.

Tip: Use 1-1/2 pounds of beef to 1/2 lime. Use 2 garlic cloves per 1/2 pound of meat.

Tip: It is easier to slice meat when it is half frozen.

Tip: To make steak fajitas, place beef skirt or bottom round (4 to 5 inches long, 2 to 3 inches wide, and 1 inch thick) lengthwise on a cutting board. Hold the blade of a sharp knife parallel and butterfly, cutting horizontally to 1/4 inch thick, starting with the thin wide side, but not cutting all the way through.

TIPSY FAJITAS
Serves 10

1 tablespoon lemon
  rind, grated
freshly ground pepper
1 garlic clove, chopped
1/2 teaspoon salt
4 pounds beef fajitas
2 tablespoons teriyaki
  sauce
1/4 cup vegetable oil
1/4 cup red wine
  vinegar
1 (12-ounce) can beer
1 fresh hot pepper,
  chopped
20 tortillas
Pico de Gallo (p. 86)
Guacamole (p. 85)
Lime and Cilantro
  Sauce (p. 87)

This variation of fajitas is more oriental in its bias and deserves its own recipe.

Sprinkle lemon rind, pepper, garlic, and salt evenly over meat. Place in bowl or plastic bag. Add teriyaki sauce, oil, vinegar, beer, and hot pepper. Turn meat. Marinate for 1 hour or more before cooking. Drain marinade and discard. Heat grill, and cook steaks 2 to 3 minutes on each side. Remove and slice into strips 2 inches wide and 4 to 6 inches long. Warm tortillas. Serve with pico de gallo, guacamole, and sour cream. Fajitas may be made ahead and reheated.

Variation
Grill 2 sliced onions, along with the fajitas.

Variation
Serve with Asian pesto and hoisin sauce, with cilantro sprigs as a garnish.

CHINESE PANCAKES
Makes 20 to 30 pancakes

1 cup boiling water
2 to 3 cups bread or all-
  purpose flour
sesame oil

Stir the water into 2 cups of the flour, adding more if necessary to make a rough dough. Knead dough on a floured board or in a food processor until it is smooth. Place in an oiled bowl and cover with plastic wrap. Rest 30 minutes.

Roll dough into a log 1-1/2 inches thick. Cut dough into 1-1/2-inch pieces. Roll each piece between palms and flatten into a round. Repeat with remaining balls of dough. Brush one side of round with sesame oil. Place the oiled side against another round and press together to make a pair. Roll the two rounds with a rolling pin to about 5 or 6 inches across.

Heat a heavy unoiled frying pan or non-stick pan. When pan is hot, add the pair of pancakes. Brown lightly on one side. Turn the pair and brown second side. Place on a rack. Repeat.

When pancakes are still warm but cool enough to handle, separate them. The pancakes may be served immediately or wrapped in foil and reheated. They may also be frozen, if stacked and wrapped well. To reheat, place frozen pancakes in a steamer for a few minutes, then fill. To deep fry, thaw first, fill, and fry. Makes 20 to 30 pancakes.

GUACAMOLE

Makes 2 cups

2 large ripe avocados
2 tablespoons lime or
   lemon juice
1 garlic clove (optional)
3 hot peppers, chopped
1/2 small onion,
   chopped
salt
freshly ground pepper
1/4 cup sour cream

In a food processor or with a fork mash the avocados with the lime juice, garlic, peppers, and onion. Season with salt and pepper to taste. Cover with the sour cream to prevent turning dark, before tightly covering with plastic wrap. Stir in sour cream when ready to serve.

Variation
Stir in 1 to 2 chopped, peeled, and seeded ripe red tomatoes just before serving.

Variation
Keep the avocados chunky rather than smooth.

SCALLION BRUSHES

20 scallions

Trim scallions into 3- or 4-inch lengths. To create the brush, make a 1-inch cut into the green end. Roll the onion and make another 1-inch cut, perpendicular to the first. Repeat for three and four cuts. To make a double brush, do the other end of the scallion the same way. Drop the scallions into ice water, and after a minute or two the ends will curl attractively. Will last up to a week.

PICO DE GALLO

Makes 2 cups

2 ripe tomatoes, seeded
  and finely chopped
1 medium red onion,
  chopped
2 green onions or
  scallions, chopped,
  including green
5 tablespoons vegetable
  oil
juice of 1 lemon
4 fresh green chilies,
  seeded and finely
  chopped
1 to 2 tablespoons fresh
  chopped cilantro
4 tablespoons tomato
  juice
salt
freshly ground pepper

Mix the tomatoes, onions, oil, lemon juice, chilies, and cilantro in large bowl. Add tomato juice, salt, and pepper as needed. Cover and refrigerate. Will keep up to 5 days.

Tip: *Pico de Gallo* means "Rooster's Bill" or "Rooster's Tooth."

Comment: Pico de Gallo is less liquid than salsa. Once it sits a few days the acid draws the liquid out of the vegetables and it becomes more like a salsa. If you want it drier, stir, then pour off the excess liquid.

Comment: Hot peppers vary in intensity, the milder being "broad shouldered" and coming down to a tip. The tinier and more narrow they are, the hotter they are. Choose your hotness accordingly.

Tip: Do not try to do this recipe in a food processor—it will be too liquid.

LIME AND CILANTRO SALSA
Makes 1-1/4 cups

1/2 to 2/3 cup fresh cilantro leaves, finely chopped
juice of 2 limes
salt
freshly ground pepper
1 cup sour cream, Crème Fraiche (p. 107), or 1/2 cup sour cream and 1/2 cup yogurt

Combine cilantro, lime juice, salt, pepper, and sour cream. May be made ahead several days and refrigerated until 30 minutes before serving.

MARCO POLO SAUCE
Makes 1-1/2 cups

3/4 cup oil
1/2 cup hot peppers, seeded and chopped (optional)
1/2 cup chopped fresh basil
8 garlic cloves, chopped
1/3 to 1/2 cup fresh chopped ginger (optional)
1/4 cup lemon juice or dry white wine
3 tablespoons oriental dark sesame oil
salt
freshly ground pepper

Purée oil, hot peppers, basil, garlic, ginger, lemon juice or wine, and sesame oil in food processor or blender. Add salt and pepper to taste.

Tip: It will take 4 cups of fresh basil to yield 1/2 cup of chopped fresh basil.

ITALIAN BASIL OR PESTO SAUCE
Makes 3 cups

6 to 8 garlic cloves,
  chopped
4 cups fresh basil leaves,
  packed tightly
1/2 to 1 cup imported
  olive oil
2 to 3 cups imported
  Parmesan cheese,
  grated
1/4 cup pine nuts
  (optional)

Place the garlic, basil leaves, olive oil, cheese, and optional pine nuts in a food processor or blender and process until puréed. Keep refrigerated several weeks, or freeze.

Variation
Substitute 1/2 the basil with mint or thyme; add oregano and parsley.

Variation
I enjoy adding some butter in place of or with the olive oil when serving this over rice and shrimp. I find some butter fills out the sauce and makes it fuller.

Variation
Walnuts or almonds are interesting substitutions for the pine nuts.

Variation
Try pesto with pasta, shrimp, clams, oysters, chicken, or pork tenderloin.

> **Comment:** Although an authentic Italian pesto includes pine nuts, they are very expensive and, for casual dining, not always worth what they add in consistency.

Tip: The recipe doubles, triples, etc., or may be made in small batches.

Tip: Make a large batch several times a year (especially at summer's end) and keep it in the freezer.

Tip: To store, pour additional olive oil on top of the pesto to create a film, which will prevent darkening of the sauce.

CHOCOLATE AND NUT SNOWBALL
Serves 12 to 15

1 pound semisweet
    chocolate
1 cup water
2 cups sugar
2 cups butter, at room
    temperature
8 large eggs
2 tablespoons vanilla or
    other flavoring such
    as orange cognac
    liqueur
1 cup chopped pecans
    or walnuts

Decoration

2 cups heavy whipping
    cream
4 tablespoons sugar
1 teaspoon vanilla or 1
    tablespoon cognac or
    orange cognac-
    flavored liqueur (optional)
Optional garnish:
grated chocolate or cocoa powder

Preheat oven to 350°F. Line a 10-cup ovenproof bowl with a double thickness of foil. Melt the chocolate with the water and sugar over low heat or in the microwave. Place in a mixer or the food processor; beat in the butter, then the eggs, one by one, followed by the optional flavoring, beating after each addition. Fold in the nuts.

Pour the mixture into the foil-lined mold; bake 1-1/2 hours or until a thick crust has formed on top. Remove from oven and cool. It will collapse—don't worry. Wrap well and refrigerate until solid. (It will keep in the refrigerator up to 2 weeks, and freezes well.)

Whip the cream with the sugar and the vanilla or cognac. Place the cream in a piping bag with a star tip. Remove the snowball from the refrigerator. Peel off the foil. Place flat side down on a serving dish. Pipe to cover completely with rosettes so no chocolate shows. Dust with chocolate or cocoa. Chill until served. Cut in small slices.

Variation
For 6 to 8, halve recipe and put in 5-cup ovenproof bowl. Bake 45 to 60 minutes.

Tip: For stiffly whipped cream, "whip" in a chilled food-processor bowl, using the steel knife and taking care not to overbeat. There is not as much volume, but it pipes more easily.

Tip: For optimal results, place the whipped cream in a cloth-lined strainer and let excess water drain for several hours before piping.

Tip: Avoid handling the cream-filled portion, as you will melt the cream. Push from the top, then release. Steer the tube with one or two fingers on the metal tip, not on the bag!

❧ 10 ❧

MENU FOR A SPECIAL OCCASION

A New Arrival Honored

The golden harp was being set up in Steve and Marie's home as I arrived, early, eagerly, for their baby's christening. Beckoning me past the curving harp were abundant pastels of white and pink stock, tube roses, and lilies of the field in a loose arrangement in the living room. Their sweet smells were first to greet me.

Soon the other guests arrived, radiant women adorned in the flowered dresses of the season. The house was a garden of flowers on fabric and in bloom, enchanting the eye. Throughout Sunday afternoon the harpist played, accompanied by the giggles of little girls dressed up in frilly Sunday fancy dresses chasing after little boys in white suits. The grownups remarked that they had never seen prettier children, or happier ones. Delighting in the sounds of the day, the adults praised the baby's dress and her good temper. The sun flirted with showers, forming rainbows that could be seen through the window.

The baby's grandmother stood in the spacious kitchen, happily frying chicken for the children's meal. A small child flopped at her feet, crying, and another grandchild squatted down low, cajoling her to give up her tears. Both brightened when a piece of chicken was given to them straight from the pan, crisp and hot.

In time, when the skies cleared, we went outside and formed a circle in the garden for the baptism. The baby was very good and didn't cry until the very end, when Father Ford doused her with more water than she liked. We were slightly doused too, our prayer books dampened by the misty rain cooling us down in the late hot summer afternoon. It seemed we were all blessed.

The smell of the fried chicken mingled tantalizingly with the smells of beef for the grownups and the flowers on the polished table. There the rosy beef and the pink shrimp were juxtaposed with the deep green of the asparagus, and the oranges were highlighted against the flecked wild rice. With the multicolors of braided bread and the ratatouille, the table was a masterpiece. The sounds were merry, grownups laughing. "Rain today, too, just as at their wedding," we chuckled. "Must be a good sign." The silver clanked on the dishes, the children squealed, the harp played. We lined up for repeats of dessert, adults and children alike, happy and reluctant to leave.

MENU

MENU FOR A SPECIAL OCCASION

Three-Flour Braided Bread

Marie Nygren's Shrimp and Watercress Salad

Roasted Beef Tenderloin or *Cynthia's Grilled Beef Tenderloin*

Wild Rice and Orange Salad (p. 52)

Asparagus or *Ratatouille*

Chocolate Nut Tassies or *Daffodil Cake (p. 288)*

Angel Food Cake (p. 290)

Additions for Children

Jean Sparks' Fried Chicken

The World's Best Carrot Cake

SERVES 10

LOGISTICS

The beef may be cooked a day or two ahead, as may the bread, tassies, cake, and the ratatouille (which may also be frozen). The shrimp may be cooked and peeled a day ahead, or even purchased cooked if necessary. The eggs for the shrimp and watercress salad may be cooked in advance, peeled the day of the event, then kept in a plastic bag. Then the rest of the ingredients for this and for the wild rice salad may be prepared and placed in containers ready to be assembled. The asparagus may be cooked ahead and refrigerated, then covered with the vinaigrette half an hour before serving. Fry the chicken as late as possible, or fry early in the day and serve cold. If you are serving a much larger crowd, these recipes multiply easily (*but:* be sure to note the doubling tip on the shrimp and watercress salad).

↶ R E C I P E S ↷

THREE-FLOUR BRAIDED BREAD

Makes 2 standard loaves or 6 small loaves

Basic Batter

3-1/4 cups bread flour
2 tablespoons sugar
1 tablespoon salt
2 packages rapid-rise
   yeast
4 tablespoons (1/4 cup)
   butter, softened
2-1/4 cups water
   (130°F)

Place 2-1/4 cups of the flour, the sugar, salt, yeast, and butter in a bowl or food processor. Add the warm water. Beat or process until smooth. Add the remaining 1 cup of flour and beat or process again. Divide batter into 3 bowls.

Whole Wheat Braid

2 tablespoons molasses
1-1/4 cups whole wheat
   flour

Beat or process the molasses into 1/3 of the batter, then add enough whole wheat flour, 1/2 cup at a time, to make a soft whole wheat dough. It will seem sticky because of the molasses.

Rye Braid

2 tablespoons molasses
1 teaspoon caraway seed
1 tablespoon cocoa
1-1/4 cups rye flour

Beat the molasses, caraway seed, and cocoa into 1/3 of the batter, add enough rye flour, 1/2 cup at a time, to make a soft rye dough. It will seem sticky because of the molasses.

White Braid

1-1/4 cups bread flour

Beat enough bread flour, 1/2 cup at a time, into the remaining 1/3 batter to make a soft white dough.

Knead each dough until elastic and smooth as a baby's bottom. Cover the two other doughs while working on one. Place each dough in an oiled bowl, turn, and cover with plastic wrap, or place in an oiled plastic bag. Let rise in a warm place until doubled, about 1 hour. Punch down; turn out the dough on a floured board, and divide each dough in half. Roll each piece into a 15-inch rope. On a greased baking sheet, braid together one rope of white, one of whole wheat, and one of rye. Pinch the ends to seal. Repeat with remaining dough. Cover with oiled plastic wrap and let rise until doubled, about 1 hour. Be sure ends are tucked under.

Preheat oven to 350°F. Bake for 30 to 40 minutes or until done. Cool on a rack. Freezes well.

Variation
Make 6 miniature loaves. Reduce baking time to 30 minutes, testing after 20 minutes.

Comment: If you don't have rapid-rise yeast, you may use active dry yeast and dissolve as directed on the package.

MARIE NYGREN'S SHRIMP AND WATERCRESS SALAD
Serves 10

2 bunches watercress,
   washed and dried
   well, with some stems
   removed
2 large red onions,
   thinly sliced
2 pounds medium or
   jumbo shrimp,
   cooked and shelled
4 hard-cooked eggs,
   sliced
1 to 3 tablespoons
   capers
1 cup feta cheese,
   crumbled

Dressing

2-1/2 tablespoons Dijon
   mustard
1/2 cup fresh lemon juice
1/4 cup red wine
   vinegar
2 garlic cloves, finely
   chopped
3/4 cup olive oil
4 tablespoons chopped
   thyme or basil
hot sauce, homemade or
   Tabasco
salt
freshly ground pepper

Place the watercress on a large platter or individual plates. Scatter circles of red onions on top, then the shrimp. Intersperse with the eggs and sprinkle on capers and feta cheese. Make the dressing by mixing together the mustard, lemon juice, vinegar, garlic, and oil. Season to taste with herbs, hot sauce, salt, and pepper. Pour the dressing over the salad just before serving.

Tip: To hard-cook an egg, bring a large pan of water to the boil. Prick the shell with an egg pricker. Place the egg on a spoon and gently roll it off onto the bottom of the pan. Roll a few seconds to coagulate the yolk in the center. Reduce heat and simmer 11 minutes. Remove the egg to cold water briefly and then drain. Roll on the counter to crack the shell, then peel, starting at the large end.

Tip: When doubling this recipe, cut back the onions and eggs to 2 additional onions and 6 eggs, total.

BOILED SHRIMP

Serves 4 to 6 (or enough for 1 recipe Shrimp and Watercress Salad)

2 pounds shrimp, in
   shell
water to cover
1 bay leaf (optional)
1 onion, sliced
   (optional)
freshly ground pepper
   (optional)
creole seasonings or
   shrimp boil (optional)

Place the shrimp and optional seasonings in boiling water to cover. Bring back to the boil, quickly reduce the heat, and simmer, covered, until the shrimp turn pink, anywhere from 3 to 5 minutes.

Tip: Shrimp is always better cooked in the shell. Peeled and cooked, it loses some of its flavor as well as tenderness. Veining is a matter of aesthetics and personal preference, necessary only when the shrimp have grit in their veins, which is becoming more and more unusual.

Tip: Serve with melted butter or homemade mayonnaise, such as the Béarnaise Mayonnaise (p. 258), or Pico de Gallo (p. 83), or Salsa (p. 87).

ROASTED BEEF TENDERLOIN

Serves 10

1 (3-1/2 to 5-pound)
   trimmed beef
   tenderloin
oil, butter, or fat
salt
freshly ground pepper

Preheat oven to 500°F. Tie the meat at 1-1/2 to 2-inch intervals. Rub with the oil. Place in a roasting pan in the oven, uncovered. Immediately reduce the heat to 400°F and roast 18 to 20 minutes, until it is 140°F for rare, longer for medium. Season with salt and pepper when done. Let rest 10 minutes before carving. May be served hot or cold.

Continued

Variation
Serve with Mustard Sauce (p. 107), or horseradish.

Variation
Serve with Lime and Cilantro Salsa (p. 87).

Variation
Serve with mustard-butter. Mix together Dijon or pommery mustard, room-temperature butter, and a bit of cream.

Variation
Serve with Red Pepper Sauce (p. 191).

Serving tip: A pound of peeled "tender," not including the "chain," will serve 3 people.

Tip: "Filet," "fillet," "tenderloin," and "a tender" are interchangeable names. Filet is the French spelling, fillet the American, tenderloin the common term, and tender the abbreviated form for what technically is the whole short-loin tenderloin. The average beef tenderloin, untrimmed, is 7 to 9 pounds including the butt. Rarely are those tenders sold peeled or trimmed. "Peeled" tenders are usually smaller tenders that weigh 3-1/2 to 4 pounds when sold. Untrimmed, these small tenders weigh 5 to 7 pounds. Most tenders that are sold unpeeled will include 3/4 inch of fat as well as the chain. "Cow" tenders are less expensive though not as wonderful as the beef tenderloin, but are more than satisfactory for casual grilling, large parties, hors d'oeuvres, or any time when people are drinking.

Butchering tip: The tenderloin of beef is wrapped in a mass of fat and membrane that needs to be completely removed with a sharp knife. You lose around 1/3 of the weight of the meat when it is trimmed by you or the butcher. There is very little price savings when buying trimmed (peeled) vs. untrimmed tenderloin, unless on sale.

Purchasing tip: Be sure to ask for the whole tenderloin. Some stores are selling pieces of the tenderloin, also untrimmed, in packages just marked "beef tenderloin." It is not a whole tenderloin at all but the less desirable part of the tenderloin, the butt, with its higher ratio of fat. It appears to be cheaper but is in fact more expensive. The cost of the fat is computed once all fat and membrane are removed and there are two pieces of meat. The smaller one is called the chain. I prefer removing it, and using it for another meal, such as a stir-fry, or as a "cook's treat" meal, rolled up like a small steak and wrapped with bacon when I am by myself.

Tip: The whole tenderloin has several types of meat. The larger, fat end, the butt (also called the head), is from the rump or sirloin end and is the least desirable piece, but it is still quite nice. The middle portion is the porterhouse-steak section and includes the chateaubriand and filet-steak sections. This is the best part of the tenderloin and is about 8 to 10 inches. The end, or tail, section is the rib end and includes meat for tournedos and filet mignon. (Not everyone agrees on the names for these parts, either. Some call the butt the chateaubriand.)

The variance of diameter in different parts of the meat doesn't insure uniform cooking time for the whole piece. This is fine if you want a roast that ranges from very well done (at the tail) to rare (for the large butt) and medium rare (for the center). The easier way of achieving some degree of uniformity is to flip about 2 inches of the tail under and tie the tenderloin, making it all nearly the same diameter as the center portion. Stripped of its fat, the tenderloin needs some fat for cooking. Brush it with olive oil or butter, or lay some of the removed fat or some bacon over it for part of the cooking. Zealots may lard it with narrow strips of salt pork.

Tip: The meat may be served hot or cold.

Reheating tip: May be made ahead and wrapped in foil, then reheated, 18 minutes in a 350°F oven.

CYNTHIA'S GRILLED BEEF TENDERLOIN

Serves 10

1 (3-1/2 to 5-pound) trimmed beef tenderloin

Marinade and Sauce

2 cups soy sauce
2/3 cup dark sesame oil
6 large garlic cloves, chopped
2 tablespoons fresh chopped ginger

Place the tenderloin in a nonaluminum pan. Mix together the soy sauce, oil, garlic, and ginger, and pour 1/2 of the marinade over the tenderloin. Reserve the remaining for the sauce. Cover the beef with plastic wrap and marinate overnight in the refrigerator.

Remove the tenderloin from the pan and place it on a charcoal grill over low fire, covered, or place in a pan in a 400°F oven. Cook until rare (internal temperature should be 140°F), turning if necessary. Remove from heat. If cooking in the oven, bring the remaining marinade and pan juices to the boil and pour over the meat. Serve hot or cold. May be made ahead and reheated.

Continued

Variation

Try cooking a brisket of beef on the grill. Place the brisket in a pan with the marinade. Place the pan in the center of a grill where 2 sides of the grill have hot coals. Cook 4 to 6 hours over indirect heat until very tender. Serve with Dinah's Sweet Barbecue Sauce (p. 70).

Variation

Grill a tenderloin or saddle of venison, using this marinade.

Tip: This may be sliced thin for an appetizer, in which case you can feed 20 to 30 people.

ASPARAGUS

Serves 10

4 pounds asparagus
1/2 cup butter
  (optional)

Cut off the thick ends of the asparagus. If the stalks are large, peel them from the bottom up to the first of the little offshoots. Place in a large frying pan with enough boiling water to cover. Cook until no longer raw but still rigid, usually 3 to 5 minutes for small spears, 5 to 8 minutes for large spears. Remove. Drain. Run under cold water to refresh. Reheat in the butter or liquid or serve cold in a salad.

Variation

Omit butter and serve with a mix of soy sauce, ginger, and green onions; Lemon Hollandaise Sauce (p. 33); White Butter Sauce (p. 257); or Red Pepper Sauce (p. 191).

Variation

Omit the butter. Place the still warm asparagus in a vinaigrette. Serve at room temperature.

Variation

Top hot asparagus and butter with 1/2 pound cooked and peeled shrimp, or top asparagus in vinaigrette with 1/2 pound cooked and peeled shrimp.

Variation

Add 4 tablespoons fresh herbs.

Variation

Add 2 tablespoons chopped ginger.

Tip: Asparagus, properly cooked, should be rigid enough to eat with the fingers. (I collect asparagus tongs, which can also be used.)

Tip: For 4: Use 2 pounds asparagus and 4 tablespoons of the optional butter.

RATATOUILLE
Serves 10 to 12

4 large eggplants or 6
   small ones, sliced
salt
6 zucchini, sliced
8 tablespoons oil (half
   peanut, half olive)
6 onions, sliced
3 green or red bell
   peppers, seeded and
   sliced
6 garlic cloves, chopped
2 (1-pound 12-ounce)
   cans Italian plum
   tomatoes, and juice
   or 2 (1-pound 12-ounce)
   fresh tomatoes, seeded
   and chopped
1 cup fresh herbs
   (preferably thyme,
   parsley, and basil),
   chopped
freshly ground pepper

Preheat oven to 350°F. To cook the eggplant in the oven, slice, score, and place in a colander with salt. Leave for 30 minutes. Rinse, drain, and dry well with paper towels. Brush the eggplant and zucchini slices with oil and place on an oiled baking sheet. Cook in the oven about 10 minutes. To cook in the microwave, place whole eggplants, pierced, and zucchini, pierced, in the microwave, and cook until soft, then cool and slice.

Heat 2 tablespoons of the oil in a heavy-bottomed pan. Add the onions, peppers, and garlic, and cook until soft, adding oil as needed. Add the cooked eggplant, zucchini, tomatoes and their juices, and half of the herbs to the pan and simmer, uncovered, for 1 hour, or cook in the microwave until soft. Add the rest of the herbs. Season well to taste with pepper. Serve hot or cold. Freezes well. Reheats well in microwave.

Variation
Pierre Henri continues to cook the ratatouille for another hour, until thick and creamy. It is delicious, making a wonderful bed for grilled pork or lamb chops or chicken breasts.

CHOCOLATE NUT TASSIES
Makes 24

Cream Cheese Dough

8 tablespoons butter,
  softened
1 (8-ounce) package
  cream cheese,
  softened
1 cup sifted all-purpose
  flour

Filling

2/3 cup hazelnuts,
  walnuts, or pecans,
  chopped
1/3 cup chocolate chips
1 egg
1/2 cup brown sugar
1 tablespoon butter,
  softened
1 teaspoon vanilla

Preheat oven to 350°F.

To make the dough, mix together the butter and cream cheese in a small bowl or food processor. Add the flour and blend thoroughly. Divide and shape into 24 balls. Wrap all 24 balls together in plastic wrap and chill slightly. Place each ball in a tiny ungreased fluted tart pan or muffin cup. Line the pans by pressing the dough with your fingertips against the bottoms and sides.

To make the filling, place half the nuts and half the chocolate chips in the dough-lined pan. Beat together the egg, sugar, butter, and vanilla until all lumps are gone. Pour the egg mixture over the nuts and chocolate chips and top with the remaining nuts and chips. Bake for 30 minutes in a hot oven, until the filling is set. Cool for 5 minutes on a wire rack and remove from the pans before they are cool, as the caramel will set.

Tip: To skin hazlenuts see p. 63.

Comment: This short dough is so easy to make anyone can do it! It does not roll easily, however, so is best suited to pressing in small tarts. It is easily patched.

JEAN SPARKS' FRIED CHICKEN

Serves 4

2 to 2-1/2 cups
   shortening or
   vegetable oil
salt
freshly ground pepper
1 (3-pound) chicken, cut
   up
1 cup flour

Heat the shortening to 360°F in a 12-inch skillet or frying pan, filling it no more than half full. While the shortening is heating, liberally salt and pepper the chicken. Salt and pepper the flour, and turn the seasoned chicken in the flour to coat it lightly. Turn the chicken in the flour again, tapping off any excess. Put the chicken, pieces of dark meat first, with skin side down, in the center of the skillet. Surround with the white meat, also skin side down. Allow the pieces to touch but don't crowd the pan. Cover loosely. Reduce the heat to medium high and cook 9 to 10 minutes, or until dark golden. Uncover, turn the chicken with tongs, and cook 8 to 10 minutes more, uncovered. Drain on paper towels.

Variation
To make a thicker crust, don't tap off the flour the second time.

Variation
Try a little cayenne or herbs on the chicken or in the flour.

Variation
Substitute some butter for the shortening or oil.

Variation
Serve with Cream Gravy.

CREAM GRAVY

Makes 2 cups

3 tablespoons of fat
   from meat or pan
   drippings
3 to 4 tablespoons flour
2 cups milk

Leave the fat in the skillet. Brown the flour in the fat a few minutes. Add the milk and continue stirring over heat until it boils down and is thick. Pour over potatoes, tomatoes, biscuits, or corn bread. Don't put it on crisp meat or chicken.

THE WORLD'S BEST CARROT CAKE

Makes 1 three-layer cake

1-1/2 cups whole wheat
  flour
2/3 cup all-purpose
  flour
2 teaspoons baking soda
2 teaspoons cinnamon
1/2 teaspoon salt
1/2 teaspoon ground
  nutmeg
1/4 teaspoon ground
  ginger
1 cup sugar
1 cup brown sugar,
  firmly packed
1 cup buttermilk
3/4 cup vegetable oil
4 eggs
1-1/2 teaspoons vanilla
1 (1-pound) bag carrots,
  peeled and grated
1 (8-ounce) can crushed
  pineapple, drained
1 cup pecans or walnuts,
  chopped
1 cup flaked coconut
1/2 cup raisins or
  currants

Preheat oven to 350°F. Sift together the flours, baking soda, cinnamon, salt, nutmeg, and ginger onto a sheet of wax paper. Mix the sugars together in a large bowl. Stir in the buttermilk, vegetable oil, eggs, and vanilla. Pour in the flour mixture, carrots, pineapple, nuts, coconut, and raisins or currants, stirring just until well blended.

Grease and flour three 9-inch round cake pans. Line the bottoms with wax paper; grease and flour the waxed paper. Pour the batter into cake pans. Bake for 30 minutes or until a wooden toothpick inserted in the center comes out clean. Cool in pans 10 minutes. Loosen the cake layers from the edges of the pans and invert onto wire racks. Peel off the waxed paper and cool completely.

To make the frosting, beat butter and cream cheese together in a large mixing bowl until light. Add confectioners' sugar, orange peel, and vanilla, mixing well.

Spread frosting between layers and on top and sides of cake. Cover and refrigerate overnight before cutting.

Cream Cheese Frosting

1/2 cup butter, at room temperature
1 (8-ounce) package cream cheese, at room temperature
1 (16-ounce) package confectioners' sugar
2 teaspoons grated orange peel
1 teaspoon vanilla

Tip: To frost a cake without messing up the plate, place long strips of wax paper on the plate to the edge. Frost the cake. Pull out the wax paper.

✁ 11 ✁

SINGLE PERSON'S DINNER PARTY FOR SIX

Entertaining as a Single Cook and Host

One of the most dreaded things about a divorce or the death of a spouse is the prospect of having to entertain alone afterwards. Being two for so long, how does one suddenly learn to function as "one"?

All entertaining is mainly organization. But when you are single, it is crucial. It takes lists as well as anticipating questions or problems and answering them. A party takes creativity, compassion, joy, vitality, graciousness, a desire to bless and enrich others. If you don't want to share those qualities with the people you want in your home, you won't have a good party. You won't even have a good guest list.

Perhaps the nicest thing about being single and having a party is the guest list. You don't have to find people two of you like (or who like both of you)! Gender, rather than being a crucial dinner party issue becomes less important. Recently I had a condo party and the two single men seemed quite happy nestled at the table with five women.

Decide how many people you are inviting and what you can afford to do for them. Is the budget to include all food and drinks or will people be asked to bring something? Many times people are grateful to have a place to have a party and an organizer, and are delighted to participate by bringing something. There is a lot less pressure to perform since everyone understands that a single person many times doesn't have the financial and physical resources of a married person. You may even ask people to bring their own alcohol.

Plan to serve some kind of meat that can be made in advance, frozen or refrigerated, then reheated when necessary, combining the vegetables as part of the same dish—sometimes in the stuffing or as part of a garnish. Make a time chart of when you are cooking what, how long it will take to reheat, who will be doing the reheating. Make a list of serving dishes. What gets placed in what? When? Post the list so anyone helping you can find it. Find someone to help you with the door, the coats, the greetings, the ice, the glasses. Assign your friends tasks—they usually love it.

Do not try to impress anyone through your menu. Express yourself in your home's warmth, not through tortured food that you resent because of the time and energy it took from you. No one worth knowing needs to be impressed with your culinary skills. Your ease and confidence and mastery of what you serve will be what leaves a lasting impression. (*Note:* For another single person's dinner menu, see page 149.)

ᴳMENU ᴄ

SINGLE PERSON'S DINNER PARTY FOR SIX

Orange and Carrot Soup

Stuffed Flank Steak with Mustard Sauce

or

Turkey or Veal Italienne

Sue's Make-Ahead Green Salad

Boiled Rice

Mushrooms and Okra

Party Ring-Bread

Crème Brûlée

SERVES 6

LOGISTICS

The flank steak or veal or turkey Italienne and the bread may be made a day in advance or frozen well ahead of time. Reheat, defrosted, for 20 minutes at 350°F, or until heated through. Add tomato garnish to the veal. The soup and the crème brulée may be made a day or two in advance. (The topping for the crème brulée [see alternate] may be made a couple of hours in advance.) The rice may be made a few hours ahead of time and reheated in a colander over hot water (p. 110). The greens should be washed, the vinaigrette made, and the salad tossed at the last minute. The mushrooms and okra may be made ahead and reheated, or started cooking 15 minutes before serving. If using caramel rounds, place on finished custard. If not, when nearly ready to serve the crème brulée, place in ice, sprinkle with brown sugar and run under the broiler as directed.

ℭ R E C I P E S ℭ

ORANGE AND CARROT SOUP

Serves 6

4 tablespoons butter or
   olive oil*
4 to 6 medium carrots,
   peeled and chopped
2 onions, chopped
1 leek, white part only,
   chopped (optional)
1 teaspoon curry
   powder
1 garlic clove, chopped
peel of 1 orange, grated,
   with no white
4 cups chicken stock
juice of 2 oranges
salt
freshly ground pepper
1 teaspoon brown sugar

Heat the butter or oil in a heavy pan, add the carrots, onions, and leek. Cover and cook over low heat for 10 minutes, without browning, until the onions are soft.

Stir in the curry powder and garlic and cook briefly. Add 1/2 the orange peel, the chicken stock, and the orange juice. Season lightly. Continue to cook until the carrots are just tender. Remove the solids with a slotted spoon and purée in a blender or food processor until smooth. Add the purée and the liquid back in the saucepan to reheat. Add salt and pepper to taste along with the sugar and remaining orange peel. Chill well if serving cold. Garnish with carrot and leek. May be made a day or two ahead.

Continued

When you plan to serve cold, olive oil should be used instead of butter.

Garnish:
peeled carrot, sliced
  lengthwise in 3-inch
  strips, blanched,
  curled with a
  toothpick, and put in
  cold water
leek greens, sliced
  lengthwise in 3-inch
  strips, curled with a
  toothpick, and put in
  cold water

Low-cal tip: Cook the vegetables in the microwave or a nonstick pan and omit the fat altogether.

> **Comment:** This soup is good hot or cold.

Variation
Add 1 tablespoon chopped fresh ginger with the curry powder.

Variation
Add 1-1/2 teaspoons ground cumin in place of the curry powder.

STUFFED FLANK STEAK

Makes 30 to 50 slices or serves 6 for dinner

1 to 1-1/2 pounds flank
  steak
4 tablespoons butter
3 shallots, chopped
1 garlic clove, chopped
4 ounces mushrooms,
  chopped
1 (10-ounce) box frozen
  chopped spinach,
  defrosted
1 tablespoon Dijon
  mustard
1/2 cup bread crumbs
1/2 cup imported
  Parmesan cheese,
  grated

Preheat oven to 350°F. Butterfly the flank steak. Be sure the butcher has not prescored the meat as many do. To butterfly, slice the meat vertically against the grain, with a long sharp knife. Heat the butter in a large frying pan until singing. Add the shallots, garlic, and mushrooms. Cook over low heat until soft. Squeeze the spinach until dry. Add to the shallot mixture, along with the Dijon mustard, the bread crumbs, the cheeses, and egg. Season to taste, adding salt, pepper, and herbs. Add more crumbs if necessary to hold together. Spread out the flank steak and fill with the mixture. (See tip below).

Place strips of sausage on top of the filling, leaving space between. Roll up the steak

1/2 cup Swiss or
  Gruyère cheese,
  grated
1 egg
salt
freshly ground pepper
1/4 cup fresh parsley,
  chopped
1/4 cup fresh thyme,
  oregano, or
  marjoram, chopped
1/4 pound chorizo or
  dried sausage such as
  red Italian pepperoni
  or salami, cut into
  strips
3 tablespoons oil
1-1/4 cups brown stock
1/4 cup vinegar
1 recipe Mustard Sauce
  (optional, p. 107)

like a jelly roll and tie up at 2-inch intervals very securely.

Heat the oil in a large frying pan. Brown the meat well on one side, then turn and cook until completely brown. Add the stock and vinegar. Cover with a lid or foil. Place in the hot oven and cook for 1 hour. Remove from pan, saving juices. Place a heavy pan or other weight on top of the roast to compress it, to facilitate slicing later. Refrigerate until very cold, about 8 hours. May be frozen at this point.

When ready to serve, slice cold or half-frozen meat very thin—1/8 to 1/4 inch thick and across the grain of the meat, to make an attractive pattern—into 30 to 50 slices. Serve hot or cold. To reheat, place a little of the reserved juices in the bottom of a pan to create steam, cover, and reheat 1/2 hour at 350°F.

Tip: Any leftover mixture can be frozen and used for another purpose, such as stuffing mushrooms or mixing with rice.

Tip: This will serve 6 for dinner, or provide a couple of slices each for 10 to 15 people at a cocktail party.

MUSTARD SAUCE

Makes 3 cups

3 cups Crème Fraiche
  (recipe follows)
1/4 cup Dijon mustard

Mix crème fraiche and mustard. Serve hot or cold. Beat briefly before serving.

CRÈME FRAICHE

Makes 4 cups

2 cups sour cream
2 cups heavy whipping
  cream

Whisk together sour cream and cream. Leave at room temperature a few hours or overnight, until thick. Cover and refrigerate until needed.

TURKEY OR VEAL ITALIENNE

Serves 6

2 pounds turkey or veal
    scallops or cutlets (9
    to 10 cutlets)
4 tablespoons butter
2 tablespoons oil
1 onion, chopped
1 tablespoon flour
1/4 cup dry Madeira
    (optional)
1-1/2 cups beef or
    turkey stock
1-1/2 teaspoons tomato
    paste
1 bay leaf
salt
freshly ground pepper
Garnish:
1-1/2 pounds fresh or 3
    (10-ounce) packages
    frozen spinach
8 tablespoons (1/2 cup)
    butter
3 tomatoes, peeled and
    cut into quarters,
    then eighths
1 garlic clove, chopped
1/3 to 1/2 cup heavy
    cream
6 large slices Gruyère or
    Swiss cheese

Pound the scallops thin. Then pat them dry. In a skillet heat enough butter and oil to cover the bottom of pan until sizzling. Add the scallops and sauté 1 to 2 minutes on each side. Remove and set aside. Add the onion and cook until soft. Add the flour, stir and cook until smooth. Mix the Madeira, stock, tomato paste, bay leaf, salt, and pepper together and add to the pan. Bring to the boil, stirring until smooth; add scallops, cover and simmer gently for 5 to 7 minutes or until tender.

To make garnish, place the fresh spinach, cleaned and stemmed and torn into pieces, in a large pan of boiling water for 3 minutes. Drain. Run under cold water, drain again, and chop. If using frozen spinach, defrost only (cooking is not necessary). Drain well, pressing between 2 plates to remove water. Squeeze to be sure it is totally dry.

In a skillet, melt 1 tablespoon of the butter, add tomatoes and garlic, and coat the tomatoes quickly in garlic butter without cooking. Set aside. Melt the remaining butter in a clean pan. Heat until butter turns brown like a hazelnut—watch it closely. Quickly remove pan from heat and add the spinach. Add cream to taste, stirring. Add salt and pepper to taste. The garnish may be made in advance. Arrange on a long ovenproof platter.

Remove the scallops from the sauce and drain. Set aside the sauce. Arrange the scallops on top of the spinach. Cut the cheese slices to cover the meat. This may be done well in advance and frozen or refrigerated, without the tomatoes. Bring to room temperature. Place the tomatoes around the rim of the dish. Brown under broiler or in 350°F oven for 10 minutes, until the cheese is melted and the dish is reheated through. Reheat sauce, and remove the bay leaf. Pour a little sauce around the dish and serve the rest in a separate bowl.

Tip: To bone turkey breast, place in freezer 1/2 hour, slice in thin scallops. If necessary, slice veal or turkey scallops in half vertically to make them thinner.

Variation
Substitute Marsala, dry sherry, or other dry fortified wine for the Madeira.

Variation
Omit the tomatoes if serving tomatoes elsewhere in the menu.

SUE'S MAKE-AHEAD GREEN SALAD
Serves 4 to 6

juice of 1 lime
1 garlic clove, chopped
3 to 4 tablespoons extra
   virgin olive oil
salt
freshly ground pepper
   (optional)
1 small endive, well
   washed
1 head leaf lettuce, well
   washed
1/4 cup fresh chopped
   cilantro (optional)
1/4 cup fresh oregano
   or thyme

Mix together the lime juice and garlic in a large salad bowl. Add the olive oil and mix. Add salt and pepper to taste. Tear the lettuce in pieces and dry. Add the herbs. Place salad serving spoon and fork crosswise in the bowl. Place the greens on top of the serving utensils, cover the bowl with plastic wrap, and refrigerate. To serve, bring to table and toss, stirring up dressing from the bottom of the bowl.

Variation
Garnish salads with Fried Pasta (p. 242) or tortilla strips. Vary the seasoning, using chili or curry!

Variation
Use a Vinaigrette (p. 140).

Tip: Cilantro, also called Chinese parsley and fresh coriander, is a very dominant herb, and for many people it is a cultivated taste. Use judiciously until you know the tastes of your guests.

BOILED RICE
Serves 4 to 6

1 cup uncooked long
   grain white rice
2 cups chicken stock or
   water
1/2 teaspoon salt
freshly ground pepper

To cook rice, you can always follow the package directions. But this easy method guarantees good results and tastes delicious.

Put the rice and stock or water in a 2 to 3-quart saucepan, and bring to the boil. Stir once or twice. Lower heat to a simmer. Cover with a tight-fitting lid or heavy-duty foil and cook 15 minutes. If the rice is not quite tender or the liquid is not absorbed, replace the lid and cook 2 to 4 minutes longer. Season with salt and pepper. Fluff with a fork.

Comment: For drier rice, use 2 tablespoons less water.

Tip: It is easier to cook rice in a large quantity of boiling water for 10 to 12 minutes, then drain, but unfortunately this removes all the water-soluble nutrients that have been added to the rice.

Comment: For drier rice, use 2 tablespoons less water.

Comment: To reheat rice, place in a colander over boiling water, making sure the water does not boil into or soak the rice, but only steams it. The rice will stay fluffy as long as the water doesn't evaporate. In restaurants it is kept this way for hours. Cover the rice to prevent the top layer from drying out.

Variation
Rice is a perfect foil for additions. Add 1 cup chopped pecans, canned or frozen defrosted and reheated artichoke hearts, chopped green onions or scallions, or fresh herbs to the hot rice.

Variation
If calories are of no concern, add a tablespoon of butter or olive oil to the broth.

Tip: Use 2 crumbled bouillon cubes and 2 cups water if chicken broth is not available.

MUSHROOMS AND OKRA
Serves 4 to 6

2 to 4 tablespoons
  butter
1 pound fresh
  mushrooms, cleaned
  and stemmed
1 pound fresh okra,
  tipped and sliced
salt
freshly ground pepper
1 tablespoon fresh herbs
  (optional)

Melt 2 tablespoons of the butter, add the mushrooms, and cook 5 minutes until soft. Bring a pot of water to the boil, drop in the okra, and boil 3 to 5 minutes. Drain. May be made several hours ahead to this point. When ready to serve, mix the okra with the mushrooms and heat through. Add salt, pepper, and herbs to taste.

Variation
Substitute shiitake mushrooms or button mushrooms.

Tip: This halves and doubles easily.

PARTY RING-BREAD
Makes 2 small rings or 1 ten-inch ring

1 package active dry
  yeast
2 tablespoons sugar,
  divided
1/8 cup warm water
  (105° to 115°F)
1/2 cup milk
1/4 pound butter,
  divided
2 eggs
1/2 teaspoon salt
3 to 4 cups bread flour

Dissolve the yeast and 1 tablespoon of the sugar in the warm water. Heat the milk and 4 tablespoons of the butter together until warm. Pour the milk and butter mixture into a mixing bowl or food processor. Add the remaining sugar and the eggs, one at a time, beating until smooth. Add the dissolved yeast mixture, salt, and 1-1/2 cups of the flour. Gradually add enough of the remaining flour, 1/2 cup at a time, to make a soft dough. Knead in the mixer, the food processor, or by hand on a floured board until the dough is smooth and elastic. Shape in a ball and turn in an oiled bowl, then cover with plastic wrap or place in an oiled plastic bag. Let the dough rise in a warm place until doubled.

Continued

Punch down. Turn out on a lightly floured board. Knead lightly. Melt the remaining 4 tablespoons butter. Roll dough out on a floured board to about 1/3 inch thickness. Using a 1-1/2-inch round, or a diamond-shaped or heart-shaped cutter, cut dough into rounds, diamonds, or hearts. Roll and cut scraps until all dough is used. Dip each piece in the melted butter to coat both sides. Place in overlapping layers in two greased 2-quart ovenproof soufflé dishes, charlottes, or ring molds. Cover pan with plastic wrap and a towel. Place in a warm place to rise, about 45 minutes.

Preheat oven to 350°F. Bake for 30 to 35 minutes or until lightly browned and loaf sounds "hollow" when thumped. If in doubt, test for doneness by piercing with a trussing needle to see if still doughy. Turn out on large plate and serve while warm. Or, let cool, wrap airtight, and freeze. Allow to thaw and reheat before serving.

Variation
Spread 1 cup of grated Parmesan cheese on a piece of wax paper. Dip each piece of dough into the butter as directed, then dip into the Parmesan. Proceed with recipe.

Variation
Combine 1-1/2 cups sugar and 1 tablespoon cinnamon. Dip each piece of dough into butter, then cinnamon mixture. Proceed with recipe.

Variation
To make a 3-quart ring mold: Use 1 package active dry yeast, 4 tablespoons sugar, 1/4 cup warm water, 1 cup milk, 1/2 pound butter, 3 eggs, 1 teaspoon salt, and 5 to 7 cups bread or all-purpose flour.

CRÈME BRÛLÉE

Serves 6

2 cups heavy or
   whipping cream
4 egg yolks
3 tablespoons sugar
1 teaspoon vanilla

CARAMEL
ROUNDS

1 tablespoon butter
4 to 6 teaspoons brown
   sugar

Preheat the oven to 325°F. Slowly heat the cream in a heavy saucepan until small bubbles concentrate around the sides of the pan, being careful not to burn it. Beat the egg yolks until well mixed, adding the sugar gradually. Add several tablespoons of the hot cream into the egg mixture, stirring with a wooden spoon, then add the remaining cream, stirring. Add the vanilla and stir until just blended. Pour into 6 small custard cups, or a pretty 1-quart ovenproof dish. Place a kitchen towel on the bottom of a large roasting pan, then place the custard cups on the towel and pour boiling water into the pan so that it reaches halfway up the sides, being careful not to get any water in the custard. Bake, uncovered, until set, about 30 minutes for the small cups, 45 minutes for the larger dish. This water bath keeps the custard from overcooking, as long as the water in the pan does not boil or evaporate. If it evaporates, add more water. Remove when done and refrigerate.

Make the caramel rounds (see below) and keep airtight, or when ready to serve, sprinkle with 1/8-inch layer of brown sugar. Place container(s) in a pan. Surround with ice cubes and run under hot broiler until sugar is bubbling and has a slight caramel odor. Remove and serve immediately.

Tip: Overbeating causes too much foam, which will leave air bubbles, or cause the custard to collapse.

Tip: Variations abound—fruit purées or chunks are added, as well as flavorings. Once you get the recipe down pat, experiment!

Tip: To make cooking pans for the caramel rounds, cut out circles of aluminum foil 1/4 inch larger than the top of a custard cup. Mold the foil around the rims of the cups, folding up the excess foil to create rims like small tart pans. Remove the foil from the custard cups. Butter each foil pan.

Continued

Sprinkle in 1 to 2 teaspoons sugar for each round. Place the foil pans under the broiler until the rounds are lacy and brown. Do not burn. Remove from the oven and cool. Bend back the foil and remove the hardened round. Keep in an airtight tin or container. If the rounds break, don't worry. Just sprinkle on the custard.

✶12✶

TASTY SUMMER DIET FOOD FOR FAMILY AND FRIENDS

The Skinnies and the Roundies

Just before my high school reunion, it seemed to me the world was divided into two types of people—the skinnies and the roundies. As I talked to my high school friends on the phone or in person, I tried to determine: Were they more like a Modigliani or a Rubens? Did they jog, do aerobics, eat more than one meal a day? More importantly, what size were they? My mother always said comparisons were odious, but I found myself mentally weighing myself (literally) against my peers.

The last time I visited an old high school skinny friend (remembering her mother was a darn good cook), I nearly starved to death. Her mother is beautiful at 70, and so is my friend the skinny. She runs three miles a day, four days a week, and she was pointedly polite about my protruding stomach (although I thought I could hear her thinking "tsk, tsk" as she glanced at it). She doesn't eat. She doesn't feed her family more than one meal a day, either. She gets a high from running. I get a high from chopping. One day I was ravenous at noon. She was surprised, saying, "But I thought you ate breakfast!" I wondered, "What has breakfast got to do with lunch?"

You see, most of the skinnies don't eat. They don't like food, they don't like to cook, and they don't like to admit that food is a requirement of life. Not only do they not eat, they don't cook or feed others, and they don't have food spots on their clothes. Their nails are polished and unchipped. (Have you ever noticed how the skinnies' skin doesn't look as good as the roundies'? They look too taut, and the lines in their faces are deeper. I worry about their skin.) The skinny vogue has aided and abetted their aversion to food, encouraging it to become a fetish.

Nevertheless, a month before the reunion I decided I needed to lose weight. I was afraid all the boys in my class would remember me as a skinny, having weighed 110 pounds until just a few years ago. (How many was it, now?) First I tried the sensible things. A bowl of cereal with skim milk or a boiled egg for breakfast. Low-calorie cottage cheese with slices of tomato for lunch. Poached chicken with steamed broccoli and rice or a baked potato for dinner. I sprinkled everything with herbs. Occasional fruit was my only dessert or snack. I hated it. I thought about the meals I was missing. I love food. I want to eat five times a day, if possible, small meals. I love slicing and chopping and cooking for others. I love the smells of the kitchen. I like breakfast in bed. I crave fresh food. I like to feed myself. Finally I found some recipes that satisfied my cravings and helped me lose a few pounds.

A long distance beau called, and I told him of my vows. "I," I proudly announced, hoping the declaration would spur me on as a challenge, "will be ten pounds lighter when I see you again." Instead of a crow of pleasure, I received a groan. "Oh, no," he said, "I like you Romanesque!"

With that, I threw my diet out the window. By the time of the reunion, I fit into my favorite roundies dress. I felt very comfortable in it. I got there early, quivering with anticipation at seeing people I hadn't seen for years. Like Rip Van Winkle, the years fell away. My high school sweetheart walked in the door. He'd been the high school football captain, and I suppose if you saw him today, you'd think he looked like Kenny Rogers, and that he might be considered a bit beefy—a roundy, even. I didn't notice. In fact, I didn't notice anyone's looks in particular, can't recall concentrating on their dresses or their shapes. All the women were beautiful, all the men handsome—just as I'd remembered them to be. The joy of being together overcame our mortality. We danced and laughed, and cried. I did notice one good thing, though, about the skinnies—you can't tell they have lines in the dark.

However, I do know so many people these days who are worried about being round that I indulge them with a skinny, but delicious, dinner such as this one.

၆ M E N U ၆

TASTY SUMMER DIET FOOD FOR FAMILY AND FRIENDS

Elegant Zucchini and Red Bell Pepper Soup

Chinese-Style Asparagus and Chicken Breasts

Brown Rice or John Markham's Szechwan Noodles

Refreshing Cucumber and Yogurt Salad

Merijoy's Honey Whole Wheat Rolls (optional)

Tiny Meringues

SERVES 6 TO 8

LOGISTICS

All of this menu may be made in advance. It is good hot or cold. The rolls and the meringues (which I add to the menu for the nondieters) will keep for months frozen. (I think all dieters need a little sweet something. A tiny meringue or two will keep the chocolate away.)

Make the soup one or two days in advance. It may be reheated if the day is chilly or served straight from the refrigerator. The salad may be made 4 to 5 hours in advance, and the rice cooked. Thirty minutes before serving, place the rice in a colander over boiling water (see p. 110). If serving the pasta (for a few more calories it really perks up the menu!), it may be made one to two days ahead, served cold, or reheated in the microwave or for 10 minutes in a large frying pan. The chicken may be made a day or two ahead, served cold, or reheated in the microwave or in a heavy covered skillet about 10 minutes over medium heat. It is heavenly made just before serving, however, and once chicken and asparagus are prepared to the point of cooking, may be cooked in less than 10 minutes. The salad may be served right from the refrigerator and the meringues straight from the freezer.

Note—several of the recipes in this menu have seeds. You might want to drop all but one garnish.

ꗞ R E C I P E S ꗞ

ELEGANT ZUCCHINI AND RED BELL PEPPER SOUP

Serves 8

4 to 5 zucchini, peeled
   and sliced (about 3
   cups)
1 onion, chopped
6 cups chicken stock,
   canned or fresh
4 red bell peppers,
   roasted and peeled
   (p. 191)
1 cup plain yogurt
1 to 2 teaspoons ground
   cumin seed
salt
freshly ground pepper
Garnish (optional):
1 teaspoon cumin seed,
   toasted

To make the soup base, bring the zucchini, onion, and stock to the boil, and simmer 25 minutes. In a food processor or blender, purée the roasted bell peppers and yogurt. Add the soup base in batches along with about 1 teaspoon of the ground cumin until smooth. Taste for seasoning and add salt and pepper and more cumin if necessary. Reheat without boiling or chill to serve cold. Garnish with cumin seed when serving. May be made one or two days in advance.

Variation
If you are not trying to be a skinny, try sour cream in place of the yogurt. Use fresh cilantro, chopped, in place of the cumin.

Variation
For a poached fish soup, add 2 pounds of a fresh white fish, such as grouper or flounder, skinned and boned and cut in 2-inch pieces, to the finished soup. Bring to the boil, reduce heat, and simmer 2 to 5 minutes, until the fish is just cooked.

Tip: This is beautiful served in a glass bowl.

CHINESE-STYLE ASPARAGUS AND CHICKEN BREASTS

Serves 6 to 8

1-1/2 pounds fresh, thin
  asparagus
3 tablespoons olive or
  salad oil
6 chicken breasts,
  boned and skinned,
  cut in 1-inch strips
5 tablespoons soy sauce
2 teaspoons sugar
  (optional)
2 tablespoons dark
  sesame seed oil
Garnish:
toasted or black sesame
  seeds

Cut off the end tips of the asparagus to the point where they are not "woody." Unless they are pencil thin, peel the asparagus to the bottom of the first flower. Slice diagonally in 1-1/2-inch lengths. Bring a pan of salted water to the boil, drop in the asparagus, and cook a few minutes, until they are barely tender and still crisp. Drain. Run cold water over to stop the cooking.

Heat the oil in a frying pan and add the chicken. Toss over high heat until cooked but still moist, about 3 to 5 minutes. Mix together the soy sauce, optional sugar, and sesame seed oil. May be made a day or two in advance. When ready to serve, put the chicken, asparagus, and sauce in the pan and bring to the boil, tossing until heated through. Toss with sesame seeds. Good hot or cold, as a main course or a salad.

Variation
Serve over sesame noodles or rice.

Variation
Add lots of chopped fresh ginger, and green onions or scallions, sliced in the Chinese style on the diagonal.

Variation
Serve inside a warmed tortilla or Chinese pancake (p. 82).

BROWN RICE

Serves 8

2 cups brown rice
4-1/2 cups liquid
    (water, broth, juice)
2 tablespoons butter or
    olive oil
2 teaspoons salt
    (optional)

Place the rice, cups of liquid, butter, and salt in a 3-quart saucepan. Bring to the boil; stir once or twice. Reduce heat, cover, and simmer 45 to 50 minutes, or until rice is tender and liquid is absorbed. Fluff with a fork.

Tip: When cooking brown rice, always follow package directions, as varieties differ. When directions are not available, use the above easy method. If using canned stock or broth, decrease salt to 1 teaspoon or to taste.

Tip: Brown rice retains its bran coat and its germ, so it takes longer to cook and tenderize. It is much more nutritious than white rice, which has had the bran and germ removed. Nowadays nutrients are added back to white rice in most, but not in all states and countries.

Serving tip: Rice may be made ahead and refrigerated, or frozen and reheated in the microwave, or placed in a colander over a pan of boiling water (be careful not to immerse the rice).

Tip: About Rice: Three basic groups of rice are grown in the United States. *Long grain* is four to five times as long as the grain is wide; its grains are fluffy and separate when cooked. *Medium grain* is shorter and thicker than long grain, and has a tender, soft texture when cooked. *Short grain* is also called "round" grain; the grains stick together when cooked. *Brown rice* is rough rice straight from the mill; only the hull has been removed. Any of the groups of rice can be brown. Brown rice needs to be cooked longer. *Parboiled, "converted,"* or *precooked rice* is rice that has undergone a steam-pressure process prior to milling; its grains are fluffy and separate when cooked. *Arborio* or *Valencia* are types of imported short grain rice that are particularly good to use when making risotto.

JOHN MARKHAM'S SZECHWAN NOODLES
Serves 6 to 8

4 garlic cloves, peeled
1/4 cup roughly
   chopped fresh ginger
   root
1/2 cup white wine
   vinegar
1/3 cup peanut oil
5 tablespoons smooth
   peanut butter
2 teaspoons hot red
   pepper flakes
1 teaspoon Szechwan
   peppercorns, ground
   to a fine powder
   (optional)
1 cup soy sauce
salt
freshly ground pepper
2 teaspoons sugar
1 pound thin spaghetti
   or vermicelli
Garnish:
1 bunch green onions or
   scallions, including
   green ends, chopped
1 cucumber, seeded and
   grated or julienned in
   the food processor

In a food processor or blender, purée the garlic, ginger, vinegar, 1/4 cup of the peanut oil, the peanut butter, pepper flakes, optional ground peppercorns, and soy sauce until you have a saucelike consistency. Taste and add salt, pepper, and sugar as needed. Bring a large quantity of water to the boil. Add noodles and cook 8 to 10 minutes until *al dente*. Drain and toss with a little peanut oil to prevent sticking. Refrigerate sauce and noodles separately, in plastic bags, and toss together before serving. May be made up to 2 days in advance. If serving hot, reheat the noodles with the sauce. If serving cold, may be tossed with the sauce and refrigerated.

Tip: Szechwan peppercorns, which are an optional seasoning, can be bought in health food stores, Asian grocery stores, or in the fancy-food sections of grocery stores.

Tip: Grind Szechwan peppercorns in a small chopper.

REFRESHING CUCUMBER AND YOGURT SALAD

Serves 6 to 8

4 cucumbers, peeled or
   unpeeled, sliced
2 cups plain or low-fat
   yogurt
4 tablespoons fresh
   mint, chopped
   (optional)
salt
freshly ground pepper
mint leaves

Stack the cucumber slices and cut down each stack twice, dividing the slices into four quarters. Toss with the yogurt. Add the optional mint, and season to taste with salt and pepper. Garnish with mint leaves.

Tip: Dried mint may be used, but quite judiciously.

MERIJOY'S HONEY WHOLE WHEAT ROLLS

Makes 2 dozen rolls or 1 loaf

1 package active dry
   yeast
2 tablespoons honey,
   divided
1/4 cup warm water
   (115°F)
2 cups milk, heated to
   lukewarm
1 tablespoon butter,
   melted
2 teaspoons salt
2 cups whole wheat
   flour
3 cups bread flour,
   sifted
1 egg white
1/2 teaspoon water

Dissolve the yeast and 1 teaspoon of the honey in the warm water. Place the warm milk in a large mixing bowl or food processor with the butter, the remaining honey, the salt, and the yeast mixture. Add all of the whole wheat flour. Beat until smooth. Add enough white flour, 1/2 cup at a time, to make a soft dough. Knead until the dough is elastic and smooth as a baby's bottom. Shape into a ball and place in an oiled bowl, turning the dough to coat, then cover with plastic wrap or place in an oiled plastic bag. Let rise in a warm place until doubled, about 1 hour.

Preheat oven to 375°F. Punch down the dough. Let rest 5 minutes. Shape into rolls and place 1/2 inch apart on greased baking sheets. Beat the egg white with water until foamy and brush on rolls. Let rise again uncovered until doubled. Bake at 375°F for 20 to 30 minutes, or until golden.

Variation

Sprinkle the rolls with 3 tablespoons sesame seeds after brushing with the egg white.

Tip: Rolls can be frozen and will keep for months.

TINY MERINGUES
Makes 30 to 35

4 egg whites, at room
  temperature
1/8 teaspoon cream of
  tartar
1 cup sugar

Preheat oven to 200°F. Oil a baking sheet, or line it with parchment paper. Beat the egg whites with the cream of tartar until stiff peaks form. Add half the sugar, 1 tablespoon at a time, continuing to beat until the meringue is very stiff and shiny. Fold in the remaining sugar.

Spoon or pipe the meringue mixture into tiny rounds or cigarettes on the prepared pan. Bake until the meringues are dry throughout, but not brown, about 1-1/2 to 2-1/2 hours. To test for doneness, press one with fingers. If it crumbles with no sogginess, the meringues are done. When they are completely dry, the meringues may be kept covered in an airtight container, or frozen and served straight from the freezer.

Variation
Dust with ground sieved chocolate or cocoa.

Variation
Sandwich 2 together with drained lemon yogurt or whipped cream.

Variation
Serve with strawberries, raspberries, or peaches.

Tip: The length of time to cook the meringues varies considerably with the humidity of the day. When cooked, a meringue will be crisp throughout, and crumble when pressed firmly. Test one to be sure.

✗13✗

A LOBSTER FEAST
FOR FRIENDS

Advice on the Art of Eating Lobster

I didn't eat a lobster, properly, until after my sophomore year in college. I was living in a boarding house in Cambridge, Massachusetts, that had no resident manager. We were a diverse lot—some MIT students, some Harvard, others who were researchers and/or graduate students. None of us had any money. There were four girls in my room, and even at that the rent seemed high. We all chipped in and contributed $18.50 a month for dinners, and thought it too much.

Jean was a nonresident who would come by for dinner, paying a slightly higher rate—I think 85 cents a meal. The rumor was that Jean was from a wealthy Main Line family, but had chucked family and fortune to be a sculptor at the Museum School in Boston. She was renowned for a red boatneck sweater, which she wore inside-out over a frequently worn shirt. She was older than the rest of us, and quite worldly. We were in awe. She smoked a cigar. She was our own Gertrude Stein, a genius in our midst.

One of her assets was a sailboat. One day in late summer as many of us as could fit piled into a beat-up car and drove to Marblehead, Massachusetts, for my first day of sailing and my first freshly caught lobster. We had a long day on the water, the sun keeping company with a slight breeze. When the sun went down, we were struck with a ravenous hunger, and as Jean brought us back to the dock, she told us how to eat lobster.

"Never," she said, "eat a lobster above one pound. The small ones are the sweetest. They are also affordable; a larger one might not be." We walked into a small restaurant with white tablecloths but not much else in the way of pizzazz. A slight smell of beer lingered in the air. Jean's short dark hair was still ruffled by the wind. She disdained combs. The rest of us were flushed with the wind and sun, but tidy enough. Jean was treated royally. The owner was as delighted to see her as if she were in a ball gown, and we were gathered in the embrace of his enthusiasm.

"I'm here," she exclaimed, "to teach these children how to eat lobster." He nodded assent, and they discussed the perfect menu. "First," she said, "a very dry martini." Hands folded in front of him, the owner nodded, as if he knew the menu by heart, which he most assuredly did. Still, they treated it as if it were serious business.

"Next," she said, "a crisp green salad. And, then, with the lobster, a baked potato. Sour cream on the potato, and plenty of butter for the lobster." Nearly through with her order, she jabbed a finger in the air, "And bibs," she said, "we all need bibs and big white cloth napkins."

I don't know what the drinking age at the time was, but that martini was potent enough to insure my avoidance of them from then on. But the rest of the meal was perfect. The salad was crisp with just enough dressing clinging to the greens to coat them lightly. The potato was soft and fluffy inside the thick jacket in which it was cooked. Sour cream was oozing from the split up its center. The lobsters, a small one for each of us, with a few extras for second helpings for the hearty eaters, were brought out, once bibs had been tied around our necks. With them we were served melted clarified butter—real butter, not margarine—and mallets.

Mallet in one hand, lobster in the other, Jean proceeded to teach us how to eat lobster, first tearing off the claws, then cracking them, and pulling out the tender meat. Then she twisted off the tiny pincers on the bottom, and taught us to suck them between our teeth. Arnie, one of the boys who lived on the floor above me, thought the pounding was great fun and pounded all our claws for us, while the rest of us ate the pincers. Pincers consumed, we pulled back off the body, ate the green tomalley inside, and proceeded to the separated tail. We cracked the tail, sliced and ate it, dipping it in the butter. We savored the rest of the lobster, wiping our fingers on the snowy white napkins. Those with room left reached for seconds, and so the evening went, until all the food was gone. I slept a good part of the way home, while the others sang driving songs, aided, no doubt, by the martini.

Here is a lobster dinner I love to make for friends.

MENU

A LOBSTER FEAST FOR FRIENDS

Thymed Red Pepper and Corn Chowder
Boiled Lobster
Best Baked Potatoes
Grated Turnips with Leeks and Peppers or *Quick Broccoli with Garlic*
Sue's Make-Ahead Green Salad (p. 109)
Crispy Egg-white Rolls
Fruit Tarts

SERVES 4 TO 6

LOGISTICS

Everything in this menu but the lobster may be made ahead. And the guests enjoy the flurry of activity and excitement that goes with cooking the lobster! The corn chowder may be made one or two days ahead and refrigerated. The rolls and tart shells can be baked ahead and frozen or refrigerated. If frozen, defrost rolls and tart shells, then glaze and fill shells 1 to 2 hours before serving. The potatoes and vegetables can be cooked ahead then reheated. And the salad, true to its name, can be made ahead, ready for tossing.

When serving the chowder, have the water in the lobster pot boiling and the oven preheated to 350°F for the potatoes and the rolls. Put in the potatoes about 15 minutes before eating. The lobster can go in as you sit down. Have the defrosted rolls wrapped in aluminum foil and place in the oven after the lobster has cooked 5 minutes. Start to reheat the vegetables in a frying pan. The salad may be served with or after the lobster.

ℭ RECIPES ℭ

THYMED RED PEPPER AND CORN CHOWDER

Serves 4 to 6

1/4 cup salt pork or
    bacon, cubed
1 onion, chopped
1 red bell pepper,
    seeded and chopped
1 cup chicken stock
2 cups fresh, frozen, or
    canned corn kernels,
    drained
2 teaspoons thyme,
    chopped
1 bay leaf, crumbled
1 cup milk
1 cup heavy cream
salt
freshly ground pepper
Garnish:
sprigs of thyme

Fry the salt pork or bacon in a heavy casserole. Remove and set aside. Add the onion and pepper to the hot fat and cook until the onion is soft. Add the stock, bring to the boil, and reduce the heat to a simmer. Add the corn, thyme, bay leaf, milk, and cream. Bring back to the boil, reduce to a simmer, and simmer a few minutes until the corn is cooked. Return the salt pork to the pan. Taste for salt and pepper. Serve hot, garnishing with the thyme. May be made ahead one or two days and refrigerated.

Variation
For an elegant soup, add chunks of boiled lobster.

Variation
Add a dash of ground cumin seed.

Variation
Add chopped fresh tarragon or chives.

Continued

Variation

Roast and peel the red peppers (p. 191) before using, saving some for a garnish.

Variation

Add 1/4 cup white wine to the stock and stir in 1/4 cup Cheddar cheese at the end.

Variation

Add 2 medium potatoes, peeled and cut in 1-inch cubes, to the chowder with the stock. Cook until potatoes are done, then add corn and proceed as directed.

BOILED LOBSTER

Serves 4 to 6

6 (1 to 2-pound) lobsters, alive

Bring a large pot of water to the boil. Add the lobsters, headfirst, immediately reduce the heat to a simmer, and cover. Simmer until the lobsters turn color, then continue to cook 8 minutes per pound. Remove from heat. Drain, slit tail and crack the claws, and serve immediately.

Clarified ("Drawn") Butter

1 cup (1/2 pound) butter

Melt the butter over low heat. Remove from the heat and let stand several minutes, until the milk solids settle on the bottom. Skim the salt, if any, from the top and discard. The next layer is the butter fat, the clarified butter. Remove to a container. Discard the milk solids.

Variation

Add a squeeze of lemon to the clarified butter.

Variation

Make a low-calorie dipping sauce of 1/2 cup lime juice and up to 1 tablespoon of butter. Heat together and serve. Garnish with twisted slices of lime.

Leftover tips: Crack any leftover shells containing meat and remove the meat. Use in a salad or add to the leftover corn chowder and reheat gently for a spectacular meal the next day.

Comment: Even those lobsters kept in a holding tank may be old and underfed. Know your purveyor, and ask how long the lobster has been in the tank. Once home, live lobsters will last several days in the refrigerator, out of water. Female lobsters have a broader tail shell than males do.

Comment: Killing any live thing is disquieting for most of us. Lobsters, in particular, are disturbing to kill, as their muscles continue to move long after they are dead. There is no one way to kill a lobster that suits everyone's sensibilities. I favor plunging the lobsters into boiling water, headfirst. Many people believe inserting a knife in 2 sharp perpendicular thrusts at the back of the head of the lobster is more humane. Suit your own conscience.

Tip for larger lobsters: Cook a 2-1/2 to 5-pound lobster for 20 to 25 minutes, and a 6 to 10-pound lobster for 25 to 35 minutes.

Comment: A 1-pound lobster is a little too small for a healthy eater, although I personally find it enough for myself. A 1-1/2 to 2-pound one is a better choice when entertaining. I always try to get a lobster or two extra, to give a feeling of abundance to the meal. Leftover lobster meat can be used in a salad, or added to any leftover soup as a next-day treat. The pale green substance inside the lobster is the liver, called the tomalley, and is a favorite of mine. It is totally edible, as is the red roe of the female lobster. The stomach sac is a little sac that should be discarded. Before serving, slit the tail and crack the claws to drain excess fluid.

BEST BAKED POTATOES

Serves 6

6 baking potatoes
salt
freshly ground pepper

Preheat oven to 500°F. Wash and dry the potatoes. Prick several times with a fork and place on a baking sheet. Bake for 1 to 1-1/2 hours until done. Serve with plenty of salt and pepper. Although potatoes lose some quality when baked ahead a few hours, they still are satisfactory reheated at 350°F for 15 minutes.

Continued

Variation

If time is too short to bake the potatoes, cook the potatoes according to individual microwave directions. Place in 500°F oven for 10 more minutes to get a crisper skin and a baked feeling.

Serving tip: Serve with butter and/or sour cream, chives, and crumbled bacon pieces.

Health tip: Try extra virgin olive oil rather than butter, or top with plain yogurt or cottage cheese.

GRATED TURNIPS WITH LEEKS AND PEPPERS
Serves 10 to 12

2 medium-sized turnips,
   peeled and grated
1 leek, white part with
   small portion of the
   green, julienned
1/3 cup butter
1 red bell pepper,
   julienned
1 green bell pepper,
   julienned
1 tablespoon mixed
   fresh herbs (basil,
   thyme, marjoram,
   and lemon balm),
   chopped
salt
freshly ground pepper

Bring a pot of water to the boil, add the grated turnip, bring back to the boil, and boil 5 minutes, then drain well. Melt half of the butter in the pot, add the leek, and sauté until tender. Mix the drained turnips in with the leek. In another pan, melt the remaining butter, add the peppers, and sauté until tender. Add to the pot with turnips and leek. May be done ahead to this point. When ready to serve, season with herbs, salt, and pepper, and heat over low heat, tossing until heated through.

Variation

Reduce quantities to the minimum—1/2 of each kind of pepper, 1 leek, 1 turnip—to serve 4 to 6.

Tip: There is a vegetable called a "yellow turnip," or rutabaga. This is not the same vegetable.

QUICK BROCCOLI WITH GARLIC
Serves 4

1 head broccoli
1/4 to 1/2 cup butter or
  olive oil
2 garlic cloves, chopped
salt
freshly ground pepper

Trim off the tough ends of the broccoli stalks. Peel the rest of the stalk to just below the florets, then cut the stalk off and slice 1/4 inch thick. Bring a frying pan or large saucepan of water to the boil, add the sliced broccoli, and cook 3 minutes over high heat. Break the head into florets and add them to the stalks to cook 2 minutes more. Rinse with cold water to set the color and refresh. Drain. Set aside until time to serve. Heat the butter or oil in a frying pan, add the garlic, and cook a few minutes. Set aside. When ready to serve, reheat the pan, add the broccoli, and toss over medium heat until coated with the garlic and butter or oil. Season with salt and pepper.

Variation
Add 1/2 cup grated imported Parmesan cheese to the frying pan when reheating with the garlic.

CRISPY EGG-WHITE ROLLS
Makes 48 small rolls

5 to 7 cups bread or all-
  purpose flour
2 packages rapid-rise
  yeast (see tip below)
2 tablespoons sugar
2 teaspoons salt
3 tablespoons butter or
  shortening, at room
  temperature or
  melted
2 cups hot water
  (130°F)
3 egg whites

Mix together 3 cups of the flour, the yeast, sugar, salt, and butter or shortening in a mixing bowl or food-processor bowl. Add the hot water and mix well. In a separate bowl, whip the egg whites to a firm but not very stiff peak. Fold the whites into the dough. Add enough of the flour, 1/2 cup at a time, to make a soft dough. Knead until elastic and smooth as a baby's bottom. Shape into a ball. Turn the ball in an oiled bowl and cover with plastic wrap, or place in an oiled plastic bag. Let rise, uncovered, in a warm place until doubled.

Continued

Pull off dough in egg-size pieces and roll into balls. Place on greased baking sheets, leaving space to rise. Let rise in a warm place until doubled, about 45 minutes.

Preheat oven to 400°F. Bake on the middle rack for 25 to 30 minutes, to a lovely golden brown. Cool on a wire rack. The rolls may be frozen, thawed, then reheated for 15 minutes at 350°F.

Bread tip: To speed up rising, place the bowl of covered dough in a pan of water heated to 140°F. Alternately, it is possible to raise breads in some microwaves providing the dough never gets heated above 110°F.

Comment: The new rapid- and quick-rising yeasts are highly active strains of yeast that can replace dry yeast in equal measure. When used according to the package directions, these yeasts reduce bread-making time by about half. These steps call for adding the yeast directly to a portion of the dry ingredients. Liquids heated to a very warm temperature (125° to 130°F) are then added to the dry ingredients. Active dry yeast can either be dissolved in warm water (105° to 115°F), which is the traditional method, or mixed with a portion of the dry ingredients before dissolving with very warm water (120° to 130°F). Many recipes for quick-rising yeasts need only one rising. Check package directions and adapt the recipe if speed is crucial.

FRUIT TARTS

Makes 30 tarts or 1 (9-inch) flan ring

1 cup sifted all-purpose
   flour
1 teaspoon salt
1-1/2 tablespoons sugar
5 tablespoons butter
1/2 teaspoon grated
   lemon peel
1 hard-cooked egg yolk,
   mashed
1 raw egg white

Sift the flour, salt, and sugar into a food processor or large bowl. Cut in the butter until pea-sized. Add the lemon peel, yolk, and egg white, and mix to form a smooth ball. Flatten the dough into a circle, wrap, and chill until it is firm enough to roll. Preheat oven to 350°F.

To shape: To make tart shells, divide dough into 30 pieces and press into individual tart shells. To make a large tart, roll the slightly chilled pastry between sheets of wax paper

To fill:
**3/4 cup apricot or
currant jam
1 tablespoon water
1/2 teaspoon lemon
juice
2 to 2-1/2 cups assorted
fruits (such as small
strawberries, red and
green grapes, kiwi,
raspberries, and
starfruit), sliced**

until 10 inches in diameter, then remove top piece of wax paper. Place the 9-inch flan ring or pie pan on a baking sheet. Gently flip the dough over into the flan ring or pan. Remove the second sheet of wax paper. Gently settle the dough into the ring or pan, without stretching. Trim off the excess dough. Chill the dough on the baking sheet, for at least 15 minutes.

To prebake: Preheat oven to 350°F. Crumple a piece of wax paper, then spread it out to the top edges of each tart pan or pie pan. To weigh down, fill the paper with raw rice or dried peas. Place the filled tart ring on the baking sheet in the preheated oven. Bake for 20 minutes. Carefully remove the rice or peas, then the paper. (The rice or peas may be used again the next time you prebake a pie crust.) Return the tart shells to the oven and bake until done, about 20 minutes. Cool on a rack. Put the jam in a pan with the water and lemon juice. Bring to the boil and boil to a thick syrup, the right consistency for brushing, and strain. To glaze, dip a pastry brush in the hot liquid and brush the pastry. Move to a serving plate with a doily and arrange the fruits alternately in the precooked shells and glaze with more apricot or currant jam according to the color.

Tip: The empty shell may be made ahead, wrapped, and stored carefully to avoid breakage, then frozen.

Tip: Use apricot-jam glaze for yellow and green fruits, red currant for red fruits.

⚹ 14 ⚹

MENU FOR TWELVE FLORIDA EXILES

Key West's Famous Dessert

Recently, I went on a quest for a true Key lime pie, that flavorful, airy confection spoken of with reverence by those few who have savored the real thing. This select group is primarily composed of Floridians exiled from the Keys, whose social standing seems to be based not on their money, background, or polo ponies, but on whether or not their grandmothers had a Key lime tree.

One such illustrious personage once declared, "The women in my family for three generations have made Key lime pies, and they swear it cannot be made from regular limes. We've not made a lime pie since my mother-in-law's tree died." Now, either that was a pretext on his wife's part to avoid baking a pie crust, or the difference was so vast that what we regular earthlings settle for was not worth the effort of the initiated.

I myself have always preferred lemon meringue pie to nearly every other pie. I've dutifully eaten my share of those other alleged Key lime pies, with their graham cracker crusts, heavy cream on top, and laden green with food coloring. Usually they are a disappointment, particularly those in restaurants. But the thought had always lurked in the back of my mind: I'd never had the real thing. Perhaps there really is a magic to the Key lime itself that sets it apart from the others.

Imagine my pleasure, then, at finding myself in the Keys one summer. There, I was informed, the original and true lime is Key lime, brought to Florida in 1835 by Dr. Henry Perrine. It comes from thorny trees grown from seed, which require little care, and it is the same as the Mexican and West Indian lime. The limes are smaller in diameter and slightly higher in acid than what we find in the supermarkets. These market limes are hybrids that came to Florida from California at the turn of the century and are called "Persian," "Tahiti," or "Bears" limes.

The most obvious difference is that the Key lime is allowed to ripen on the tree until it turns yellow. All limes are yellow when ripe, but by then they are too soft to ship—that is why we buy and use our Persian limes green, when they are most acidic and tasty. The juice of both is pale yellow, tinged with green.

Robert, a wonderfully eccentric fruit grower who has more than two hundred kinds of fruit growing in his operation, had a Key lime tree. When he admitted that he couldn't taste the difference between the Key lime and the Persian lime, we were all shocked, horrified even. For this we had flown to Miami, driven for hours, eaten at mediocre restaurants in quest of the legendary pie?

He shrugged off our protests with a "you'll see for yourself"— and then picked us dozens of Key limes along with dozens of Persian limes picked the same day from a nearby grove.

Once home, we studied pie recipes. Key lime pies originated around the time of the Civil War. They were a natural use of the plentiful limes and the new and important milk product, Borden's canned Eagle-brand sweetened condensed milk. This high-quality milk, which required no refrigeration, was a boon to Florida's settlers. The rest is history. The "real" thing is always made with sweetened condensed milk, is yellow, and has a traditional pie crust (graham cracker crusts, popular as they are, are a modern innovation).

Eagerly, we baked two pies—side by side, using the same recipe, but one with Key limes, the other with Persian limes. We called in our friends for the taste test. "Which one do you like?" we asked. "Which one is the Key lime?" The votes were exactly divided: 50 percent liked one pie better than the other and thought it was the Key lime; 50 percent liked the other pie better even if it turned out not to be the Key lime. It was discouraging. But I loved them all!

We repeated the test three times and included some Key Westians in our survey, until we finally put our finger on what the real difference was. It was not so much flavor as texture and acidity. The Key lime pie had a softer texture and a softer color. We wondered if another Key lime tree might have produced a tarter Key lime—we really didn't want to believe our own senses, even though all the pies were delicious really. So the next time I find Key limes, I'll repeat the test—as you can. I'm sure it's worth testing and retesting as a confirmed Key lime pie lover!

(Note: Haitian limes are now being sold as "Key" limes. They are picked smaller and slightly greener than Key limes, and create a similar texture, but they are more acidic and tart.)

MENU

MENU FOR TWELVE FLORIDA EXILES

Chilled Cucumber and Apple Soup

Elliott Mackle's Key West Paella

Red Leaf Salad with Vinaigrette or Greek Salad (p. 202)

Beer Bread or Cuban Bread (store-bought)

Two Key Lime Pies or
Mango Ice Cream, with Blueberries or Sliced Mangoes

SERVES 12

LOGISTICS

The soup may be made several days in advance. The pie crusts may be baked a day in advance, and filled and finished the morning of the party or up to 2 hours before the guests arrive. The bread may be made ahead and frozen. All the vegetables, meats, poultry, and fish should be cut up and generally prepped several hours in advance if possible. The ice cream may be made several hours in advance, and the fruit prepared. One or 2 hours before the guests arrive, brown the chicken for the paella. Refrigerate. Cook the onions, garlic, pork, tomato, and paprika. Add the rice, salt, and saffron. About 45 minutes before serving, boil the broth for the paella and proceed with the rest of the recipe. Guests enjoy seeing the dish put together, but if this is not your style, the whole paella may be made a few hours in advance, refrigerated, then reheated for 20 to 30 minutes until heated through, loosely covered with foil in a 350°F oven. It won't be perfect but will still get oohs and aahs.

ᑕ R E C I P E S ᑐ

CHILLED CUCUMBER AND APPLE SOUP
Makes 2-1/2 quarts

1 onion, chopped
1 cup chicken stock
6 medium cucumbers
1 Granny Smith or
    Golden Delicious
    apple
1-1/2 cups plain yogurt
1/4 cup fresh parsley
1/4 to 1/2 cup fresh
    mint, chopped
salt
freshly ground pepper
Garnish:
yogurt and/or mint
    leaves

Heat the onion and the chicken stock in a heavy pan and bring to the boil. Boil 5 minutes. Seed and halve the cucumbers. Peel and core the apples. Place together in a blender or food processor and blend or process until smooth, adding the stock. Cool down, then blend or process in the yogurt. Chill until ready to serve. Chop the parsley and mint, and add to taste. Whisk briefly if the soup has separated. Adjust seasoning, adding salt and pepper to taste. Garnish with yogurt and mint leaves. May be made several days in advance. Doubles easily.

Tip: Chilling causes the flavor to recede. Always taste after chilling and correct the seasoning then.
Serving tip: Measure soup bowls and ladles, being sure 1/2 to 3/4 cup per person is sufficient for your servings. If not, double recipe.

ELLIOTT MACKLE'S KEY WEST PAELLA

Serves 12

1/2 pound dried
    Spanish pork chorizo,
    good red Italian
    pepperoni, or salami
1 pound large or jumbo
    shrimp
1 frying chicken or 3
    pounds chicken
    thighs
salt
freshly ground pepper
1/2 cup olive oil
1 large onion
1 garlic clove, finely
    chopped
1/2 pound lean pork,
    cut into 1-inch cubes
1 large fresh or canned
    tomato, peeled,
    seeded, and chopped
1 tablespoon paprika
1 tablespoon lemon
    juice
1/3 to 1 tablespoon
    saffron* (optional)
1 can chicken broth
2-1/2 cups rice,
    preferably imported
    short grain rice such
    as Arborio or
    Valenciano**
1/2 red or green bell
    pepper, finely
    chopped
1/2 cup shelled fresh or
    frozen green peas

Preheat oven to 400°F. Skin and slice the sausage into 1/8-inch rounds. If desired, peel the shrimp, leaving the tails intact, or remove only the legs and leave shells on. If using a whole chicken, cut into 8 pieces. Dry the chicken pieces and season with salt and pepper. Heat 1/4 cup of the olive oil in a large skillet until singing,*** then add the chicken, skin side down, and brown on 1 side. Turn and brown second side. Remove the chicken and set aside.

Soak the optional saffron thread in the lemon juice and a little of the chicken broth.

In a paella pan, casserole, or large ovenproof skillet, heat the remaining 1/4 cup of the oil until singing. Finely chop the onions and garlic, add to the oil, and cook until soft. Add the pork, sautéing briefly. Peel and seed the tomato. Chop roughly. Add to the pan with the paprika. Cook, stirring, until most of the juice evaporates. Add the rice, salt, and saffron with its soaking liquid to the onion mixture, and cook, stirring 1 minute. In a separate pan, mix the chicken broth with enough water to make 5 cups and bring to a boil. Pour it onto the rice and onion mixture. Bring back to the boil quickly, stirring constantly. Remove from heat and arrange the chicken, sausage, pork, and bell pepper over the rice. Scatter the shelled peas over all. Set in the lowest part of the oven and bake 10 minutes, remove, scatter the fish, lobster and shrimp over, and return to the oven and cook for five more minutes or until the liquid has evaporated.

Add the mussels, clams and/or scallops. Return to the oven and cook 5 minutes more

1 pound red snapper,
   flounder, sea bass, or
   orange roughy, in
   1-inch cubes
1 or 2 Florida lobster
   tails, shelled and cut
   into 1-inch
   medallions (optional)
1 to 1-1/2 pounds
   mussels, clams, and/
   or scallops
2 tablespoons parsley,
   chopped

until the liquid has evaporated. Remove from the oven and let rest 5 to 10 minutes draped with a towel. Chop the parsley and sprinkle over the paella. The paella may be made a few hours in advance and reheated as directed in logistics (p. 136).

Variation
Serve chilled, as a main course salad. It's wonderful! Use more salt and pepper when serving chilled.

    *   *Comment:* Saffron, the stamen of a crocus, is costly to produce and very expensive. Therefore, it may be hard to find at your local grocery store. Be sure to ask for it, as it is frequently locked up. Indian grocery stores usually have some, as do specialty gourmet shops. You may leave it out, but you will have to use more salt and pepper, and you will miss its flavor and color. The strength varies considerably with the quality.

    ** *Comment:* This recipe may be made with a converted rice, like Uncle Ben's, quite satisfactorily. But if you can find Arborio or Valenciano in your grocery store, by all means use it.

  *** *Comment:* To prepare oil for cooking meat, be sure it is heated to just sizzling, which causes it to "sing."

Comment: Paella is a traditional Spanish dish, made in a special pan. A frying pan is a good American substitute. I've substituted Florida ingredients for the traditional Spanish ones.

Comment: Florida lobsters are really a type of crayfish (also called rock lobster or South African lobster). Usually you see just the tail available for sale, and frequently it is frozen. If it is exorbitantly expensive, bypass.

Continued

Tip: Crush saffron before soaking. The lemon juice gives a lighter red color.

Tip: Chorizo is a flavorful, mildly spicy, dried, traditional Spanish sausage. Substitute a good dried pepperoni if it is not available.

Low-cal tip: To reduce fattiness, prick the skinned sausage several times with the tip of a knife before slicing it, then simmer for 5 minutes and drain on a paper towel. Delete the optional pork from the recipe. You'll lose some flavor but it's acceptable.

RED LEAF SALAD WITH VINAIGRETTE

Serves 12

3 heads Red Leaf
   lettuce, washed and
   dried
1 head Bibb lettuce
1 double recipe
   Vinaigrette with
   Herbs (p. 141)

Remove any tough stalks and veins. Tear into large bite-sized pieces. Keep refrigerated until ready to serve. When ready to serve, toss with vinaigrette and herbs.

Variation
Leave lettuce in pieces large enough to provide a bed for mushrooms. Place marinated mushrooms (p. 248) on lettuce. Omit other vinaigrette.

VINAIGRETTE

Makes 1 cup

1/4 cup red wine
   vinegar
1 teaspoon Dijon
   mustard
3/4 cup oil
salt
1/2 teaspoon sugar
   (optional)
freshly ground pepper

Mix vinegar and mustard in a bowl. Whisk in the oil. Taste for seasoning and add salt, sugar, and pepper as needed. If kept in an airtight container, vinaigrette will stay fresh almost indefinitely in the refrigerator.

Variation
Add 1 garlic clove, chopped.

Variation
Add 1 to 2 tablespoons fresh herbs, chopped, and/or 1 to 2 green onions or scallions, chopped.

Tip: If dressing is too oily, add salt and sugar before adding more vinegar.

Variation
Add 1 teaspoon dark sesame seed oil to the dressing.

Variation
Add 1 to 2 tablespoons fresh chopped ginger to the dressing.

BEER BREAD

Makes 1 loaf

3 cups self-rising flour*
1/4 cup sugar
1/8 teaspoon salt
1 (12-ounce) bottle beer,
   or nonalcoholic beer
1/2 cup butter, melted

Preheat oven to 350°F. Grease one 8 × 5-inch loaf pan. Line with a strip of wax paper and grease the paper. Place flour, sugar, and salt in a food-processor bowl or mixer. Beating or processing, add the beer. Mix until smooth. Pour batter into the prepared loaf pan and top with melted butter. Bake for 45 to 50 minutes. Bread may be made ahead and frozen.

Tip: You may grease with oil or butter.

Comment: The beer has nothing to do with the rising; it's the baking powder in the flour. The beer just gives a yeasty flavor, so nonalcoholic beer does as well as alcoholic.

*See p. 37 for substitutions for self-rising flour.

KEY LIME PIE
Makes 1 pie
(make at least 2 pies for 12 servings)

1 (14-ounce) can
    sweetened condensed
    milk
4 egg yolks
1/2 cup fresh lime juice
9-inch shallow-dish pie
    crust, prebaked (see
    instructions below)
4 egg whites
6 to 8 tablespoons sugar
1/2 teaspoon cream of
    tartar (optional)
Garnish:
1 lime, sliced

Preheat oven to 350°F. Mix together condensed milk, egg yolks, and lime juice in a mixing bowl. Beat 1 egg white stiff. Fold into the mixture and turn into the prebaked pie crust. Beat remaining 3 egg whites to a stiff peak, gradually adding sugar and cream of tartar. Spread meringue over filling to the inner edge of the crust and bake on the middle rack of the oven for 20 minutes or until egg whites are golden brown. Chill before serving. Garnish with lime slices.

Tip: Beating in a copper bowl gives greater volume and more stability, and allows you to omit the cream of tartar.

Tip: To get 1/2 cup lime juice, you will need from 2 to 3 Persian limes, or 4 to 5 Key limes, or 8 to 10 Haitian limes.

Variation
If you want a tarter pie, add 1 to 2 tablespoons finely grated rind.

BEGINNER'S 1-CRUST PIE DOUGH
Makes dough for 1 crust

1-1/4 cups all-purpose
    flour
1/2 teaspoon salt
8 tablespoons
    shortening
3 to 6 tablespoons ice
    water

Mix the flour and salt together in a bowl. Cut in the shortening with a pastry blender or fork until the mixture resembles cornmeal. Add some of the ice water (see p. 000), a little at a time, to 1/3 portion of the mixture. Set aside. Repeat, adding more water until all the portions are moist. Gather the dough into a smooth ball and flatten into a round. Wrap well with plastic wrap and chill.

Rolling out doughs: Flour a board, wax

paper, or pie cloth and use a floured or stock-inged rolling pin to roll out pastry. Place the dough round in the center of the floured surface. Starting in the center of the dough, roll to, but not over, the top edge of the dough. Go back to the center, and roll down to, but not over, the bottom edge of the dough. Pick up the dough and turn it a quarter circle. This will keep it round and prevent it from sticking. Repeat your rolling, and repeat the quarter turns until you have a round 1/8 inch thick and 1-1/2 inches larger than your pan. Fold into quarters. Place the pastry in a pie pan with the tip of the triangle in the center and unfold. Trim the pastry 1 inch larger than the pie pan and fold the overhanging pastry under itself. To decorate, press the tines of a fork around the edge. To make a fluted pattern, use two thumbs to pinch the dough all around the edge so that the edge of the dough stands up. Place in the freezer or chill in the refrigerator for 30 minutes before baking.

To prebake: Preheat the oven to 425°F. Crumple a piece of wax paper, then spread it out to the edges of the pie pan. To make a weight, fill the paper with raw rice or dried peas. Bake for 20 minutes. Carefully remove the paper and rice or peas. (The rice or peas may be used again the next time you prebake a pie crust.) Fill the crust with a filling and bake according to filling directions. If the filling requires no cooking, bake the pie shell 10 minutes more before filling.

Tip: The recipe may be doubled for a 2-crust pie.

Comments on Making Pie Crust

Pie crusts are best made in advance. As little as half an hour resting in the refrigerator before baking will help prevent shrinking and bouncing back, but 12 hours or several days will

Continued

make a startling difference. The gluten in the dough relaxes and tenderizes.

Temperature   The room, work surface, and the ingredients should be cold—65° to 70°F is the ideal temperature until you gain your confidence. Pastry should be chilled before it goes into a hot oven, so the flour is set before the butter melts, and thus the pastry will not slip and slide when baking.

Speed   The faster you make your dough and the quicker you roll it out, the less opportunity you have to lose control of the dough. Practice helps.

Equipment   A rolling pin should have a solid barrel longer than the diameter of the pie. A smaller barrel will cause you to overwork the dough. Cloth covers for pins are very helpful.

Work with a small shaker full of flour, a pie brush (to brush away the excess), and a pastry scraper or knife to scrape the dry dough off the counter. Your hands (I call them God's tools), 2 forks or knives, long metal spatulas, and a pastry blender or a food processor can be used to cut the fat into the flour.

Prebaking   Prebaking, or "baking blind" is a way to prevent soggy bottom crusts. "Short" crusts, because they have so much fat in them, manage to hold their shape when they are prebaked. But other doughs tend to shrink or slide and need weights in them to hold up the sides and to keep the bottom down. Use crumbled wax paper or lightly greased aluminum foil and fit into the dough in the pie pan to cover the bottom and sides. Then fill the paper with dried beans, uncooked rice, or metal "pie weights." Chill the crust for at least 30 minutes, then bake in a hot oven until it is partially or completely done, depending on whether the filling will need cooking. When the shell is done to the proper point, remove the weights. (They are all reusable as pie weights. I've had my rice and beans for 20 years!) If the crust is underdone the paper tends to stick, so it should be carefully pulled away.

Flour

Flour varies radically from region to region. And you can't always depend on the brand because the same company will sell different types of flour to different regions of the country; even the package sizes sometimes differ.

The best flour to use for pie doughs is soft winter wheat flour because you need a flour that is not high in gluten. In the North it is called pastry flour. In the South, it is the standard all-purpose. (My favorite is White Lily.) The more gluten in the flour, the tougher your crust will be. Winter wheat absorbs water differently from summer wheat, requiring less, and it is the water that toughens the gluten, thus making for a tougher finished pie crust.

It is difficult to tell when buying flour what the gluten content is because it is not labeled. However, the higher the protein count, the higher the gluten is, so if nutritional information is marked on the flour package, look for the protein count. Bread flour usually has about 14 grams protein per cup, all-purpose winter wheat 9, and cake flour (such as Swans Down), has about 8 grams; however, in some cases cornstarch may have been added to cake flour so the protein count can be misleading.

Fats

Butter   Butter makes the most flavorful pie crust. It is also the hardest fat to handle as it melts easily, and if overworked it makes a tougher crust. My solution is to use half butter for a particularly flavorful crust, and half vegetable shortening.

Margarine   Margarine is not good for a pie dough. It doesn't have the flavor of butter or the tenderizing quality of shortening.

Shortening   Hard shortening is 100 percent fat, which makes it the best fat for a light crust. I prefer Crisco.

Oil   You can use oil, but it will make a mealy crust that I don't find as desirable.

Lard   Fresh lard makes a light and flavorful crust.

Acid   Acid is a good friend of pie doughs. A little lemon juice, vinegar, or sour cream will make a great difference in a crust.

Egg   Egg yolk tenderizes, egg white crisps.

Water   Water should be ice cold, since cold retards the development of gluten. A wet pie crust is easier to roll and shape than a "short" one. If you have to roll out a dough and are having trouble with it, and the temperature is right, the chances are you don't have enough water in it. On the other hand, too much water, or water in a dough that has been overworked (or perhaps not rested), will make it tough and incline it to shrink. Crusts that don't use water are called "short crusts," meaning the gluten strands are shortened by fat (i.e., shortening)! These crusts don't shrink or toughen if overworked, and can be prebaked without weights. They are the simplest to make of all the crusts, like making a cookie dough. However, they are hard to roll out and move, so you do better by pressing them into their forms.

Sugar   Sugar sweetens and tenderizes the dough up to a certain degree.

The process

Making the dough   The finer you cut the fat into the flour, the crumblier, but more tender, the crust will be. The larger the pieces of fat are, the flakier the crust! I, therefore, add my fat in two stages. First, cut all the fat you are using into large pieces; then add half the fat, cutting it in quickly by hand or using the food processor in quick pulses, until the fat particles are the size of green peas. Next, add the rest of the fat, cutting it in quickly, until the first batch is reduced to the size of cornmeal and the second batch now resembles peas.

It is at this point that overworking can occur. With your fingers or a fork, add some of the water to 1/3 of the flour/fat mixture, to form a dough. Push the dough to the side, add more water to a second portion, push aside, and follow with a third addition of water to the remaining flour/fat mixture. Pull the whole mixture together, smooth, and shape into a flat round (a ball makes it harder to roll), before wrapping and refrigerating it. The larger and flatter the round, the faster the dough will chill, the faster the gluten rests, and the easier it is to roll out the dough. When using vinegar, lemon juice, or sour cream in a pie crust, mix it with the water in the recipe, if any is called for, before adding to the flour.

Patching   Whether using frozen pie doughs or working from "scratch," your dough may crack or tear. If it does, wet your finger or your pastry brush, and brush the dough where you want to patch, then patch with another piece of dough.

Scraps   If you have scraps of dough, stack them up on top of each other in layers, then roll out to make a flaky pastry.

Don't wad scraps up into a ball or overwork scraps. A trick for using up the extra scraps is to sprinkle them with cinnamon and sugar, bake, and store in a tight container or the freezer. They're wonderful as snacks.

Frozen pie crusts   These are available at the store. Pet Ritz seems very reliable, as do some of the generic crusts. One of the troubles encountered is the cracking of the dough. Patch with water when possible. If completely broken up, layer the pieces of dough as described under "scraps," then roll out when at room temperature between pieces of wax paper. Although it also works to use these doughs for top crusts, getting them to be perfect is a bit of a challenge.

Two-crust pies   When dividing your dough, make one piece larger for the bottom crust. Dampen the rim of the bottom crust before putting on the top one, then seal the two together. Be very careful to avoid stretching either dough so they stay together in baking.

Pricking   When not baking a crust with pie weights or filling, be sure to prick the crust at regular intervals with a fork to prevent bubbling up.

Graham cracker crusts   These are a nice substitution from time to time.

Varying fillings   When you are a little bored with your traditional pie filling, try adding your own touch—a little grated ginger or chopped candied ginger; or a bit of orange, lemon, or lime rind; or a dash of brandy or one of the flavored liqueurs.

MANGO ICE CREAM

Makes 3 quarts

Boiled Custard

1/3 cup sugar
1 teaspoon cornstarch
1/3 scant teaspoon salt
3 egg yolks
1-1/2 cups milk
3 tablespoons light corn
   syrup

To make the custard, sift the sugar, cornstarch, and salt into a heavy saucepan or into the top of a double boiler. Lightly beat the egg yolks and add along with the milk and corn syrup. Blend thoroughly. Cook over low heat, stirring constantly, until the mixture coats a spoon. Chill.

Mango Cream

9 large mangoes, to
    make 4-1/2 cups
    strained mango pulp
1 to 1-1/4 cups sugar
juice of 2 lemons
1-1/2 cups boiled
    custard, chilled
3 cups heavy whipping
    cream
ice cream salt
Garnish:
5 cups sliced mangoes
    or blueberries

To make mango cream, peel the mangoes, remove the flesh from the stones, roughly chop in food processor using steel blade; or chop in a blender, a few pieces at a time; or by hand. Put through a sieve. Measure. Stir in 1 cup sugar and the juice of one lemon. Stir in the custard, then the whipping cream. Taste and correct flavor with lemon juice or additional sugar, keeping in mind that the ice cream will be less sweet after freezing. Freeze, preferably in an ice cream churn. Let stand for at least 30 minutes but preferably up to 2 hours to mellow.

Tip: 1 mango usually equals 1/2 cup mango pulp cream.

Tip: Ripe mangoes are extremely soft and juicy, with the sweetest having skins rosy red in places. The flesh of the mangoes is not easily separated from the pit. With a sharp knife make a vertical cut all the way around the fruit. Peel the skin back, cut the flesh in vertical slices, then run the knife between the pit and the meat of the mango.

Tip: Salt is added to the ice to lower the freezing point of the brine solution. Mix one part rock salt with eight parts ice. Be sure to fill the freezer tub above the mixture in the cream container. When mixture is frozen, drain off brine and pack the freezer tub with three parts ice to one part salt. Garnish with fruit.

Variation

For a molded dessert, pour into an oiled or plastic wrap–lined 12-cup batter bowl or bombe. Let freeze for several hours. Unmold and garnish with fruit.

Tip: To unmold, dip the bombe mold in hot water for a few seconds to release ice cream.

⤞ 15 ⤝

SINGLE MAN'S DINNER

A Man Alone

The longer he lived alone, the more he spent on food and the less he enjoyed it. He had complained about his wife spending so much on food for the family, and now he spent nearly that much on himself alone. But he couldn't cook for himself. He'd never had to.

He had gone from his mother to his wife, with no time for himself, to take charge of his own food, his own life. Now he didn't know how. The only thing he knew how to cook was his favorite cheesecake pie. Otherwise, he bought cartons of frozen food. One, in particular, he stocked up on. How his wife would laugh if she could spy into his freezer.

Before, at home, she would wipe off the place mats before setting the table, and would try to find something pretty to put in the center. Some magnolia leaves, perhaps, with those decoy ducks her mother had given her, or pine cones she had picked and kept. Or sea shells. She always tried to have something on the table, something to cheer them all up. Now she was gone.

He ate out a lot. That's what was so expensive. He couldn't stand the bare walls, the quiet room. Even when the TV was on, it was quiet in a way it had never been when he lived with the family around. It was hard being a man living alone, getting to know a whole new set of friends.

149

It wasn't as hard as being a woman, though, he knew that. He watched women alone. They were a lot more lonely than he was. There were more of them, and they didn't have his money, his power. Still, they were all alone, just like he was. How could they cook for themselves? Great smells would come to him through their doors in his apartment building.

He sat on an outdoor terrace of a nice restaurant overlooking the park and watched the people go by. He ordered veal scallopine, a favorite of his, and wondered why was he here? Why didn't he fix his own scallopine at home? He finished the meal. He stared at a father, across the street, walking under the trees, with his son nearly up to his waist. The boy was trailing behind, then running ahead, the autumn sun casting a halo around his hair as he ran and stopped. His hand reached up and met his father's hand reaching down. Neither looked at each other as they did it, walking together now.

The man paid his check. He knew he would never hold his little son's hand again. Little boys grow up or they can be gone in some other way.

He walked home, knowing he had to get his life in order, knowing he had to learn to feed himself, to love himself, a man alone. He could cook, he knew it. He'd start with his favorite foods—like the scallopine. He picked up the phone and invited some new friends over to dinner for the next evening. He could make his cheesecake pie tonight.

❦ M E N U ❦

SINGLE MAN'S DINNER

Parmesan Dip

Lavash or Flatbread (store bought)

Veal or Turkey Scallopine

Quick Broccoli with Garlic (p. 131) or Brussels Sprouts (p. 53)

Marie's Country Cherry Tomatoes

Green Rice

Sunken Fudge Brownies or Glenn and Elise's Oreo Cheesecake

SERVES 4 TO 6

LOGISTICS

The cheesecake or the brownies, for the less experienced cook, may be made in advance several days, or frozen. The Parmesan dip and Lavash may also be made several days in advance or frozen (store-bought flatbread or crackers may be substituted for the Lavash). Reheat the defrosted dip 15 minutes before guests arrive. Serve, together, in the living room 1/2 hour before dinner.

Start cooking the green onions and peppers for the rice 45 minutes before serving time or make the whole recipe earlier in the day and reheat, covered, 5 minutes before placing the tomatoes in the oven. The butter-and-bread-crumb mixture for the tomatoes may be made a day ahead of time and sprinkled over the tomatoes several hours before serving. The vegetables may be cooked earlier in the day and reheated in a heavy saucepan 6 to 8 minutes before eating, when starting the scallopine, or in the microwave. Place the tomatoes in the oven when starting to sauté the scallopine.

ℭ R E C I P E S ℚ

PARMESAN DIP

Makes 4 cups

1 (10-ounce) package
  frozen chopped
  spinach or turnip
  greens
1-1/3 cups grated
  Parmesan cheese
1 large onion, chopped
1 garlic clove, chopped
4 ounces cream cheese,
  softened
1 cup mayonnaise
3 canned or fresh hot
  peppers (optional),
  chopped
salt
freshly ground pepper
1 teaspoon paprika

Preheat oven to 350°F. Defrost and squeeze dry the spinach or greens. Mix together 1 cup of the Parmesan cheese, the chopped spinach or turnip greens, onion, garlic, cream cheese, mayonnaise. Chop the optional red pepper and add to the mixture. Season with salt and pepper to taste. Place in a greased casserole dish, top with the remaining 1/3 cup of the Parmesan cheese, and sprinkle with paprika. Bake until hot and bubbly. Freezes well, both before and after baking. Serve with Lavash or crackers. Holds well in a chafing dish.

Variation

Try substituting 1 (14-1/2-ounce) can artichoke hearts, drained and chopped, or 1 (14-ounce) can crabmeat, drained, or 2 cups mushroom *duxelles* for the spinach.

Comment: For individual hors d'oeuvres, this can also be spooned or piped onto bread rounds or squares and run under the broiler until hot and bubbling.

LAVASH

Makes 8 flatbreads

1 package active dry
  yeast
1 tablespoon sugar

Preheat oven to 350°F. Dissolve the yeast and sugar in the warm water. Place 3 cups flour in a food-processor bowl. Add salt, butter,

1 cup warm water (110°
　to 115°F)
3 to 5 cups bread flour
1-1/2 teaspoons salt
1/4 cup melted butter
1 garlic clove, chopped
egg wash of 1 egg
　beaten with 1
　tablespoon water
sesame seeds

yeast mixture, and garlic. Add enough flour, 1/2 cup at a time, to make a soft dough. Knead until elastic and smooth as a baby's bottom. Turn in greased bowl. Cover with plastic wrap, place in a warm but not hot place, and let rise until doubled. Punch down and divide into 8 pieces. Roll each piece out very thin, to about 8-1/2 × 11 inches and place on a greased baking sheet. Brush with egg wash and sprinkle with sesame seeds. Bake about 20 to 25 minutes, or until golden brown. Break into pieces. May be made several days in advance or frozen.

Tip: This thin crisp bread is a real party favorite. Present it standing up in baskets. It's great with dips. Also, try it as a cracker for soups. Each guest breaks off what he or she wants to eat.

VEAL OR TURKEY SCALLOPINE

Serves 4

1 pound veal or turkey
　scallops or cutlets,
　pounded thin (about
　6 scallops)
salt
freshly ground pepper
1/4 cup flour
2 tablespoons oil
4 tablespoons butter
juice of 2 lemons
Garnish:
1 lemon, sliced

　Season veal or turkey with the salt and pepper. Dust with the flour. Heat the oil and 2 tablespoons of the butter in a large skillet until sizzling hot. Dry the meat and add in batches. Brown on one side, for 1 to 2 minutes, turn, and brown on second. Remove from the pan to hot platter and repeat until all the meat is browned. Add the rest of the butter to the pan and let it turn brown in the pan. Add the lemon juice to taste. Bring to a quick boil and pour over the veal. Serve right away, garnished with lemon slices.

Variation
Add 2 tablespoons fresh chopped parsley or herbs to the pan with the lemon juice.

Variation
Add 2 tablespoons capers to the pan with the lemon juice.

Continued

Variation
For a butter sauce, add 3/4 cup butter to the pan and let turn brown before adding lemon juice.

Variation
Omit the extra butter and the lemon and serve with 1 cup Marinara Sauce (p. 182).

Tip: For tender veal, soak in milk overnight, drain, and proceed as directed.
Tip: Veal and turkey scallops may also be sold as cutlets in the grocery store. They are about 1/4 inch thick.

MARIE'S COUNTRY CHERRY TOMATOES

Serves 4

1-1/2 pints cherry tomatoes, stemmed
1/4 cup butter or olive oil
2 green onions or scallions
1 garlic clove, peeled
1/4 cup fresh parsley
1 teaspoon thyme
1/2 cup bread crumbs
salt
freshly ground pepper

Preheat oven to 450°F. Place the tomatoes in a single layer in a lightly oiled, shallow baking dish. Melt the butter. Chop the onions and their trimmed tops, the garlic, parsley and thyme, and toss with the butter and the bread crumbs. Season to taste with salt and pepper. Sprinkle the bread crumb mixture over the tomatoes. Bake 6 to 8 minutes or until the tomatoes are tender.

Variation
Substitute mushroom caps for the tomatoes, or use 1/2 tomatoes, 1/2 mushroom caps.

Tip: For a fancier look, slice off 1/4 of the tomatoes from the blossom end to make a cap. Set aside. Top with bread crumb mixture and replace cap before baking.
Tip: May be made ahead, cooked 4 to 6 minutes, then reheated 4 to 6 minutes when ready to serve, or reheated in the microwave.
Tip: The butter-and-bread-crumb mixture can be made a day ahead of time and sprinkled over the tomatoes several hours before serving.

GREEN RICE

Serves 6

2 tablespoons vegetable
  oil
3/4 cup green onions or
  scallions
1/2 cup finely chopped
  green bell pepper
1 cup long grain rice
1 teaspoon salt
freshly ground pepper
2 cups boiling chicken
  stock or broth
1/4 cup parsley

Preheat oven to 350°F. Heat the oil in a large skillet. Slice the green onions and their trimmed tops. Add to the oil with the bell pepper and cook until soft. Place the un-cooked rice in a 2-quart baking dish. Add the cooked onions and green pepper, salt, pepper, and stock; stir, then cover with tight-fitting lid or heavy-duty foil. Bake in oven for 25 minutes or until rice is tender and liquid is absorbed. Chop the parsley and toss in lightly with a fork before serving. May be made ahead, covered, and reheated in microwave or in oven.

Tip: Vegetables can be made earlier in the day.

SUNKEN FUDGE BROWNIES

Makes 3-1/2 dozen 2-inch brownies

1/2 pound (1 cup)
  butter
1/4 cup peanut oil
2 cups sugar
1-1/4 cups plain all-
  purpose flour
3/4 cup unsweetened
  cocoa powder
1/2 teaspoon baking
  soda
1/2 teaspoon salt
4 eggs
2 teaspoons vanilla
1 cup chopped nuts
Chocolate Frosting
  (recipe follows)

Preheat oven to 350°F. Grease a 13 × 9 × 2-inch baking dish; set aside. Melt butter in a saucepan. Add the oil. Mix together sugar, flour, cocoa powder, soda, and salt. Stir into butter/oil mixture until smooth. Stir in eggs and vanilla just until smooth. Stir in nuts. Pour batter into prepared dish. Bake in 350°F oven for 30 minutes or until brownies just start to pull away from edges of dish. Cool in dish on wire rack. Frost with Chocolate Frosting. May be made in advance or frozen.

Tip: These brownies sink a bit in the pan when perfect and moist. If you want them unsunken and a bit drier but still tasty, bake 5 to 10 minutes longer.

CHOCOLATE FROSTING

3 squares (3 ounces)
   unsweetened
   chocolate
1 tablespoon butter or
   margarine
3 cups sifted powdered
   sugar
1/4 cup hot water

In a saucepan, combine chocolate and butter or margarine. Heat and stir just until melted. Stir in powdered sugar and enough hot water to make frosting of spreading consistency.

GLENN AND ELISE'S OREO CHEESECAKE

Makes 1 cheesecake

Crust

8 ounces Oreo cookies,
   crushed into crumbs
6 tablespoons butter,
   melted

Batter

2 pounds Philadelphia
   cream cheese
2/3 cup sugar
4 eggs
1 tablespoon vanilla
6 ounces Oreo cookies,
   cut into thirds
Garnish:
1/2 cup Oreo cookies,
   crushed into fine
   crumbs

Preheat oven to 350°F. Line the bottom of a 10 × 3-inch solid cake pan with a round of wax paper. Mix together the crushed cookies and the butter and press on the bottom only. Bake in hot oven 5 to 8 minutes. Reduce the temperature to 275°F.

Meanwhile, in a food processor or with a mixer, beat together the cream cheese and sugar. Add the eggs, one by one, beating after each is added. Add the vanilla. Fold in the Oreos. Pour into the pan containing the pre-baked crust and place the cheesecake pan in a larger pan. Pour enough hot water into the larger pan to come halfway up the outside of the cheesecake pan (this is called a *bain marie*). Place in the 275°F oven and bake for 3 hours. Cover with foil if cake starts to color. Remove from oven, cool, and chill 8 hours or freeze. Turn out onto a plate, remove the wax paper, then quickly flip over on another plate. Garnish by sprinkling the crumbs over a lace doily placed on top of the cake. Remove the doily, leaving a pattern of crumbs.

Tip: Do not use a cheesecake pan with a removable bottom as water will get into it, unless you wrap the outside in a double layer of sturdy foil.

Variation

To make an Oreo Cheesecake Pie, use 1/2 the ingredients. Preheat oven to 350°F. Line the bottom of a 9-inch pie pan with crumbs. Place in oven and bake for 5 to 8 minutes. Reduce temperature to 275°F. Beat cream cheese and sugar. Add the eggs, one by one, beating after each is added. Add the vanilla. Fold in the Oreos. Pour mixture into pie pan and bake 45 to 50 minutes or until done. Garnish as above.

✺16✺

A NEARLY SINLESS MENU

What Are Home-Cooked Meals For?

My 105-pound, very attractive friend arrived having had a couple of drinks. "Can I fix you some dinner?" I asked, being a bit hungry myself and ready for real food. "No," she said, "I'm being good. Last night I ate a great chocolate dessert at the restaurant!" As if NOT eating dinner was being good. Since when did being good have anything to do with dinner?

This whole fad of not eating at home and going on a binge in a restaurant undermines the fundamental joy of food. Food should be nurturing, a means of sharing with friends and family at home, and creating bridges for communication and exchanging memories. What a switch from when I was a child, and you had to eat what was in front of you, whether you wanted it or not. If you weren't punished for not eating all your food, you were at least made to feel guilty about all the starving children in China who didn't have enough to eat—as if that food from your plate could mysteriously have been delivered to a child in China. And you didn't get dessert if you didn't eat the main course. Surely, somewhere in between there is a sensible balance.

Another dear friend is very worried about her husband's cholesterol. Once every couple of months I have a craving for country-cooked greasy foods, which I satisfy at home. The other day, she joined us when we were eating a lunch of turnip greens and corn-bread made with fatback.

She declared how good it was, and how much her husband would love it. "Don't you fix turnip greens any more for him?" we asked. "NO!" she said. "I keep him on a strict diet. But he goes out three times a week with his cronies, and that's when they eat all this rich, fattening food." We asked if fixing it occasionally at home—enough to satisfy his cravings for what was familiar—would stop him from eating incorrectly those three times a week. "NO," she said, "he wants it when he goes out to eat."

What a shame! The food that satisfies him, makes him happy, makes him feel nurtured, is what he gets away from home. What he eats at home *is* tasty—she's a good cook. Her efforts in her own kitchen at home have reduced his cholesterol, and he is now in good physical shape. But they have decided between them that the restaurant is the place for special occasions for him, and home is the place for what he feels is punishment food—the healthy food. She can feel good about keeping him healthy, because she doesn't actually feed him or see him eating the food she knows is bad for him. Thus he can "sin" out of the home, with his fat-laden meals.

I have another friend, whom I call a cook-on-a-perch since he doesn't cook every day, as I do. He mostly eats out. He complains about my using canned chicken stock in an everyday soup. Dilettante cook that he is, he can look down his nose at those of us who feed family and friends day in and day out, and say, "No canned chicken stock, pul-leeze. It is too salty." When salty canned stock is reduced by boiling, it can be too salty. But when it is simmered gently and briefly, or diluted, it is not. More importantly, it is much better than no stock at all in the soup, or eating out! Moreover, the number of restaurants that use homemade chicken stock is very small—all but the finest use a prepared product!

This same man who complains about the salt in my canned chicken stock knows which brand of potato chips are his favorite, and is a connoisseur of beers. It isn't salt he objects to—it is salt on real food. I know people who eat high-salt frozen foods that are low in calories (promoted as being "slim" or "lean" foods) but that are also often high in cholesterol or additives. My potato-chip friend also loves ice cream.

The egg is currently getting a bad rap from the cholesterol-conscious. Yet while the simple egg is still the best form of nutrition for a starving family, many low-income families don't know how to cook an egg and frequently spend much too great a proportion of their income on so-called fast foods and eating out. They'd rather have a fatty hamburger any day than eat an egg at home.

A solution? I don't have one that everyone will accept. I am for balanced meals and for not overeating any one thing. Unless your medical doctor has put you on a special diet, I'm for having meat loaf and mashed potatoes one night, and grilled chicken and steamed vegetables the next. I'm for eating at home and serving a meal that satisfies as well as nourishes. And, if "sin" is the issue, let it be chocolate—the whole family deserves an occasional chocolate bash!

MENU

A NEARLY SINLESS MENU

Mushroom and Rice Soup

Steamed Fish
or Grilled Herbed Swordfish Steak

Colorful Vegetables

Roasted Red Pepper Sauce

Whole Wheat Bread

Barbara St. Amand's Grape Delight (p. 9)
or Sinful Chocolate Cake (p. 202)

SERVES 4

LOGISTICS

The bread and chocolate cake may be made the day ahead or frozen. The Red Pepper Sauce may be made a day or two in advance and kept tightly covered in the refrigerator. Fix the soup up to a day ahead or start cooking 1/2 hour before serving time. The vegetables may be cut and placed in foil ahead of time. Put in a preheated oven 25 minutes before serving. Five minutes later place the fish on the hot grill. The grapes may be made at the last minute or several hours ahead.

☙ R E C I P E S ❧

MUSHROOM AND RICE SOUP
Serves 4 to 6

3 tablespoons butter
2 medium onions
1/2 pound mushrooms
2 tablespoons flour
5 cups chicken stock
1 tablespoon white long
   grain rice
1 bay leaf
salt
freshly ground pepper
1/2 teaspoon mint or
   parsley, chopped

Chop the onions and the mushrooms. Heat the butter in a heavy soup pot, add the onions and mushrooms, and cook until soft. Stir in the flour until smooth. Pour in the stock, stirring, and bring to the boil. Add the rice and bay leaf, turn down the heat, cover and simmer for 15 to 20 minutes. Remove bay leaf, taste, and add salt and pepper as necessary. To serve, sprinkle mint or parsley over each serving.

Variation
To reduce calories, use 1 tablespoon oil or butter to cook the onions and mushrooms and cook until soft or cook them in the microwave or in a nonstick pan.

Variation
Try using shiitake or wild mushrooms in this soup.

Variation
For Oyster and Mushroom Soup, substitute cooked wild rice or brown rice for the uncooked white rice, add 1/2 pint of drained oysters to the hot soup, and cook until the edges of the oysters just begin to curl. Omit the mint. Serve with oyster crackers or hot garlic bread.

Tip: Salt after you've tasted, particularly with canned broth, which is quite salty. This is one recipe where fresh is superior to canned.
Tip: This soup reheats well, doubles easily.

STEAMED FISH
Serves 4

2 to 2-1/2 pounds
   whole fresh fish, such
   as red snapper or
   trout, scaled and
   cleaned
2 stalks green onions or
   scallions, cut in
   1-inch slivers
3 slices fresh ginger, the
   size of quarters,
   slivered
1/4 to 1/2 cup soy
   sauce

Put the fish in a wide, shallow dish with a 1-inch high rim. Place the dish on a rack in an electric frying pan or a wok that you have filled about 2 inches deep with water, making sure the water does not come up the sides of the dish. Spread 1/2 the green onions and ginger strips over the fish and pour soy sauce over. Cover the pan and steam fish for 20 minutes or until tender and moist. Remove the dish from the wok, and pour off excess liquid. Sprinkle with the remainder of the green onions, and pour the soy sauce over the fish.

Variation

Traditionally the Chinese pour a bit of hot sesame oil or sizzling hot vegetable oil over the fish after it has steamed.

Variation

Sprinkle the fish with 1/2 to 1 teaspoon Chinese five-spice powder before placing on dish.

GRILLED HERBED SWORDFISH STEAK
Serves 4

4 (1-inch) thick
   swordfish, tuna,
   amberjack, or other
   fresh fish steaks, 1/3
   to 1/2 pound each
3 medium shallots
2 tablespoons oil
3 garlic cloves, chopped
3 tablespoons fresh
   lemon juice
2 tablespoons fresh
   chopped herbs

Put the swordfish in a glass dish. Chop the shallots and mix with the oil, garlic, lemon juice, and herbs and pour mixture over the fish. Marinate for 2 hours, turning once.

Remove the fish from the marinade. Place on a hot grill and cook 4 to 5 minutes on first side, turn, grill on second, until done.

Variation

Place on an oiled broiler pan and broil 3 to 5 inches from the heat.

Variation

Serve with Red Pepper Hollandaise (p. 33), Roasted Red Pepper Sauce (p. 164), Aioli (p. 25), White Butter Sauce (p. 257), Ratatouille (p. 99), or Pico de Gallo (p. 83).

Tip: Broil or grill after measuring the thickness of the steak. Cook approximately 10 minutes per inch of thickness.

COLORFUL VEGETABLES

Serves 4

1 carrot, peeled
1 yellow squash
1 zucchini
1 red bell pepper
1 green bell pepper
1 onion, sliced
2 garlic cloves, chopped
1 tablespoon olive oil
1 tablespoon chopped
   fresh basil, thyme, or
   oregano
salt
freshly ground pepper

Preheat oven to 350°F. Cut the carrot, squash and zucchini into 1/2 inch julienne sticks 2 inches long. Seed the bell pepper and cut into sticks the same size. Blanch the carrot strips in boiling water 3 to 5 minutes, bring back to the boil, and boil 3 minutes. Mix together the carrots, squash, zucchini, red and green peppers, onion, and garlic in 2 layers on a large sheet of aluminum foil. Dot with the oil, and sprinkle with the herbs. Fold over and seal the foil. Twenty-five minutes before serving, place the foil envelope on a baking sheet. Bake in the preheated oven until vegetables are crisp yet tender, about 25 minutes. Unwrap, season to taste, and place vegetables in serving dish.

Variation

Place the vegetables and herbs in a microwave dish with cover or plastic wrap, or place them in a large microwave-proof plastic bag and microwave until crisp tender, about 5 minutes. Add oil if desired.

Variation

Use butter in place of the oil. Grate vegetables 1/8 to 1/4 inch thick.

Variation
Add 1 tablespoon chili powder or 1 tablespoon ground cumin seed.

Variation
Serve chilled, with 1 cup Vinaigrette (p. 140).

Tip: May be done ahead, kept in container, and reheated.

ROASTED RED PEPPER SAUCE
Makes 3 cups

2 cups roasted, chopped
   and seeded red
   peppers
6 large black olives
6 to 8 anchovy fillets
2 tablespoons parsley
1-1/2 tablespoons olive
   oil
1 tablespoon fresh
   lemon juice
salt
freshly ground pepper

Peel, seed and chop the peppers. Pit and chop the olives. Place in a food processor with 6 of the anchovies. Chop the parsley and add. Puree. In a food processor or blender, purée together the peppers, olives, 6 of the anchovies, and parsley. Beat in the olive oil and lemon juice. Add salt and pepper to taste. Add more of the anchovies if desired. Serve at room temperature. Will keep, refrigerated, up to a week.

Tip: 3 roasted, peeled red peppers make 1 cup.

Tip: Roasted red peppers may be purchased in jars and cans. Drain before chopping.

Variation
Good on spaghetti or pizza dough.

Variation
Rather than purée the mixture, just finely chop and mix together the peppers, olives, anchovies, and parsley. Add the olive oil and lemon juice. Season. Serve on crackers as a spread. Serve chilled.

WHOLE WHEAT BREAD
Makes 2 loaves

2 packages rapid-rise
    yeast
1 tablespoon salt
1 tablespoon sugar
3 tablespoons honey
3 tablespoons cooking
    oil
2-1/2 cups all-purpose
    or bread flour
about 3-3/4 cups whole
    wheat flour
2 cups water heated to
    140°F

Mix the yeast, salt, sugar, honey, oil, and 2-1/2 cups of the all-purpose or bread flour and 2 cups of the whole wheat flour. Add the hot water to the flour mixture.

Knead to a soft dough, adding flour as needed. Shape into a ball. Turn in an oiled bowl and cover with plastic wrap or place in an oiled plastic bag and let rise in a warm place until doubled, about 1 hour. Punch down. Shape into 2 rounds or long loaves and place on a greased baking sheet. With a sharp knife, slash tops in a decorative design. Let rise again until doubled.

Preheat oven to 350°F. Bake on the middle rack of the oven approximately 35 to 40 minutes, until done. Cool on a rack.

Tip: You may want to use an egg white wash to glaze the top of the bread. Use 1 egg white and 1 tablespoon water beaten until frothy. Glaze the top of the bread after you make the decorative design.

☙ 17 ❧

A GREAT SUNDAY DINNER

Mama Ricci

When Donna Seibert married an Italian, Alfredo Ricci, and lived in Rome, Italy, she wound up with a bonus—Mama Ricci's Italian cooking. And I wound up with two of the best recipes to come out of Italy! Each Sunday, Mama Ricci fixes a large Italian dinner to eat around two o'clock.

Visiting Rome, I woke up early one morning and took a long walk down to the Roman Forum, to see the little prisons where Paul and Peter had been kept nearly 2,000 years ago. Then I walked back to a bar-restaurant at the nearby piazza and sat in the shade and read, drinking a diet Coke in the rising heat of the day, watching the cluster of elderly Italian men at the next table, listening to their gossip and their comments on the passing women.

By the time I started walking to meet Donna, my skin felt that dampness that foretells a miserably hot day. I got lost, or rather, passed twice by the church where we were supposed to meet. I had forgotten that in Italy a non-Catholic church might not be an imposing structure, and that I should look for the specific number, not a large sign or building. Everyone I asked for directions kept sending me to the American church.

Donna was late, too, as her car had broken down, and so she

had left it parked somewhere in Rome. We welcomed the serenity of the church, where at last we connected, glad to see each other after a lapse of years. Still, there is a type of hunger that I call Church-hunger, stronger than any other, and I was distracted and ready to eat, anticipating Mama Ricci's cooking!

As we took the taxi home we caught up further with each other's lives for the year since we last met. Mama Ricci, in true Italian fashion, is devoted to her only son and his family, and comes over every weekend, staying from Friday to Sunday. She spoils the children, baby-sits, and cooks.

Donna, like so many women, American and Italian, works, and dinners during the week always include pasta made from scratch, but they may not be as elaborate as Mama Ricci's cooking. This Sunday, Alfredo's grandmother was there as well, relishing the children's cries and enjoying the day, as Mama Ricci prepared the meal. There was a flurry of activity as we walked in, the children rushing to greet us while Mama Ricci and Grandmother Ricci dashed around to pick up toys and indulgences.

Donna and I set the table looking out onto the balcony, where flowers and herbs carefully tended by Donna year-round flourished.

At last we ate. It had seemed forever since breakfast. During melon season, no meal in Rome is complete without prosciutto wrapped around slices of melon. Then we had a pasta I'd never seen before, called *mezze maniche rogate* (a large-holed pasta), sauced with a homemade tomato sauce of fresh tomatoes and garlic, a little sautéed ground veal, and fresh marjoram.

Next came a veal roast, roasted in wine, with a blush of pink in its center, served with the succulent juices from its cooking, greens somewhat like turnip greens, and potatoes like I'd never had before.

The potatoes were crisp on the outside, buttery and flavorful, tinged with the flavor of fennel. The dish was unaffected and faultless—as only a simple dish made by an excellent cook can be. As we sat at the table, Donna translated as I laboriously extracted the recipes from Mama Ricci. It wasn't that she minded sharing them, she was just amazed I didn't know how to make them, and surprised that I thought them more astounding than the arugula salad that followed, or the dessert Donna had bought from the local pastry shop.

After the meal, Donna and I chatted in the kitchen while doing dishes, and she told me of her favorite chicken recipe. I jotted it down, next to Mama Ricci's, thinking I'd never get a veal roast as good.

When I got back in my own kitchen, weeks later, I made those potatoes, even though the summer heat spoke against lighting the oven. I had to see if they were as wonderful as I remembered them. They were. They are. They are perfect with Donna's chicken. Thank you Donna and Mama Ricci!

☾ MENU ☽

A GREAT SUNDAY DINNER

Melons with Prosciutto (p. 189)

Tomato Bruschetta
or *Marie's Country Tomatoes (p. 154)*

Wilted Spinach Salad

Donna Siebert's Roman Chicken

Mama Ricci's Potatoes

Artichokes and Mushrooms

Raspberry-Peach Pie or Rhubarb Pie

SERVES 4 TO 6

LOGISTICS

The chicken may be made a day ahead, or way ahead, frozen, then defrosted. The pies may be made a day ahead. The potatoes may be made a few hours ahead and reheated. The tomato bruschetta may be made a few hours ahead and reheated. The artichokes and mushrooms may be made ahead and reheated. The melons may be prepared several hours ahead, closely covered, and kept refrigerated until needed, as may the tomatoes. The salad may be made ahead but tossed at the last minute.

RECIPES

TOMATO BRUSCHETTA

Serves 6

1 loaf Italian bread
2 garlic cloves
3 tablespoons extra
   virgin olive oil
3 medium tomatoes
1/4 teaspoon freshly
   ground pepper
1/2 cup imported
   Parmesan cheese
1/2 cup fresh basil

Preheat the broiler. Halve the bread lengthwise, and cut crosswise on the diagonal into 1 inch slices. Place slices of bread cut side up on a baking sheet and broil until lightly browned. Chop the garlic and mix with the olive oil and brush over one side of the toast. Peel, seed and chop the tomatoes and spread evenly over the toast. Season with pepper. Grate the Parmesan and sprinkle on top. Broil for about 30 seconds, just until the tomatoes are heated through. Chop the basil and sprinkle over the tomatoes.

Tip: This works fine with stale bread. The extra-virgin olive oil makes a big difference.

WILTED SPINACH SALAD

Serves 4 to 6

2 pounds fresh spinach,
   stemmed, washed,
   and dried, in bite-
   sized pieces
5 slices bacon
1 small onion, chopped
1 to 2 teaspoons sugar
1/2 cup red wine
   vinegar
1/2 teaspoon Dijon
   mustard
salt
freshly ground pepper

Place the clean and dry spinach in a serving bowl. Fry the bacon until crisp. Remove from the pan, crumble, and set aside on paper towels. Remove all but 5 tablespoons of the fat from the pan. Add the onion and cook until soft. Stir in the sugar, red wine vinegar, and mustard, and heat quickly until sugar is dissolved. Taste for seasoning and add salt if necessary. Pour hot dressing over spinach, add freshly ground pepper, and garnish with crumbled bacon.

Tip: Dressing may be made in advance but should be heated before pouring over spinach.

DONNA SIEBERT'S ROMAN CHICKEN
Serves 4 to 6

3 tablespoons olive oil
1 (2-1/2 to 3-pound)
   chicken, cut up, or 8
   chicken thighs with
   skin on
3 garlic cloves, chopped
1 teaspoon hot red
   pepper, chopped
1/2 cup fresh rosemary,
   chopped or dried
1/2 cup dry white wine
   or 1/4 cup lemon
   juice
1 cup chicken or beef
   bouillon
10 capers
1 tablespoon fresh
   oregano or marjoram,
   chopped
2 anchovies
1 cup red wine vinegar
salt
freshly ground pepper
Garnish:
2 sprigs fresh
   rosemary (optional)

Heat the olive oil in a large pan. Add the chicken, skin side down. Brown, turn, and brown other side. Drain off excess fat. Add 1 of the garlic cloves, the hot pepper, 1/4 cup of the rosemary, and the wine. Bring to the boil and boil to reduce. Add the bouillon and capers. Cover and simmer until done, about 45 minutes. With a mortar and pestle, blender, or food processor, make a paste of the rest of the garlic, the anchovies, the other 1/4 cup rosemary, and the oregano or marjoram. Mix in the red wine vinegar and steep all together, 20 to 30 minutes. When the chicken is cooked, remove and keep warm. Add the steeped mixture to the hot broth and bring to the boil. Let boil vigorously to reduce by half. Season with salt and pepper to taste. Pour the sauce over the chicken and serve hot. Garnish with the rosemary.

Variation
Garnish with a "gremolata": 1/2 cup basil, 1/2 cup parsley, chopped, 2 cloves garlic, chopped, and 2 tablespoons lemon peel, grated.

Variation
For chicken cacciatore, substitute 1-1/2 cups Marinara Sauce (p. 182) for the chicken stock and white wine. Add 1/3 cup of the wine vinegar. Taste and add more vinegar if needed. Add 8 ounces black olives, pitted. Omit the capers and anchovies.

Tip: Marjoram and oregano are interchangeable herbs. The first is cultivated, the other "wild."

MAMMA RICCI'S POTATOES

Serves 4 to 6

3 pounds potatoes,
    peeled and cut in 1 to
    1-1/2-inch chunks
4 tablespoons olive oil
4 tablespoons butter
2 tablespoons fennel
    seeds

Preheat oven to 250°F. Put the potatoes in a saucepan of cold water and bring to the boil. Boil for 1 minute. Drain. Heat a roasting pan with the olive oil and butter, and add the drained potatoes. Place in the oven and cook 1/2 hour. Add the fennel seeds, and turn up heat to 400°F. Continue baking, stirring from time to time. Remove when golden and crisp, about 1/2 to 1 hour.

ARTICHOKES AND MUSHROOMS

Serves 4 to 6

12 ounces mushrooms,
    preferably button,
    cleaned
4 tablespoons butter
1 (9-ounce) package
    frozen artichoke
    hearts
1 to 2 tablespoons
    lemon juice
3 tablespoons imported
    Parmesan cheese
3 tablespoons fresh
    herbs (thyme,
    marjoram, parsley),
    chopped
salt
freshly ground pepper
Garnish:
sprigs of fresh herbs

Quarter or slice the mushrooms, depending on size. Melt 3 tablespoons of the butter in a large frying pan. Sauté the mushrooms, stirring occasionally, until soft. Defrost the artichokes at room temperature if possible or in microwave oven. Drain. Add the artichokes to the mushrooms, with more of the butter if needed, and heat through. Set aside if necessary. When ready to serve, reheat vigorously, adding the lemon juice. Grate the cheese and chop the herbs. Toss. Season to taste with salt and pepper. Garnish with sprigs of fresh herbs.

Tip: Many frozen vegetables, such as artichoke hearts, do not really need to be cooked further, just reheated, as they are already cooked when blanched for freezing.

RASPBERRY-PEACH PIE

Makes 1 pie

1 recipe 2-crust pie
  dough, chilled
  (p. 175)
1/3 cup all-purpose
  flour
1 cup sugar
2 cups fresh or frozen
  peaches, thawed,
  drained, reserving
  juices
2 cups fresh or frozen
  raspberries, thawed,
  drained, reserving
  juices
1/2 cup hazelnuts,
  pecans, or walnuts,
  chopped
1 tablespoon rum
  (optional)
2-1/2 tablespoons
  butter

Preheat oven to 375°F. Roll out dough for the bottom crust as directed (p. 143), and place in a 9-inch pie pan. Trim. Chill.

To make the filling, mix the flour and sugar together. Add the drained fruit, nuts, and optional rum. Stir in 1/2 of the drained juices. Toss together with your hands until well mixed. Place the filling in the crust. Dot with the butter.

To add a top crust, brush lip of bottom crust with water to adhere. Press on a lattice crust, or top with a full crust, pierced or decorated. Brush with glaze. Bake for 3/4 hour in hot oven, or until crust is golden and juices are bubbling.

Glaze

sugar dissolved in water

Variation
Substitute blueberries for the raspberries.

Comments on Making Dough Designs

Leftover dough is ideal for making pastry designs. For example, cut out leaves, hearts, diamonds, or other shapes with a cookie or pastry cutter. I frequently make a freehand pattern, such as apples, or pears. Once you feel secure, try making standup shapes. The most popular, and easiest, of these is to make a strip of dough—any width will do, but about an inch is an easy place to start—about 3 inches long. Make a series of slashes on one side, roll up, pull down the edges, and you have a rose! To adhere, brush with egg white, egg yolk, milk, or water on top of the crust, then place the design on top. In order for all dough designs to retain their shape they must be well chilled before going into the oven.

Making decorative edges

Decorating the rim of pies is a snap. There are many pretty variations. The easiest is simply a pinched edge. To do this, make a "v" with the thumb and pointing finger of one hand, placed next to the rim. Insert the pointing finger of the other hand and pinch in, move a "v" length away on the rim and repeat until top rim of the pie is uniformly done.

Another popular rim is made with a fork. Just press the back of a fork around the rim.

For a snappy design if you have extra dough, brush the rim with water or egg, and add your favorite cutouts the size of the rim—leaves, hearts, diamonds, apples, etc. Chill well.

To make a lattice crust for a double-crust pie, use a knife or a pastry wheel and cut strips of equal width—anywhere from 1 to 3 inches wide—from the portion of the dough you have reserved for the top crust (the strips should be longer than the diameter of the pie pan). Chill about 1/2 hour. After you have filled the bottom crust, weave the strips over the filling, pressing firmly at the rim before decorating the edges. Chill again.

Jam glazes for fruit tarts

The simplest way to dress up a fruit tart is to use a jam glaze. The traditional ones are red currant for red fruits and apricot for green or yellow fruits, but any jam or jelly can be used— raspberry, strawberry, wine jellies, etc. Melt the jam or jelly over low heat. If thick and full of fruit, add a little water. If very sweet, add lemon juice. Strain, reserving fruit for some other use. Place strained mixture back in a saucepan and melt. Add water or lemon juice to get to the desired consistency for brushing. Bring 'to the boil. Using a pastry brush, brush the fruit once it has been arranged decoratively in the precooked pie shell. Such glazes are used for an apple tart when the apples have been cooked in a bottom round or a freeform crust, as well as for raw fruits, such as berries or kiwi in a prebaked crust.

Continued

Dough slipping or shrinking

If you have trouble with your double crusts slipping, you may be stretching your top crust, or it may not be adhering properly. To correct, before putting on the top crust, cut out a strip of dough slightly wider than the rim of the pie pan, brush the edge of the pie crust with water, affix the strip of dough, brush with water to adhere again, then cover with the top crust, press all together, flute, and decorate the pie.

RHUBARB PIE

Makes 1 pie

1 recipe 2-crust pie
   dough, chilled
   (p. 175)
1/3 cup flour
1-1/2 cups sugar
1/4 teaspoon ground
   cinnamon
6 long stalks rhubarb,
   trimmed and cut in
   1/2-inch slices (or 1
   pound package
   frozen)
1 tablespoon finely
   grated lemon peel
1 to 2 tablespoons
   freshly squeezed
   lemon juice

Glaze

egg, beaten with water
water

Preheat oven to 425°F. Roll out dough for bottom crust as directed (p. 143) and place in a 9-inch pie pan. Trim. Chill.

To make the filling, mix the flour, sugar, and cinnamon in a large bowl. Add the rhubarb, lemon peel, and lemon juice. Toss together with your hands until the rhubarb is coated evenly. Spoon the filling into the pie crust.

To make top crust, roll out remaining dough as directed (p. 143). Brush lip of bottom crust with water to adhere. Press on top crust. Press the edges of bottom and top crust together. With a scissors or knife, trim evenly along the edge of the pie pan. Decorate the edges and top. Brush the pastry with the egg to glaze. Slash to vent. Bake for 15 minutes in hot oven. Reduce temperature to 350°F and continue baking for 40 minutes, or until the crust is golden. If edges get too brown, cover with foil. Remove pie from oven and cool for at least 1 hour on a wire rack. Serve barely warm or at room temperature.

Variation

Add 1-1/2 tablespoons fresh ginger, chopped.

EXTRA SPECIAL 2-CRUST PIE DOUGH*

Makes dough for 2 crusts

2 cups all-purpose flour
1 teaspoon salt
2 teaspoons sugar
  (optional)
4 tablespoons butter,
  cut up and chilled
8 tablespoons vegetable
  shortening, cut up
  and chilled
1/4 to 1/2 cup ice water

Double the ingredients for basic single-crust pie dough (p. 142) or use these ingredients for a richer pie.

Divide the dough into 2 smooth balls and flatten. Wrap individually with plastic wrap and chill. Roll out doughs (see p. 142). Trim the pastry 1 inch larger than the pie pan.

Variation

Use 2 teaspoons vinegar or lemon juice (optional), mixed with 1/4 cup ice water or 1 egg (optional), mixed with 1/4 cup ice water.

Tip: Vinegar/lemon juice (any acid, really) make a dough lighter and more tender. Egg makes pie crust more tender. Sugar adds color; flavor; toughens.

*See p. 142 for basic pie dough.

⚹18⚹

FISH FOR FRIENDS

First Fish

It was a cold and choppy day when we set out from shore to go fishing, and if I hadn't said I'd go, I would have stayed at home. But I was committed and made the best of it. I had dressed for the occasion with a sweatshirt and blue jeans over my bathing suit, socks up to my knees, and tennis shoes, not rubber sandals. But I wished I'd had galoshes.

Suddenly, after an hour of misery, the weather lifted and the motor stopped smelling so vile, and the boat stopped rocking. The sun greeted us as an old friend, tanning us with warmth and radiance above the reflected sea. With the sea and sun as our only comrades, my friend Lee McCown and I lolled under the clear sky, laughing and talking and reading short stories and making up limericks, giggling at the globs of protector cream on our noses and tummies. And we caught a few fish.

Most of them were small bluefish. The larger ones we either didn't know how to catch or they weren't coming in that close to shore. I landed my first fish at the end of the day. We packed all the fish in ice, and a willing fisherman cleaned them for a small consideration on the tiny dock. It was my time to cook, and we were eager.

When the sea and sun marry with laughter, there's a tired hungry completeness that seasons the food. Coupled with the smell of sea on clothes and hair, and the pride of achievement, anticipation dances on a high wire before the meal.

I broiled my bluefish in a flat enamel plate/lid, with a little wine and butter. I was proud of my fish, my first fish, and carried him arrogantly to the table. Somehow, I slid and stumbled and my fish gently slithered out onto the floor. I nearly wept. Lee, dear soul, knew my anguish, and slipped a spatula under my fish and placed him back on the platter, saying, "We won't eat the skin on the bottom where he touched the floor." My tears dried on their way to my cheek, and we looked out the window at our friend the sun traveling down the sky and talked and marveled at the specialness of simple fresh fish.

⸒ M E N U ⸒

FISH FOR FRIENDS

Broccoli and Red Bell Pepper Salad

Baked Fish with Marinara Sauce

Cabbage

Corn on the Cob

Cold Baked Onions (p. 5)

Corn Bread (p. 54)

***Old-Time Shortcake with Peaches or Strawberries
or Lemon Meringue Pie***

SERVES 6

LOGISTICS

Start the marinara sauce 1 to 1-1/2 hours before serving, or make ahead. Bake the onions 1 to 4 hours before serving or the day ahead and refrigerate. Make the pie earlier in the day. Roast the peppers, peel and prepare, or prepare salad completely ahead. Surround onions with pepper salad. Cook cabbage, set aside. Meanwhile cook corn bread and keep warm. Bring the water for the corn to the boil. Measure the fish for thickness and place in oven at appropriate time for its size. While the fish is in the oven, make the shortcake and prepare the fruit, and add corn to water or microwave. Place shortcake in oven when fish comes out.

RECIPES

BROCCOLI AND RED BELL PEPPER SALAD

Serves 4 to 6

3/4 cup mayonnaise
1 tablespoon red wine vinegar
1 broccoli head, cut into florets, stalks peeled and sliced
2 red bell peppers, roasted, seeded, peeled, and chopped
3 scallions or green onions, including green tops, chopped
10 slices bacon, cooked until crisp, crumbled
1/4 cup pecans or walnuts, chopped
salt
freshly ground pepper

Whisk together the mayonnaise and vinegar to make the dressing. Toss the broccoli, bell peppers, onions, bacon, and nuts in a large bowl. Add the dressing and toss again. Season to taste with salt and pepper. The salad will keep in the refrigerator for a day or two.

Quick variation
Substitute fresh seeded and julienned red bell peppers (not roasted).

Variation
The bell pepper may also be one of the bottled variety, which includes its sister, canned pimiento.

Tip: Although the easiest way to cook bacon is in the microwave, my favorite way is to spread the slices on a metal baking sheet with sides and place in a 350°F oven until crisp on one side, turn the slices, and finish cooking. Drain on paper towels on a rack. It can take up to 20 minutes, but the bacon is so crisp it snaps.

CABBAGE

Serves 6 to 8

1 (2-pound) cabbage, trimmed
1 cup water
8 tablespoons butter
salt
freshly ground pepper

Cut the cabbage into 6 to 8 wedges. Bring the water to the boil and add the cabbage and the butter. Boil for 15 to 25 minutes, until the cabbage is tender but has a little "give." There should be 1 cup or so of water left in the pot. Taste for seasoning, boil down if necessary, and pour over the cabbage. Season with salt and pepper. Serve cabbage, with its juices.

CORN ON THE COB

Serves 6

6 ears corn
salt
freshly ground pepper
1/4 to 1/2 cup butter

Shuck and silk the corn. Place in a large quantity of boiling water and boil 3 to 7 minutes until done. Drain and season with salt, pepper, and butter.

Variation
Try different butters: cumin butter, coriander butter, herb butter, shallot butter.

Tip: Cooking corn in the microwave is marvelously easy. Leave the shucks and silk on. Place in microwave and time according to manufacturer's directions. When the corn is cooked, pull back the shucks but leave them attached. Use a paper towel if corn is too hot to handle and remove the silks. Season with salt, pepper, and butter. Serving with the shucks on makes a lovely festive touch, particularly nice on a large platter or for eating outdoors.

BAKED FISH WITH MARINARA SAUCE

Serves 6

1 (3 to 3-1/2 pound) sea
  bass, sea trout, red
  snapper, or fresh
  bluefish
2 garlic cloves, sliced
2 bay leaves, crumbled
1/2 cup fresh thyme or
  parsley
1 recipe Marinara Sauce
  (see below)

Stuff the fish with the garlic cloves and 2 tablespoons of the herbs. Place the stuffed fish in a plastic bag or refrigerator dish and refrigerate until ready to cook.

Preheat oven to 400°F. Measure the thickness of the fish and place it in an oiled dish. Pour the marinara sauce around the fish. Bake 10 minutes per inch of thickness.

Variation

Substitute 3 smaller fish. Cook according to thickness.

Variation

Stuff each of 6 freshwater trout (10 ounces each) with 1/2 a chopped garlic clove, a large sprig of fennel, or 2 tablespoons chopped fennel. Measure and bake as above.

Comments on Buying and Cooking Fish

A fresh fish has a perfume that is subtle and enticing, not overpowering. A fish when flaky is nearly too done—it should cling lightly to the bone with the suppleness of an arching cat. Just before it flakes, the moisture is trapped inside the flesh, a steam ready to push the flakes apart to be released in your mouth.

Unfortunately, in the marketplace the word "fresh" has changed in meaning. There is no standard definition for "fresh" except that the fish cannot have been frozen and must not be in a state of decomposition, according to the Georgia Consumer Protection Agency of the Georgia Department of Agriculture. However, if it smells strong it will taste strong. And oily, fatty fish smell even stronger when they are more than a couple of days old.

The closer to a frozen state a fish stays, the fresher it will seem. That is why fish are iced down when caught, and they can be kept over and under ice for as long as a couple of weeks. The constant flow of ice and fresh water from the ice as it melts over the fish keeps the fish fresh. It stops the bacteria from multiplying, thus reducing odor and decomposition.

If you need to keep a fish longer than two days, freeze it. The best way is to surround it with water, so the fish is in the middle of a block of ice. If this is too bulky for your freezer, dip the fish in water, lay it flat on freezer wrap or a tray, place in the freezer, and when a thin layer of ice encloses the fish, dip it again in water. When the second layer is frozen, wrap tightly in freezer wrap.

Almost any fresh fish can be cooked several ways. Rather than weighing a fish, measure it vertically at its thickest point and cook it for 10 minutes per inch of thickness with very high heat, or in any of the following ways:

To broil   Measure the fish and place on a buttered or oiled baking pan, or on a rack on the pan. Baste with melted butter, oil, or a sauce, and add a little lemon or wine. Heat the broiler and place the fish 2 to 4 inches from the heat source. When the fish has cooked on one side, test by pressing to see if done, turn and brush again with the butter or sauce, and continue to cook until the total time based on thickness per inch. If you have a very thin fillet, you will not need to turn it.

To deep fry   Heat oil 360° to 375°F. Measure thickness of fish, and place in the hot fat and cook according to thickness, whether you have floured and crumbed it or not. If you have battered the fish, the batter acts as an insulation and the time might vary slightly. Test one little piece first, battered, to see how it does.

To sauté or pan fry   A skillet on the heat is indeed quite hot. Melt a thin layer (approximately 1/4 inch) of butter or oil in a heavy frying pan to sizzling hot. Cook your fish according to thickness, turning once after the first side is golden brown. You may need to change butter if it burns after cooking one batch of fish. It's usually hard to do more than one good-sized fish in a pan.

Charcoal grilling   The thickness rule applies to any heat 400°F or over, whether the fish is in one of those fancy fish holders or straight on the rack. Be sure to oil the fish first—it will want to stick—and brush with oil frequently while it is cooking. Throw some herbs into the fire a few minutes before

Continued

the end, to add flavor to the fish. If you place the fish on aluminum foil or wrap it in seaweed, add a few minutes to the cooking time so the heat can penetrate.

Baking   Measure fish, place on rack or in a pan in a pre-heated 400°F oven, and bake 10 minutes to the inch, not turning. If the fish is stuffed, measure it after stuffing.

Braising or poaching   Usually the fish is placed in a flavored liquid. Begin timing the measured fish once the liquid has returned to the boiling point, then reduce heat to a simmer.

Steaming   Steam the fish covered on a rack or in a steamer for 8 to 10 minutes per inch once the steaming liquid has come to a boil. Lower heat to a simmer after adding fish.

MARINARA SAUCE
Makes 4 to 5 cups

1/2 cup olive oil
6 garlic cloves, chopped
3 onions, chopped
1 large carrot, chopped
3/4 cup red wine
  vinegar
1/4 cup lemon juice or
  red wine
2 (28-ounce) cans
  tomatoes, or 4
  pounds fresh
  tomatoes, peeled and
  chopped
1 to 1-1/2 tablespoons
  basil
1 tablespoon thyme,
  fresh or dried
1 tablespoon oregano,
  fresh or dried
sugar
1 teaspoon salt
1/2 teaspoon dried red
  pepper flakes or fresh
  hot pepper, chopped
freshly ground pepper

Heat the oil in a large, heavy pot, add the garlic, onions, and carrot, and cook until soft, stirring occasionally. Add the vinegar and lemon juice or wine, bring to the boil, reduce heat, and simmer until most of the liquid has cooked away.

Roughly chop the canned tomatoes or peel and chop the fresh. Chop the herbs if fresh. Add the tomatoes, their liquid, 1 tablespoon of the basil, 1/2 the thyme, and 1 teaspoon of the oregano. Simmer, partly covered, until thickened, stirring occasionally, about 45 minutes to 1 hour. Add the remainder of herbs to taste. Taste for seasoning and add sugar, salt, and chopped peppers to taste. Can be made ahead.

Variation
Serve over pasta.

Variation
Serve with roasted pork tenderloin.

Tip: Make a triple recipe and freeze in 1/2-pint containers.

OLD-TIME SHORTCAKE WITH PEACHES OR STRAWBERRIES

Serves 6 to 8

Filling

1/4 cup sugar
1 quart strawberries, sliced, or 4 peaches, peeled and sliced
1 cup heavy whipping cream

Shortcake

1/4 cup sugar
2-1/2 cups self-rising flour
1/3 cup butter, cut in pieces
3/4 cup heavy whipping cream
1 egg

To make filling, sprinkle 1/4 cup of the sugar on the strawberries, more or less according to taste. Stir briefly, cover, and refrigerate 1 hour or more. Whip the cream and place the whipped cream in a sieve over a bowl, to drain and thicken.

Preheat oven to 450°F. To make the shortcake, sift the sugar with 2 cups of the flour. Use a food processor, a pastry blender, or 2 knives to cut in the butter until the mixture is coarse. Mix together the 3/4 cup of cream and the egg. Mix with the flour mixture, using a quick on/off motion in the food processor, or by hand rapidly with a fork. Pull together into a rough dough. Flour a surface with the rest of the flour. Pat or roll out the dough 3/4 inch thick. Cut into eight 2-1/2 to 3-inch rounds, or shape into rounds with your hands. Place on a lightly greased cookie sheet. Bake on the second rack of the oven for 8 to 10 minutes, or until lightly browned. If not brown after 10 minutes, but risen and light, run briefly under the broiler until dappled with brown. Cool on a rack. Split the biscuits. Fill with whipped cream and fruit.

Tip: The shortcake should be made within a few hours of serving, or made ahead and frozen, then defrosted at room temperature.

Continued

Variation for 4
Filling: Use 1 to 2 tablespoons sugar, 1/2 quart strawberries or 2 peaches and, 1/2 cup heavy whipping cream.
Shortcake: Use 1 tablespoon sugar, 1-3/4 cups flour, 1-1/2 tablespoons butter, 1/3 cup heavy whipping cream, and 1/2 egg (beaten to mix).

Tip: There's not much that can be done with the other half egg except glazing a pastry or enriching some store-bought mayonnaise.

LEMON MERINGUE PIE

Makes 1 pie

1 recipe 1-Crust Pie
 Dough (p. 142)

Lemon Filling

1 cup sugar
1/2 cup cornstarch
1/4 teaspoon salt
1-1/4 cup water
4 egg yolks
2 tablespoons butter
2 teaspoons finely
 grated lemon peel
1/2 cup lemon juice

Meringue

4 egg whites
1/2 teaspoon vanilla
1/4 teaspoon cream of
 tartar
1/2 cup sugar

Preheat oven to 350°F. Roll out dough for the bottom crust as directed (p. 143) and place in a 9-inch pie pan. Trim. Chill. Prebake (see p. 143). Cool on a wire rack.

To make the filling, combine the sugar, cornstarch, and salt in a medium saucepan. Gradually stir in the water until well mixed. Cook and stir over medium-high heat until thick. Reduce heat and cook, stirring 2 minutes more. Beat the egg yolks. Pour about 1 cup of the hot mixture into the yolks, stirring constantly. Return all of the egg yolk mixture to the saucepan. Cook and stir 2 minutes more to cook the eggs, but do not let them boil. The sauce should be very thick. Add the butter, lemon peel, and lemon juice to the hot mixture. Pour the hot filling into the cooled pastry shell.

To make the meringue, beat the egg whites with the vanilla and cream of tartar until soft peaks form. Gradually add the sugar, 1 tablespoon at a time, beating until the mixture forms stiff peaks. Spread the meringue over the hot lemon filling. Be sure to spread the meringue to the outside of the crust to seal in the filling and prevent shrinkage. Bake for 12 to 15 minutes in hot oven, until the meringue is golden brown. Cool before serving.

Variation
Fruit is a traditional part of the holidays. You can spruce up this pie with it by adding 1/2 cup candied fruit with a high ratio of reds and greens to the sauce after incorporating the butter, lemon peel, and lemon juice. Fold an additional 1/3 cup candied fruit into the meringue after it has formed stiff peaks.

✦19✦

A HOT SUMMER FEAST

Roman Banquet

This hot, sultry July morning I woke up yearning for a melon like the ones I found for the wedding supper I fixed July 7 in Rome, Italy, when friends decided to marry there. A perfect melon is sweet, cool, thirst-quenching, juicy, a foil for Italy's beloved Parma ham, prosciutto. In fact, I craved not just the melon, but the result of the marriage of opposites, a ripe tender wedge of melon wrapped with the slightly salty, richly flavorful aged prosciutto, which cloaks the melon like a sheer flesh-colored gown.

The Italian melon looks like a small cantaloupe, a bit larger than a softball, and its perfume announces its presence even before you cut it. I have never had a melon like it in Atlanta.

I prepared this prenuptial wedding feast for beautiful Cynthia Stevens, the talented producer of my television show, who married Atlanta's long-time bachelor, Cliff Graubart. Lenore Conroy, with help from her husband Pat, had done most of the shopping for the 35 people we were expecting for dinner at their home in Rome. But there was still shopping to be done, so we walked, plastic bags in hand, across the Tiber to an outdoor market. There we bought branches of fresh rosemary, bunches of basil and marjoram, Lenore sniffing, critiquing, and holding out for the very best. We searched the stalls for two more melons, holding them to our noses to be sure they were fragrant.

At another stall, the man who sold us the cherries exclaimed, "they are better than a night of love." Seeing our reddened faces he quickly declared he was not flirting, just telling us how good they were. Tasting one, we thought they were good, although perhaps not "that" good, but good enough to send Cliff and Cynthia on their way.

At the poultry shop we picked up the chickens, Cornish hens, and quail, all split up the backbone for us. The poultry man asked if the hens were for a very traditional Italian dish for these birds, called "diablo." "No," we exclaimed, horrified, "for a wedding." Fresh bread completed our task, and we trudged home loaded with sacks, stopping to reshift our bundles on the narrow streets full of Old World charm.

When we returned, Pat was proudly boiling water for the stuffed spinach tortellini for the cold pasta salad and had already removed the seeds from a mound of tiny green Italian olives. The coupling of the olives and the tortellini was aided by a salad dressing of oil and vinegar and fresh herbs in abundance as well as heaping quantities of freshly grated Parmigiano Reggiano Parmesan and slices of ham.

The poultry was marinated in lemon juice, which had been squeezed by the Conroys' young daughter, then drizzled with olive oil before being roasted in the tiny oven. The birds were lovely, their skin brown and crisp, with the flesh moist. All were piled in a beautiful stack and sprinkled with herbs and the reduced juices. (The oven blew the fuse twice, and we had to stop and do other things.)

We sliced heart-red tomatoes and splashed them with rich olive oil. We peeled the roasted sweet red peppers and tore them into strips, to be mated with aged balsamic vinegar.

As we worked, we listened to calls through the open window from the convent next door, which had been turned into a prison for men. "I want a lawyer," wailed one man, followed by a different echo, "I want a woman." All the time a guard paced the catwalk with his Uzi machine gun, and the birds—swallows—circled overhead with a taunt of freedom.

The inmates were blessedly silent by the time we were ready for dinner, and the sun was blushing good night as we toasted Cynthia and Cliff, Pat Conroy orated a history of their life and love, and the story was so tender it brought us to tears. We finished the evening sucking the cherries from their pits and thinking the melons, not the cherries, were really better than a night of love.

MENU

A HOT SUMMER FEAST

Melons with Prosciutto
Pat Conroy's Spinach Tortellini Salad
Roasted Red Bell Pepper Salad
Arugula and Tomato Salad
Lemon-Roasted Cornish Hens with Grilled Zucchini
My Cream Puffs and Whipped Cream
Fresh Cherries

SERVES 12

LOGISTICS

The recipes, written for 12, are in multiples of 4 and thus may be reduced accordingly to serve 4 or 8 people. Check the proportions to suit your needs. The cream puffs may be made ahead and frozen. The day of serving, defrost and recrisp them in a hot oven, then fill them as close to serving time as possible. The spinach tortellini salad may be made up to a day ahead, as may the red pepper salad. The melons and prosciutto may be wrapped several hours in advance and kept, tightly covered with plastic wrap and refrigerated, until needed. The hens may be cooked a day or several hours in advance, refrigerated then reheated, as may the zucchini. The arugula and tomatoes may be prepared without salad dressing and kept tightly covered, ready to serve; pour salad dressing over at time of serving.

CRECIPESC

MELONS WITH PROSCIUTTO

Serves 12

3 ripe cantaloupes, cut
  in 8 wedges, rind
  removed
3/4 pound prosciutto,
  shaved

Clasp the chilled melon with strips of prosciutto, using a toothpick to hold together if necessary.

Variation
Substitute figs, partially cut into quarters and opened out like a flower, with prosciutto laid over, for the melon, or wrap pear slices or mango slices with prosciutto.

Variation
Rather than wrapping the melons with the prosciutto, arrange the prosciutto on a platter like the petals of a flower. Arrange the melon in the center. Top with Gremolata (p. 170).

PAT CONROY'S SPINACH TORTELLINI SALAD

Serves 12

1 pound spinach
  tortellini stuffed with
  Parmesan cheese
1-1/2 cups imported
  Parmesan cheese,
  grated
1 cup green olives,
  chopped

Cook the pasta according to package directions. Toss with the cheese, olives, ham, and vinaigrette. Add salt, pepper, and optional herbs, and serve—or may be made ahead and chilled but bring to room temperature before serving.

1/2 pound cooked ham, sliced in small finger-sized strips
1-1/2 cups Vinaigrette (p. 140)
salt
freshly ground pepper
4 tablespoons fresh chopped basil or thyme (optional)

Variation
Use prosciutto in place of the ham.

Variation
Add 2 cups roasted, peeled, and sliced red peppers.

Variation
Serve on a bed of spinach.

> *Comment:* Spinach tortellini stuffed with Parmesan may be made at home; however, the fresh and packaged store-bought kinds are very acceptable and can easily be found in supermarkets. Other varities of tortellini will work, too!

ROASTED RED BELL PEPPER SALAD
Serves 12

10 red peppers, roasted and peeled (p. 191)
2 cups Vinaigrette (p. 140)
salt
freshly ground pepper

Tear the peppers into strips, saving the juice. Toss peppers and their juice in the vinaigrette. Taste for seasoning. May be made several days in advance.

Variation
Add 2 to 3 tablespoons fresh chopped basil or parsley.

Variation
Add 1 to 2 tablespoons ground cumin or fresh chopped ginger to the vinaigrette.

Variation
Serve on lettuce leaves or spinach leaves.

Variation
Add 2 to 4 garlic cloves, crushed.

Variation
Toss with cooked pasta and serve hot or cold.

Tip: Jars of roasted red peppers may be bought in Italian specialty shops or gourmet stores. They are not as good as your own, but will do.

Tip: To roast red peppers, place whole peppers on a foil-lined baking sheet or broiler pan. Place 3 inches from the heat and cook until charred, turning so all sides are nearly black. Remove. Place in a plastic bag to steam off skin. Cool. Remove skin, stem, cut in half and remove seeds.

ARUGULA AND TOMATO SALAD

Serves 12

3 bunches arugula,
  (approximately 1 cup)
3/4 cup olive oil
3 tablespoons red wine
  vinegar
1-1/2 teaspoons Dijon
  mustard
10 to 12 ripe tomatoes,
  cut in wedges or 36
  cherry tomatoes,
  halved
salt
freshly ground pepper

Wash and dry the arugula, remove the tough stems and arrange on the outside of a platter. Whisk together the olive oil, vinegar, and mustard. Add salt and pepper to taste. Toss the tomatoes gently in the salad dressing. Strain and place the tomatoes in the center of the arugula, drizzling the strained dressing over the arugula.

Variation
Add 2 to 3 tablespoons chopped fresh basil or thyme.

Variation
If you can find fresh Buffalo Mozzarella in your grocery store, crumble and sprinkle it over the tomatoes, or slice and top with whole basil leaves.

Comment: Sometimes you'll find arugula among the salad greens, sometimes among the herbs in the store. It is available from mid-February to December. It has a wonderful, almost nutty, "bitey" flavor and is delicious by itself.

LEMON-ROASTED CORNISH HENS

Serves 12

12 Cornish hens, split (1
   to 2 pounds each)
6 tablespoons olive oil
12 to 14 lemons, juiced
   (2 cups juice)
1 cup bread crumbs
2 pounds ricotta,
   drained
6 tablespoons rosemary,
   chopped
16 garlic cloves,
   chopped
8 tablespoons lemon
   rind
salt
freshly ground pepper
6 cups chicken stock,
   preferably fresh or
   homemade (see tip
   for quick stock)

Preheat oven to 400°F. Mix together the olive oil, lemon juice, and half the rosemary. Place the hens in the marinade, skin side down, overnight or as long as possible. Combine the bread crumbs, ricotta, lemon rind, the rest of the rosemary, and garlic cloves. Taste and season with salt and pepper. Loosen the skin of the birds from the meat, while still leaving it attached, then ease the stuffing under the skin. If the skin tears, it may be sewn up with a trussing needle and string.

Place the hens, skin side up, in a baking pan with the marinade, and roast 1 hour at 400°F. When done, remove from the pan. (May be done ahead to this point, and reheated until crisp under broiler.) Degrease the juices. To make the sauce add the stock to the pan and bring to the boil, stirring the sides and bottom to deglaze the pan. Boil to reduce, tasting occasionally until flavorful, about 20 minutes. I prefer this sauce without further thickening, but if you wish, thicken with flour dissolved in water.

Variation for 4 to 6
4 to 6 Cornish hens, split; 2 tablespoons olive oil; 6 to 8 lemons, juiced (1 cup); 1/2 cup bread crumbs; 16 ounces ricotta, drained; 3 tablespoons rosemary, chopped; 8 garlic cloves, chopped; 4 tablespoons lemon rind; and salt and freshly ground pepper.

Variation
This quick lemon-broiled or grilled recipe is very easy. For each hen, marinate in the juice of 1 lemon mixed with 1/2 tablespoon olive oil and 1/2 tablespoon rosemary. Place a heavy weight (such as a marble slab or a heavy pan weighted with a brick) on top of the hens. Refrigerate for several hours or overnight. The goal is to have the hens completely flat and level. Place under hot broiler or place on hot grill, skin next to heat, for 1/2 hour,

turning once. Slice in two up the breastbone. Make sauce as above. Serve with grilled zucchini. Also good served chilled.

Stock: Make a quick stock by chopping the backbones and giblets (not the liver). Add 3/4 cup water and 1/4 onion, chopped, for each backbone. Bring to the boil. Reduce heat and simmer, covered, 1 hour. Strain. Reduce to 1/2 cup per bird.

> *Comment:* To split the hen, place it on a cutting board, breast side down. Split the hen by cutting down either side of the backbone, remove the backbone (but save for stock, see below), then crack the hen on either side of the breastbone at the ribs by pressing down with the heel of your hand so that it will lie flat.

> *Comment:* A whole Cornish hen is too much food for some people, myself included. But a skimpy portion can be embarrassing. I roast an extra hen for every few people, then cut the extras in quarters, available for second (or third!) helpings. More marinade is not needed for 1 or 2 extra birds.

GRILLED ZUCCHINI
Serves 12

12 zucchini
6 tablespoons olive oil
salt
freshly ground pepper
1/2 cup chopped fresh
  herbs, such as thyme,
  marjoram, and
  parsley (optional)

Remove the stems of the zucchini. Slice lengthwise into 1/4-inch oval slices, leaving the skin on the outside for color, place on a foil-lined broiler pan. Brush with oil. Place 6 inches from broiler or on a hot grill. Cook until dappled with brown. Turn. Season with salt and pepper and fresh herbs. May be made ahead to this point. When ready to serve, re-heat in hot oven. Arrange under the hot Cornish hens like the spokes of a wheel.

Variation for 4
Use 4 zucchini, 2 tablespoons olive oil, salt, freshly ground pepper, and 2 tablespoons optional fresh herbs.

Tip: It is better to omit the herbs than to use dry.

MY CREAM PUFFS
Makes 40 small puffs, 24 medium, or 12 large puffs

Dough

1 cup all-purpose or
   bread flour
1/4 teaspoon salt
1/2 cup butter
1 cup water
4 eggs

Glaze

1 egg, beaten

Sift the flour with the salt onto a sheet of wax paper. Melt the butter in a saucepan. Stir in the flour and cook, making a roux. Remove from heat and stir in the water. Place over heat and stir constantly until the mixture comes together in a paste. "Dry" over high heat for 4 to 5 minutes by stirring until the flour is cooked and the dough looks like buttered mashed potatoes, with no white particles of uncooked flour. The bottom of the pan should have a light crust of dried dough.

Remove from the pan and place in a food-processor bowl fitted with the metal blade, or in a mixing bowl. Add the eggs, one by one, processing after each addition in the food processor or beating well with an electric mixer. Process or beat until shiny and smooth. The mixture should drop from a spoon like thick mayonnaise. Add the last egg a little at a time. If too much egg is added, the mixture will be too runny, causing it to collapse in baking.

The dough may be made in advance to this point, shaped, and cooked later as below. Any leftover dough may be kept wrapped in the refrigerator for several days, or frozen; it should be brought to room temperature or warmer before being baked.

To make cream puffs: Preheat the oven to 375°F and grease and flour a baking sheet. Shape the dough with 2 spoons or pipe through a pastry bag into 24 tablespoon-sized rounds for medium-sized puffs (12 tablespoons for large), leaving room for expansion during baking.

To glaze: Brush the puffs carefully with beaten egg, being careful not to drip any on the baking sheet.

Place the baking sheet on the second rack from the top of the oven. Bake until the dough is puffed, golden, and firm. To test for doneness, remove one puff from the oven and set it aside for 1 to 2 minutes; meanwhile continue cooking the rest. If the puff is firm after 2 minutes and does not collapse, the puffs are done and should be removed. Prick each one at the side of the base with a trussing needle or fork. Place back in the oven for a few minutes to get rid of the steam and keep the pastry crisp. The size of the puffs determines the time needed for baking—15 to 20 minutes for small puffs, 25 to 40 minutes for medium to large puffs. If not eaten the day they are made, refrigerate or freeze and recrisp briefly in the oven before filling.

Cream puffs: Fill with 2 cups heavy whipping cream, whipped with 2 tablespoons sugar.

To garnish: Dust with confectioners' sugar or sifted chocolate.

≈20≈

POT ROAST SUPPER

Grandmother's Pot Roast

When I think of Republicans, I think of my grandmother's pot roast sandwiches at the time of the great Republican convention of 1952, when my grandmother had come to stay with us. A devout, religious woman who knew God was not an old man in the sky, she nonetheless could not shake the opinion that God was a Republican.

Grandmother was so riveted by politics and news that the television was on all the time, day and night. Our new television was enshrined in the middle of the living room, and for the first time we were allowed not only to eat in front of the television, but also to stay up later than our bedtime to watch the convention.

The morning of the nomination for the Republican candidate, she got up in the cool of the morning and put on the pot roast, turning and browning it in hot fat. The night before (a hot night that was also a late night for television), she had started some homemade bread, leaving it to rise in the cool basement. She knocked it down and shaped it, letting it double again as the meat was browning, and then baked it. The smell of freshly baking bread was added to the tantalizing smells of cooking meat, when we came down for our oatmeal.

Grandmother was a wizard with the lowly potato, and boiled up a batch of them, some to be put in to finish with the juices of the pot roast, some for later. All day we sniffed that meat and the lingering smell of baked bread emanating from the loaves put out to cool on the racks in the tiny kitchen.

She called her candidate "Mr. Republican." He was Senator Robert Taft, the son of the 27th President of the United States, William Howard Taft. He was in contention for the nomination against General Dwight D. Eisenhower, who had flirted briefly with the Democrats and wasn't even, to my grandmother's way of thinking, a Republican for sure.

My grandmother had supported Taft for three elections. He ran for president in 1940, 1948, and 1952, losing each time. She hated Thomas Dewey, his opponent in 1948, as much as she had hated Franklin Delano Roosevelt—and she was so convinced of the rightness and reason of the Republican party's political stance that she couldn't even bear the *names* of the Democrats. As a child, I vaguely remember a parade or commemorative service for the dead president, Franklin Delano Roosevelt, but I didn't understand the politics. I thought they were saying a rose was dead, and I started to cry. My grandmother yanked my hand and pulled me away from the scene of activity, sniffing, "Pretty names don't make pretty people." She also said that Truman's name was a lie—he wasn't a "true man." A Democrat could do no good.

The convention of 1952 was a spellbinder. We sat in front of that television until long into the night, watching the black-and-white figures parade up and down, hearing the state roll calls, and keeping count on a sheet provided by the newspaper so you could tally up the votes. It was endless—and tense. The world was watching. Sometime during the night we ate thick sandwiches of pot roast and slices of buttered bread, and drank Grandmother's famous iced tea. We were engrossed with the drama and power of a televised convention played out in front of our eyes. We became part of the ground of politics.

It was hot, beastly hot, I remember. We had no air conditioners then—did anyone?—and the screened windows and doors were wide open. Finally, at the end, General Eisenhower, to her indignation, won a narrow victory over Taft, and my grandmother knew her candidate would never be president.

She knew she couldn't sleep, between the heat and her sorrow. Nor could we, hyper with the activity long past our bedtime. She took cold potatoes and sliced them, making us a potato sandwich

with the fresh bread, using plenty of salt and pepper. Then she took our sheets and pillows out to the front lawn and spread them out. We lay under the stars and we ate our picnic sandwiches as she talked to us about the rightness of the world and God's sorrow with the Republicans. At dawn she woke us so the neighbors wouldn't see us camping out, and made us breakfast of bread dipped in sugar and milk.

ᎶMENUᎩ

POT ROAST SUPPER

Rainy Day Soup (optional) or Steamed Garlic Vegetables (p. 6)
My Grandmother's Pot Roast
Garlic and Cumin Bread
Greek Salad or Make-Ahead Green Beans (p. 72)
Sinful Chocolate Cake or Lemon Bars

SERVES 6

LOGISTICS

The cake or lemon bars as well as the bread may be made ahead and frozen and defrosted, or cooked early in the day. The pot roast and soup are best made a day ahead and reheated in the microwave or simmered on top of the stove until cooked through to reheat. Place the bread in a 300°F oven when starting to reheat the roast. If you are making the steamed vegetables instead of the soup, they may be made early in the day and reheated 5 to 10 minutes in a frying pan over high heat or served cold. The Greek salad may be nearly completed, ready to finish tossing when serving.

CRECIPES C

RAINY DAY SOUP
Serves 6 to 8

3 to 5 tablespoons olive
  oil
2 leeks, white part and a
  touch of green, sliced
2 onions, sliced
2 carrots, peeled and
  sliced
8 garlic cloves, chopped
2 medium zucchini,
  peeled and sliced
3 cups chicken stock,
  boiling
1 (1-pound 12-ounce)
  can Italian plum
  tomatoes, with juice
1/2 to 1 tablespoon
  dried red pepper
  flakes or fresh
  chopped hot peppers
1/2 cup rice
salt
freshly ground pepper
1 tablespoon thyme,
  chopped
1 tablespoon fresh basil,
  chopped
2 cups fresh spinach,
  turnip greens, or kale,
  sliced
1 cup imported
  Parmesan cheese,
  grated

Heat enough of the olive oil to cover the bottom of a large pan. Add the leeks, onions, carrots, garlic, and zucchini, and cook 15 minutes over low heat. Add the chicken stock and bring to the boil. Chop the tomatoes and add with the peppers, reduce heat, cover, and cook 1/2 hour. Bring to the boil again, add the rice, salt and pepper to taste, thyme, basil, and spinach greens, and cook 15 to 20 minutes or until the rice is done. Serve with the Parmesan, or add as desired. May be made ahead a day or two, refrigerated, then reheated.

MY GRANDMOTHER'S POT ROAST

Serves 6

1 (3-pound) beef chuck
   roast
3 tablespoons drippings
   or oil
2 onions, sliced
2 garlic cloves, chopped
2/3 cup red wine
   vinegar
1/3 cup canned beef
   bouillon or stock
6 medium potatoes,
   peeled and quartered
2 tablespoons flour

Dry the pot roast with paper towels. Heat the drippings or oil in a heavy casserole until sizzling. Add the dry meat and brown rapidly on both sides. Remove. Add the onions and cook until soft. Add the garlic and return the meat to the pan. Pour the vinegar over the roast and add 1/2 the stock. Bring to the boil. Add the potatoes to the pan. Reduce to a simmer and cook, covered—20 minutes to the pound for rare, 10 minutes more to the pound for well done. If potatoes are not done when meat is, remove meat and cook potatoes through. You may cook this in the oven at 350°F for the same amount of time. When ready to serve, remove meat and potatoes, whisk the flour until smooth with the remaining stock and add to the pan. Bring to the boil and boil rapidly until liquid is reduced somewhat and the gravy is thick. Strain if necessary.

This dish reheats well, and is best made in advance in the microwave or simmered, then reheated for 15 minutes on top of stove, or served cold on fresh bread.

Variation
From 4 to 6 peeled quartered carrots may be added with the potatoes.

Variation
Substitute Burgundy wine for the vinegar, add 1 pound sautéed sliced mushrooms, and you have a variation of beef Burgundy, the classic French bistro dish.

Variation
Add 2 green peppers, chopped, omit stock, substitute 2 pounds Italian tomatoes, chopped, for all but 1 tablespoon of the vinegar, and you have another variation.

Variation
Grandmother liked to serve pot roast cold on sandwiches as well as hot with her tart gravy.

Tip: The vinegar is a tenderizer.

GARLIC AND CUMIN BREAD
Makes 1 loaf

4 garlic cloves
1 package rapid-rise dry
  yeast
1 teaspoon salt
1-1/2 tablespoons sugar
2 teaspoons ground
  cumin seed
3 cups bread flour
4 tablespoons butter
1 cup milk
To finish:
1 to 2 tablespoons black
  caraway seeds
1 egg mixed with 1
  tablespoon water

Place the unpeeled garlic cloves in the microwave and cook on high for 30 seconds to 1 minute, or place separated cloves in a pan of boiling water for 18 to 20 minutes until soft. Cool under running water, pop out of peel. Chop finely in the food processor or by hand. Mix the yeast, salt, sugar, cumin seed, and 2 cups of the bread flour, and place in a bowl with the garlic. Meanwhile, heat the butter and milk together to 125°F. Pour onto the flour mixture to incorporate, then knead to a soft dough, adding flour as needed. Kneading takes about 1 minute in the food processor, 8 to 10 minutes by hand. Shape into a ball.

Put the dough in a greased bowl and turn it to coat, cover with plastic wrap, and let rise in a warm place until doubled, about 1 hour. Punch down. Shape into a round and place on a greased baking sheet. Cut a design on top of the dough with a sharp knife. Do not cover. Let rise again until doubled, uncovered.

Preheat oven to 375°F. Brush dough with the egg mixture, and top with caraway seeds. Bake on middle rack of oven for approximately 30 minutes, until done. Cool on a rack. Freezes and doubles well.

Variation
For two loaves, double the recipe.

Tip: If you can bear the tedium of roasting the cumin seed and grinding it yourself, it is much better than store-bought ground cumin seed.

Tip: Rather than letting the bread rise for the first rise in a greased bowl, use an oiled plastic bag. No bowl to wash!

Tip: If bread browns too quickly, slip a piece of foil on top to cover.

GREEK SALAD
Serves 12 to 14

10 cups romaine and
   iceberg lettuce,
   washed and torn into
   bite-sized pieces
3 cucumbers, peeled
   and sliced
4 medium tomatoes,
   very ripe, in wedges,
   or 2 pounds halved
   cherry tomatoes
5 green onions or
   scallions, chopped
12 pepperoncini
20 black Greek olives
2 cups feta cheese, in
   pieces
3 cups Vinaigrette
   (p. 140)
3 tablespoons fresh
   oregano, chopped

Arrange the lettuce on a large platter or on 6 individual plates. Top with even amounts of the cucumbers, tomato wedges, green onions, and pepperoncini. Sprinkle on the olives and the feta cheese. Pour on the vinaigrette when ready to serve. Top with chopped oregano.

Tip: Pepperoncini is the name of the jars of medium-hot peppers.

Tip: The Greek pepperoncini pickles called for here are also good in Cajun dishes, I have discovered.

Variation for 6
Do a half recipe: 5 cups lettuce, 1-1/2 cucumbers, 2 tomatoes, 3 green onions or scallions, 6 pepperoncini, 10 black Greek olives, 1 cup feta, in pieces, and 1 cup vinaigrette.

Tip: It would take about 2 pounds lettuce to make 10 cups torn lettuce pieces.

SINFUL CHOCOLATE CAKE
Serves 6 to 8

16 ounces semisweet
   chocolate chips
1 teaspoon hot water
1-1/2 teaspoons sugar

Preheat oven to 350°F. Grease the bottom of an 8-inch springform pan. Line with wax paper and grease the paper. Melt the chocolate chips in the water over low heat or

1-1/2 teaspoons all-
   purpose flour
1/2 cup butter, melted
4 egg yolks
4 egg whites
1 cup heavy whipping
   cream, whipped
grated chocolate

in the microwave. With a wooden spoon, beat in the sugar, flour, and butter. Add egg yolks one by one, beating well after each addition, until batter is smooth. In a separate bowl, preferably copper, whisk the egg whites until stiff peaks form. Fold a large spoonful into the chocolate mixture, then fold that mixture into the whites. Pour the mixture into the prepared pan and bake 15 minutes only. The cake will look very uncooked in the center. Remove to a wire rack and let cool completely. The cake will collapse in the pan while cooling. Remove from the pan, remove paper, wrap well with plastic wrap, then chill or freeze.

When ready to serve, slice the cake with a hot knife into 6 to 8 wedges, leaving the cake whole. Spread a very thick layer of whipped cream over the top of the cake. Smooth, and sprinkle with the grated chocolate.

Tip: To make a design with the chocolate, make a stencil or cutout of a leaf, heart, etc. Place in the center of the cake. Dust with chocolate or cocoa around it. Carefully lift up the stencil.

LEMON BARS

Makes about 3 dozen bars

2-1/2 cups flour, divided
1 cup butter, softened
1/2 cup confectioners'
   sugar
2 cups sugar
1/2 cup lemon juice
4 large eggs
peel of 1 lemon, grated
   (optional)
confectioners' sugar

Preheat oven to 350°F. Mix together 2-1/4 cups of the flour, the butter, and confectioners' sugar in a large bowl until a soft dough forms. Remove and press dough into a 13 × 9 × 2-inch baking pan. Bake 20 to 25 minutes in preheated oven or until lightly browned. Remove from oven.

Beat the sugar, lemon juice, the remaining 1/4 cup of flour, the eggs, and the optional lemon peel until well mixed. Pour over hot crust. Return to the oven and bake an additional 20 minutes or until set. Cool on wire rack and cut into bars. Center will be soft, like a custard or pie filling. Sift confectioners' sugar over tops. Freezes well.

⚡21⚡

MENU OF COMFORT FOODS

A Peanut Butter Sandwich to Go

Whenever she wanted to run away—from a job, a man, her children—she made a peanut butter sandwich and thought about the time she'd run away from home with a peanut butter sandwich and a Coke. She had been about 10, a gawky, skinny creature with glasses so thick and strong they reduced her eyes to dark beads.

She thought she didn't have a nice personality and was sure that no one in her family really liked her or had time for her.

Her parents quarreled all the time when they were together. She thought her father was leaving them all soon. He always said he was going to.

It seemed to her it was her fault her parents fought all the time. Maybe if she left—if there would be no one there who was always spilling things or fighting with her brothers and sisters, and if he didn't have her messy room to contend with—maybe then he would stay. She didn't think he liked having any of them, but her least of all. They all said she was the most difficult child.

One day, to her surprise, her dad brought home a bicycle for her. They didn't have a car, so he'd picked it up in the nearby shopping center, thrown his briefcase in the basket, and pedaled the bicycle home on the dusty highway. He had been in high spirits as he pedaled in. Proud of himself in some vain, male way. He was pleased to be able to give her such a present, as nice a bicycle as her friend had.

It had been a happy day. Everyone in the neighborhood had come out to see the bike. She had ridden it some since then, although she was afraid of so much—of leaving it at home, thinking it might not be there when she got back, even if she went to a friend's house for the afternoon.

Later, on the kind of day that was hot when you ran or biked, and cold if you stood still or were in the shadows, she decided to ride away. She spent her life in shadows, it seemed to her—listening to angry words, watching angry scenes, hearing the baby's cries mixed in with her mother's.

She packed her lunch very carefully. She took the store-bought white bread out of the package without making a mess. She spread one slice with peanut butter, then covered it with a second, and cut it in two. She wrapped it in wax paper, and then placed it in the brown bag, along with a banana. She added some gingersnaps from an open box, poured some Coke into her school thermos, and then put the brown bag, all packed, in the basket where her father's briefcase had been, so long ago, on a happier day.

Her parents were still shouting when she left the house, and no one asked her where she was going. She knew where she was going.

There was a house a few miles up the highway, a big house, with white columns. She imagined the kind of people who lived there, people with enough money for a car, people who liked little girls, people who would want her.

She pedaled up the hill past her house, looking down on the highway from above, then crossed the road that led to the exit ramp. Cars zoomed past her on the ramp as she pedaled down. Once on the highway itself, there were fewer cars. It was the middle of a hot Saturday, and she was pushing out to the country. She rode a good long while on the flat, even surface before she got hungry. Maybe the white house wasn't as close as she thought. She'd only seen it from the highway. Maybe it wasn't the next exit, maybe it was much further.

She pulled over onto the dirt strip next to the highway. She peeled open the wrapping around her sandwich and started to eat. It tasted like the banana. She should have known—bananas always give their smell and their flavor. The sandwich was hot and dry, and stuck in her throat. She drank some Coke. It was hot, too. The banana had gotten squashed, somehow. Probably by the thermos.

Maybe the people in the house already had children. They probably wouldn't want another. She got back on the bike and pedaled to the next exit. There was no house visible from her side of the highway. She labored up the ramp, ever so tired, and crossed over. There was no house there at all.

She turned back for home, weary and broken in spirit. It was longer going home than it had been leaving, and she had thrown away the rest of her sandwich. She was sorry, and longed for it, even if it tasted like the banana. The rest of the Coke had fizzled out of the thermos and made the cookies soggy and inedible.

It was late when she walked in, and the heat of the day was gone. No one said hello. No one had missed her. She didn't ride her bike much after that. Her dad left soon after and never came home again.

As life went on, she found other foods that comforted her the way peanut butter did and soon she learned that food was not only a way of consoling herself, but of nurturing others. When she moved to another country, she served American meat loaf, macaroni, and greens to her exiled friends. When she was left alone, she cooked onions to comfort her in her loneliness. And always, she kept gingersnaps on hand and a jar of peanut butter. All of them, when she needed them, soothed and comforted her.

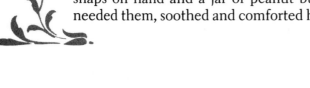

Ꮟ M E N U Ꮛ

MENU OF COMFORT FOODS

Baby Peanut Butter Sandwiches

Spicy Black Bean Soup

Everyday Meat Loaves
or *Mint Julep Meat Loaf*

Jean Van den Berg's Herbed Tomatoes (p. 7)

Macaroni and Cheese

Greens in Brown Butter

Caramelized Onions

Apple Crisp
or *Old-Fashioned Gingersnaps*

SERVES 6

LOGISTICS

The soup, meat loaf, macaroni, cookies, and apple crisp may all be made a day or two ahead, or even frozen then reheated, but the macaroni and apple crisp are a bit better when freshly made. The caramelized onions may be made up to a week ahead and reheated. The tomatoes and dressing may be prepared ahead and refrigerated until time to serve. The greens may be blanched ahead, ready for tossing over heat a few minutes before serving. The peanut butter sandwiches may be made any time.

᧕ R E C I P E S ᧕

BABY PEANUT BUTTER SANDWICHES

Makes 6 to 8 bite-size sandwiches

2 pieces white store-bought bread
2 to 3 tablespoons peanut butter
jelly (optional)

Spread 1 slice bread with peanut butter. Add jelly if desired. Top with second slice. Cut into small squares and serve with drinks.

SPICY BLACK BEAN SOUP

Serves 6 to 8

1 cup dried black beans, picked through
2 onions, chopped
4 garlic cloves, chopped
1 to 2 hot chili peppers, seeded and chopped
4 stalks fresh cilantro, tied together with string
1 quart chicken stock
1 (4-ounce) piece of cooked ham or ham bone or streak-o-lean or salt pork
salt
freshly ground pepper
juice of 1 lemon
sour cream

Cover the beans with water and soak 3 to 4 hours or overnight. Drain. Place in a large pot with the onions, garlic, hot peppers, cilantro stalks, stock, and ham or pork. Bring to the boil. Reduce heat and simmer until the beans are soft, about 2 hours, occasionally skimming off the fat. Remove the stalks and the pork. With a slotted spoon, place the beans in a food processor or blender and process until smooth. Return the purée to the pan and bring back to the boil. Season with salt, pepper, and lemon juice. May be made ahead, cooled uncovered, then covered and refrigerated for up to a day. To reheat, bring back to the boil for several minutes, taking care not to scorch the bottom. Garnish with sour cream.

Variation
Use Cumin Chicken Stock (p. 220).

Tip: To soften beans rapidly, place beans in water to cover, bring to the boil, and boil 5 minutes. Set aside one hour. Drain.

Tip: To garnish with sour cream, place the sour cream in a kitchen towel over a strainer, and let drain several hours or refrigerated overnight, to remove excess water. Place sour cream in a heavy-duty zip-close plastic bag. Cut off a small corner and use as a piping bag to drizzle a design on top.

Tip: Parsley and cilantro stalks have more flavor than their leaves, particularly when cooked more than 15 minutes. Tie together to remove easily.

EVERYDAY MEAT LOAVES

Serves 6 to 8

1/3 cup oatmeal
1 cup milk
1-1/2 pounds lean
   ground beef
2 eggs, beaten to mix
1 medium onion,
   chopped
1 garlic clove, chopped
3/4 teaspoon salt
1/2 teaspoon fresh or
   dried sage, chopped
freshly ground pepper

Preheat oven to 350°F. Soak the oatmeal in the milk for 5 minutes. Add the beef, eggs, onion, garlic, salt, sage, and pepper. Mix well. Place in 6 small individual bread tins or a 9-inch loaf pan. Whisk together the ketchup and mustard. Spread on top of each meat loaf to desired thickness. Bake for 45 minutes for the miniature loaves or about 2 hours for the large loaf. Top with any remaining sauce for the last 10 minutes. Freezes and reheats well.

Topping

1 cup ketchup
1 tablespoon Dijon
   mustard

Variation
Try a combination of 1/2 pound ground veal, 1/2 pound ground beef, and 1/2 pound ground pork.

Variation
Omit the sage and add fresh basil or thyme to taste.

Tip: The oatmeal in this recipe not only "stretches" the meat, it gives it a nice texture, while the milk keeps it moist.

MINT JULEP MEAT LOAF (CHARLES CARDEN SNOW'S)

Makes 2 loaves (serving 6 each)

4 pounds lean ground
   meat
2 eggs, beaten slightly
1/8 teaspoon curry
   powder
1-1/2 to 2 tablespoons
   salt
1 teaspoon freshly
   ground pepper
1/2 cup bread crumbs
1 onion, chopped
1 beef bouillon cube,
   crushed
2 garlic cloves, chopped
1 large handful fresh
   mint leaves, dried and
   crushed
1 cup chili sauce
1/2 cup water
3/4 cup bourbon
Garnish:
fresh mint leaves

Preheat oven to 350°F. Combine meat, eggs, curry, salt, pepper, bread crumbs, onion, bouillon, garlic, mint, and 1/4 cup of the chili sauce. Form the meat mixture into two thick, oval-shaped loaves. Pour the water into a greased baking dish that has a cover. Gently place the loaf into the dish. With a tablespoon, make a deep indentation down the center of each of the loaves. Combine the bourbon and 1/4 cup of the chili sauce and fill the indentations, pouring any remaining mixture over the loaves. Cover and bake for 45 minutes to 1 hour. Uncover, spread each loaf with 1/4 cup of the remaining chili sauce, and bake uncovered until brown. Remove from pan. Garnish with mint leaves. Freeze one loaf and serve the other.

Tip: Leftover meat loaf makes a good cold sandwich.
Tip: Any ground meat will do. I like 1/2 beef and 1/2 lean lamb.

MACARONI AND CHEESE

Serves 6 to 8

1/2 pound butter
1/4 cup flour
2 cups milk
salt
freshly ground pepper
1-3/4 cup grated sharp
   Cheddar cheese
1/2 pound dry macaroni
3/4 cup bread crumbs

Melt half of the butter in a heavy sauce-pan, add the flour, stirring until smooth. Pour in the milk and bring to the boil, stirring constantly. Season with salt and pepper and blend in 1/2 cup of the cheese. Set aside, covering with plastic wrap to prevent a skin forming. Meanwhile, place the macaroni in a large pot of boiling water and cook until nearly tender. Drain. Place a layer of the drained macaroni in a buttered 6 × 12-inch oblong baking dish and top with some of both the sauce and the cheese. Repeat until all the macaroni is layered, finishing with cheese. Melt the remaining butter in a large frying pan, add the bread crumbs, and toss in the butter. Sprinkle on top of the casserole, which may be made ahead to this point. When ready to serve, bring the casserole to room temperature and place in a preheated 400°F oven until heated through, about 20 minutes. Freezes well and can be defrosted and reheated in microwave. Doubles easily.

Variation
Use another pasta, such as rainbow rotini, green fettucine, cappelletti, or even sliced wonton strips, cooking until nearly tender and proceeding as above. A fresh pasta is heavenly in this.

Variation
Add a bit of cayenne or chili pepper, or fresh chopped hot red peppers.

GREENS IN BROWN BUTTER

Serves 6

3 pounds fresh spinach
   or other greens such
   as turnips or beets,
   well washed
6 to 8 tablespoons
   butter

If the leaves are small, leave the stems on; if large, remove them. Place in a large pot of boiling water, and boil 2 minutes after the water has returned to the boil for tiny leaves, 3 to 5 minutes longer for older, larger greens.

salt
freshly ground pepper

Drain and refresh by running cold water over. Drain thoroughly and squeeze dry. When ready to serve, melt the butter in a large frying pan. Let the butter turn a golden brown, the color of a nut. Add the drained greens and turn until coated and heated through. Season with salt and pepper to taste. Serve hot.

Variation
Add 1 cup heavy cream to the pan after adding the greens.

Variation
Substitute olive oil for the butter and add chopped garlic to the pan.

Variation
Cook and chop greens before adding to butter.

Variation
Substitute frozen spinach, turnips, or kale, defrosted and drained. Reheat in butter.

CARAMELIZED ONIONS

Serves 6 to 8

8 tablespoons butter or
   olive oil
6 onions, sliced
salt
freshly ground pepper

Heat the butter or oil in a skillet large enough to accommodate the onions in 1 layer. Add the onions to the hot fat, and cook slowly until the onions are soft and a golden caramel brown—about 1/2 hour. Stir frequently. If they become watery, turn up the heat a bit, taking care not to burn them. Salt and pepper to taste. These may be made ahead and reheated.

Variation
Some people add a bit of sugar at the end.

Variation
Add some balsamic vinegar, flavored vinegar, or even red wine vinegar at the end of the cooking time, bring to the boil, and serve.

Variation
Use to spread over cooked green beans, or in a hot grilled cheese sandwich, or surround roasted chicken, lamb, or duck, or even top a pizza with them!

APPLE CRISP
Serves 6 to 8

2 pounds (5 cups)
 apples, cored and
 sliced
1/4 cup water
1/2 cup granulated
 sugar
1/2 teaspoon nutmeg
1/2 teaspoon cinnamon
1/2 teaspoon salt
1 cup all-purpose flour
4 tablespoons butter

Preheat oven to 350°F. Place the apples in a buttered casserole and sprinkle water over them. Mix together the sugar, nutmeg, cinnamon, salt, flour, and rub in the butter. Sprinkle this mixture over the apples. Cover and bake 1/2 hour, remove cover, and bake another 1/2 hour. May be made a day or two ahead or frozen and reheated.

Variation
Add 1 tablespoon finely diced crystallized ginger, 1 cup raw cranberries, and an additional 1/2 cup sugar.

OLD-FASHIONED GINGERSNAPS
Makes about 6 dozen

2-3/4 cups all-purpose
 flour
2 teaspoons baking soda
1 teaspoon cinnamon
1 teaspoon ginger
1/2 teaspoon salt
1/4 teaspoon ground
 cloves
1 cup brown sugar,
 packed
3/4 cup butter, softened
1 egg
1/4 cup light molasses
sugar

Mix together the flour, baking soda, cinnamon, ginger, salt, and cloves. Beat the brown sugar and butter until light, then beat in the egg and molasses until light. Stir in the flour mixture until just blended. Chill dough thoroughly. May be made ahead or frozen.

Preheat oven to 375°F. Shape dough into 3/4-inch balls and roll in granulated sugar. Put the balls on greased baking sheets spaced about 2 inches apart. Flatten with the bottom of a flat-bottomed coffee mug or glass, dipped in sugar. Bake 8 to 10 minutes or until cookies are set. Cool on wire rack.

Tip: At 8 minutes, the cookies will be chewy. At 10, they will be crisp.

Tip: May be made ahead or frozen.

✕22✕

MENUS USING LEFTOVERS

Leftovers

Thinking of my friend Deni Seibert caused me to tackle my
fridge after the holidays. It was crammed full of various leftovers—some watercress and turnip greens, flavored with meaty ham
hocks, in broth as solid as Jell-O; a few bits of turkey, in the broth
from the boiled-down carcass; green onion tops whose bulbs had
seen better days; several very ripe tomatoes; a hard piece of Cheddar; some candied fruit and some cream cheese.

Deni has perfected her leftovers into an art in the form of
weekly made soup. Russ, her husband, was director of Longwood
Gardens in Delaware for years, and they brought their children up
there. Deni has the ability never to be flustered, even when the
doorbell rings and some person, perhaps never met before but heard
about, is at her door saying, "I know this is rude, but I've wanted to
meet you for ever so long and found that I had just enough time
before going to the airport if I drove straight here without calling
and rang your doorbell." Deni brings them into her kitchen, makes
them feel completely at ease, and, if they are very lucky, they get
her homemade soup.

She starts a new soup fresh each week, beginning with the
Sunday meal's leftovers—a ham bone boiled up, or the bone from
whatever meat she served for Sunday dinner. Each day, through the

rest of the week, leftovers are added to her soup. The best day is Saturday. By that time the soup is chock-full of surprises—carrots from Wednesday, butterbeans from Thursday, a couple of cut-up boiled potatoes from Friday. Perhaps it is easy to be gracious if you always know you have a good soup in the fridge.

The truth is anyone can make a soup with the bits and pieces one has in the fridge. It is good to start with a broth to give a soup body. If you have a chicken or duck or turkey carcass with a little meat still clinging to the bones, you have a fine base. Better still if you have some ham hocks in jelly. If you cut up your own raw chickens every time you're preparing fried chicken or a sauté, save the backbone, neck, and gizzards, and package and freeze them until you have enough packages for a stock. Also, when I am preparing vegetables, I chuck into a freezer bag the end pieces of onions and carrots and maybe other vegetables, as well as parsley stalks, outer ribs of celery, and so on, and these all go into the soup pot. (I'm afraid I save the green onion tops for myself and char them until crisp—a cook's treat.)

But to get back to the findings in my own post-holiday fridge: in addition to making a turkey and/or ham soup, I can use up two leftover tortillas! I'll use the tomatoes in a tomato bruschetta with some slightly stale Italian bread I have on hand. The bit of cheese has a speck of mold on it, but that doesn't hurt cheese. I'll just scrape it off and use it along with the leftover meat on the ham hocks to make a *gougère*—that delicious French cheesy cream puff that my nearly-daughter Audrey and her Frenchman beau taught me how to put together (they'll often make an entire meal of a *gougère*). The leftover vegetables will also work nicely cooked together. And that eggplant can make a nice snacking appetizer, too, while I wait.

Finally, there's the candied fruit and some cream cheese. Almond crisp cookies are a good solution for leftover candied fruit, but then I also remember a recipe from Betty Rosbottom for a wonderful cheesecake that uses both candied fruit and cream cheese—and a fair amount of sour cream, I admit—but better to add to what I have and produce a scrumptious dessert than to throw away any usable ingredient. Now I've made a clean sweep. What a feeling of satisfaction!

⎛ M E N U ⎞

MENUS USING LEFTOVERS

Spring Onion Tops or *Hot Garlic Eggplant*

Omelet with Chives or *Pierre Henri's Ham and Cheese Gougère*
or *Tomato Bruschetta (p. 169)*

After-Holiday Soup

Vegetables al Dente
or *Mushrooms and Okra (p. 111)*

Christmas Cheesecake or *Almond Crisp Cookies*

SERVES 4 TO 6

LOGISTICS

Lots of choices here, depending on your refrigerator and your time schedule. Don't try to get quantities for all your recipes. Make it fun by cooking up all the "dibs and dabs" and putting everything out on the table. The family will enjoy the variety. The *gougère*, stock, cheesecake, and cookies may be frozen, ready to pull out as needed. The spring onion tops are a "treat" for the cook. The bruschetta, omelet with chives, and soup are good last-minute dishes, taking half an hour or less to pull together.

ℭRECIPESℭ

SPRING ONION TOPS

Serves 2

4 bunches spring onions
   or scallions (10 to 12
   per bunch)
3 tablespoons butter
salt

     Wash the green onions or scallions and remove any damaged green skins. Cut off the green onion tops and dry in paper towels. Place onion tops in an iron skillet with the butter. Cook over medium heat for 8 minutes. The onion tops will turn brown. Turn them, reduce heat to medium low, and brown other side. After about 10 minutes, the onion tops should become brown and stiff. Remove to brown paper or paper towel. Sprinkle lightly with salt if desired. These are good to eat right out of the pan.

    Comment: This recipe uses only the green tops of spring onions. Cooked until crisp and brown, they are a perfect finger food or side dish. Use the onions for another purpose.

HOT GARLIC EGGPLANT

Serves 4 to 6

5 tablespoons oil
1/2 cup pork, sliced in
   small strips
1 (3/4-pound) eggplant,
   peeled and cut in
   1-inch finger-length
   strips
1 teaspoon fresh ginger,
   chopped
1 garlic clove, chopped
1-1/2 teaspoons soy
   sauce
1 teaspoon sugar

     Heat 3 tablespoons of the oil in a frying pan. Add the pork and sauté until cooked. Remove from pan and set aside. Pour the rest of the oil into the pan, add the eggplant, and cook until the pulp is lightly browned on each side. Drain the eggplant on paper towels, pressing to extract excess oil. Combine ginger, garlic, soy sauce, sugar, vinegar, chili pepper flakes, and cornstarch. Pour into hot pan and heat until near boiling; add cooked pork and eggplant, and mix together until heated thoroughly.

1 teaspoon white wine
    vinegar
1/4 teaspoon dried chili
    pepper flakes
1 teaspoon cornstarch
Garnish:
1 red bell pepper

Make flowers from the red pepper by cutting a zigzag pattern around the pepper. Pull apart for garnish.

OMELET WITH CHIVES

Serves 1 to 2

2 to 3 tablespoons
    butter
3 tablespoons chopped
    fresh or frozen chives
3 eggs
2 to 3 tablespoons water
freshly ground pepper
salt

Melt the butter in an 8-inch nonstick pan at medium or high heat—see tip below. Meanwhile, whisk the eggs and chives with a little water and pepper to taste. When the butter is singing, add the eggs. Let set 5 seconds, then with a spatula pull the cooked egg from around the edges of the pan to the center. Keep the eggs over heat 20 seconds until nearly set. Slide to one side of the pan. Sprinkle with salt and a filling if you are using one. Fold in half. Let brown 5 seconds before turning out. Place a warm plate next to the pan and slide the omelet partially out, then flip. Make neat with your hands, if necessary.

Variation
Use 1/4 cup chopped ham, cheese, bacon, herbs, for filling.

Variation
Use 1/4 cup chopped cooked artichoke hearts; black olives; goat cheese; pesto and goat cheese; mixed cheeses; sun-dried tomatoes; sautéed wild mushrooms as filling—nearly anything goes.

Variation
To multiply servings, make additional omelets.

Tip: Never use milk in an omelet—it toughens the egg. Water keeps it light.
Tip: Heating units vary radically, as do pans. In the days when a heavy, traditional, omelet pan was used, a very high heat was necessary. Now, with the thinner nonsticks, a medium or even low heat will suffice. The trick is what's happening in the pan—be sure the butter is singing or sizzling noisily.

PIERRE HENRI'S HAM AND CHEESE *GOUGÈRE*

Makes 1 large gougère or 18–20 2-inch puffs

1 recipe My Cream
  Puffs Dough (p.194)
4 to 5 ounces smoked
  ham, cooked and
  chopped
3 ounces sharp white
  Cheddar or Swiss
  cheese, grated

To make the dough, see p. 194.

To make the *gougère*, preheat the oven to 375°F. Mix the ham and half of the cheese into the room-temperature dough. Butter a 12 inch pizza pan. Spoon globs of dough about 1/2 inch in diameter around the edge of the pan, touching so they form a circular crown. To make cheese puffs, spoon the globs of dough onto the pan 1 inch apart. Sprinkle the rest of the cheese on top of the dough and place in the oven. Bake until puffed and brown, about 35 to 45 minutes.

Remove to a platter and serve. May be frozen and reheated.

Variation

Use any leftover dough (without the ham and cheese) to make cream puffs, éclairs, swans, and many other pastries.

Tip: Bread flour is necessary to sustain the rise with the weight of the ham and cheese.

BASIC POULTRY STOCK OR BROTH

Makes 1 quart

3 to 5 pounds uncooked
  turkey, 1 whole
  chicken, or 1 turkey
  breast
1 quart water or water
  to cover
1/2 carrot, roughly
  sliced
1 celery stalk without
  leaves, roughly sliced
1 onion, sliced
1 garlic clove, chopped
  (optional)

Stock is simply a well-flavored liquid, made from bones, meat, and vegetables, cooked slowly together until the liquid develops body and intensifies in flavor. *Broth, bouillon,* and *stock* are interchangeable terms.

Brown stock is stock that is made by first browning meat and vegetables before adding them to the water so that the broth turns brown. *White stock* does not require the preliminary browning, and the resulting color is pale. If you use meat or a whole chicken in addition to bones, you will have a full-flavored stock. Using only bones makes a more clear,

3 to 4 stalks parsley
1 bay leaf
3 to 4 sprigs thyme
6 peppercorns
3 to 4 mushrooms,
    sliced, or mushroom
    scraps (optional)
salt to taste

gelatinous stock, flavorful enough for a sauce base, but not desirable as a soup base. The more the bones are cut up, the more gelatinous and rich the stock. If you want to use the meat for another purpose as well, after it has cooked in the broth, be sure you have cut it up into large pieces and then extract them before they become overcooked. And a word about carrots: too much carrot will add a kind of sweetness to the stock, so use judiciously. This recipe halves, doubles, or triples easily. Most cooks don't follow a recipe for stock, but just use what bones and bits and pieces they have on hand.

Cover the bones and meat with water in a large pot or stockpot. Add the other ingredients. Bring to the boil, then reduce heat to a simmer. Cover and simmer for 1 hour or until meat is done. Remove meat if desired for another purpose. Return the bones to the pot and continue to cook, covered, another hour if possible. Strain. Cool and cover. Remove the fat. Refrigerate several days or freeze if desired. Add salt to taste. For a thicker consistency or more flavorful stock, reduce the liquid by boiling down. For a thinner consistency, add water as necessary.

Variation

For brown stock, brown the bones and meat to an almost mahogany color in a hot oven or under the broiler, turning frequently, or in a skillet on top of the stove, with a little fat to keep them from sticking. Brown the vegetables the same way, taking care not to burn them. Put in a pot with optional vegetables, cover with water, and proceed as above.

Tip: To skim fat and scum, add a dash of cold water, which will cause the fat and scum to congeal. There are skimmers available in gourmet retail shops. Otherwise, cool, refrigerate, and remove congealed fat.

Tip: For a quick stock, use chicken wings and less water. Bring to the boil, simmer 1/2 to 1 hour, remove bones, and boil down stock rapidly. Skim. The wings may be saved and used to start another pot of stock, or eaten as is.

Variation
For cumin chicken stock, use 1 chicken (3 to 5 pounds), add 4 chopped garlic cloves and 2 teaspoons ground cumin.

Variation
Add 1 to 2 slices ginger (chopped) and 1 to 2 teaspoons coriander seeds.

Variation
You may omit the carrot, celery, onion, garlic, parsley, bay leaf, and thyme if you wish. The vegetables add nutrients and flavor; however, some people like to leave them out as a stock will last longer in the refrigerator if it hasn't been cooked with vegetables.

Variation
For leftover turkey stock, substitute a chopped-up turkey carcass and any leftover meat for the chicken and bones and proceed accordingly. A stock made from just the carcass may not be quite as flavorful as a stock made with meat. Feel free to substitute a can or two of broth for the water or add a bouillon cube if you want to add flavor to your soup.

Tip: Although lamb is used for a stock in lamb dishes, it is not called for in most other dishes, because its flavor is so dominant.

AFTER-HOLIDAY SOUP
Serves 8 to 10 as a starter or 4 to 6 as a main course

2 tablespoons butter
1 onion, chopped
1 garlic clove, chopped
4 cups turkey stock
1 (16-ounce) bag mixed
    frozen vegetables
1 (14-1/2-ounce) can
    tomatoes, chopped
2 to 3 cups cooked
    turkey, cut up or
    shredded
salt
freshly ground pepper

Melt the butter, add the onion and garlic, and cook until soft in a large heavy pan or Dutch oven. Add the stock, vegetables, and tomatoes. Bring to the boil, cover, reduce heat, and simmer 1/2 hour or until done. Add the turkey and reheat. Taste for seasoning, add salt and pepper if necessary.

Variation
Cut 2 tortillas in 1/4-inch strips. Fry briefly in 2 tablespoons of vegetable oil. Use as a garnish for the soup.

Tip: Of course, you can use any leftover vegetables in addition to or in place of the store-bought mixed vegetables, but I always keep a package of them in the freezer because by the time the Thanksgiving turkey's gone, so are my fresh vegetables!

VEGETABLES AL DENTE
Serves 4 to 6

2 zucchini, sliced or
   julienned
2 carrots, sliced or
   julienned
2 onions, sliced
salt
freshly ground pepper
2 to 4 tablespoons
   butter

Slice the zucchini and carrots into diagonal thin slices or cut them in julienne strips. Heat enough butter in a heavy saucepan to coat the bottom. Add the zucchini, carrots, onions, salt, and pepper. Place a sheet of wax paper directly on the vegetables, then put the lid on the pan. Cook over low heat until tender, not mushy. Add more butter if desired. May be prepared ahead of time and reheated. These proportions may be increased to serve any number of people.

Variation
Substitute yellow squash, sliced, for the zucchini.

Variation
Substitute 2 stalks celery, sliced, for the zucchini.

Variation
Add 2 tablespoons chopped fresh herbs.

Tip: Wax paper is a good insulator. It pushes the condensation back into the pan, preventing evaporation, adding to the juices in the pan, and thus helping to avoid burning due to lack of moisture. The nutrients all stay in the pan with the vegetables. Do not let the paper extend over the sides of the pan.

Tip: These vegetables are also called "sweated" vegetables since they cook in their own juice.

CHRISTMAS CHEESECAKE
Makes 1 cake

Crust

1 cup finely ground
  pecans
1 cup graham cracker
  crumbs
1 cup confectioners'
  sugar
4 tablespoons melted
  unsalted butter

Filling

1 pound cream cheese,
  at room temperature
3/4 cup sugar
3 large eggs
1/3 cup coarsely
  chopped mixed
  candied fruits
1/3 cup raisins
1/3 cup chocolate
  morsels
2 tablespoons all-
  purpose flour

Topping and Garnish

3/4 cup sour cream
1/3 cup sugar
pecan halves, candied
  cherries, and
  chocolate bits

Preheat oven to 350°F.

To prepare the crust, mix the pecans, graham cracker crumbs, confectioners' sugar, and butter on a piece of wax paper. Pack evenly on the bottom of an 8-inch springform pan and halfway up the sides of the pan.

Beat the cream cheese and sugar together until smooth. Add the eggs and beat briefly. Toss the fruits, raisins, and chocolate morsels into the flour and fold into the cream cheese mixture. Pour into the prepared pan. Place on a baking sheet and bake in hot oven 50 to 55 minutes until firm. Whisk the sour cream and sugar together in a small bowl. Remove the cheesecake quickly from the oven, spread the topping over the warm cheesecake, and return the cheesecake to the oven. Bake until the topping is set, about 10 minutes. Remove the cheesecake from the oven and let it cool to room temperature. Wrap with plastic wrap, and refrigerate at least 12 hours, preferably 2 days.

To decorate the cheesecake, make a border of pecan flowers and candied cherries and chocolate bits.

ALMOND CRISP COOKIES
Makes 24 three-inch cookies

1 cup butter
1 cup sugar
1/3 cup honey
2/3 cup all-purpose
  flour
1/3 cup heavy whipping
  cream
4 cups sliced and
  blanched almonds

Preheat oven to 350°F. Combine the butter, sugar, honey, flour, and cream in a medium-sized heavy saucepan over medium heat. Bring to the boil, stirring frequently until smooth. Cook 1-1/2 minutes, stirring constantly. Remove from the heat. Stir in the almonds. Spoon tablespoons of the mixture onto a nonstick cookie sheet, leaving 2 inches between each. Bake 8 to 10 minutes or until a rich golden brown. Remove when cool enough to handle and cool on wire rack.

Variation
Spread the bottom sides of the cooled cookies with 1 cup melted semisweet chocolate. Let stand until chocolate sets. Store in refrigerator or freezer.

Variation
To make giant cookies, grease a 6 × 8-inch foil pie pan. Add batter and bake 10 to 14 minutes. Keep refrigerated or frozen stacked between layers of wax paper.

Variation
To make miniature cookies, grease 16 (4-1/2-inch) foil tart pans. Proceed as directed above, dividing mixture evenly among greased tart pans.

✂23✂

AN INFORMAL MENU AND A WHITE TABLECLOTH MENU

Cheri

"He ordered a meal that a shopgirl out on the spree might choose—cold fish *au porto*, a roast bird, and a piping hot soufflé which concealed in its innards a red ice, sharp on the tongue."
—from *Cheri* by Colette

Cheri—the lovesick young man in Colette's novel—had earlier hailed a taxi and proceeded to a restaurant where he was known. Running into a chance acquaintance, they were shown to a table decorated with pink carnations, in a room of highly glazed blue woodwork and clinking glasses. Memories of the woman who had been his love clouded his mind. Taut with excitement, not knowing what the next day would bring, Cheri ordered the above three-course French meal—a reflection of the era as much as of his emotional state.

He talked incessantly about his love, but slyly, sometimes blasé, other times critical, even impertinent. He wove her name throughout the conversation, happy to have a chance to speak of her, enervated by the sound of her name. He ate and drank a great deal, talking to his friend, until the restaurant was emptied except for a woman busy writing letters, alone at a table, full of artificial busyness in her own loneliness.

What, I wonder, as I read and reread this scene, was this meal in 1912 like? Colette's stories, intertwining food and life, cause me to muse about how and what we eat today and why. What is today's menu for "a shopgirl on a spree"? What do the lovesick eat? Perhaps, the latest trend? Would it be American regional—Cajun or Southwestern? French or Italian—or the latest pasta? A California pizza? Whatever the choice, there is something in the nature of a meal that makes it easier to talk about love, to rejoice in the memory of a name, of a moment, that offers respite from pacing the floor.

My women friends and I occasionally play out our romantic sorrows over spicy Buffalo chicken wings, perched on stools in a crowded Taco Mac's, the calories from the fried chicken providing us with a caloric spree. We are not greeted by waitresses or waiters or maitre d's who know or care who we are. We wear blue jeans and T-shirts, and not much makeup. After getting our order, we are left to handle our sorrows alone, the wings so hot they cause tears to run down our cheeks to combine with the tears of the heart. We are more candid than Cheri, not needing subterfuge to name our losses, speak our fears. There is no clinking of glasses—only paper cups. The smell is one dimensional—the frying of the chicken with the hotness of the sauce. The room is never empty when we leave, the energies of college students lasting longer than our tales of woe. We never eat dessert there, waiting for that until we get home.

That is hardly a duplication of Cheri's menu. I think the cold fish *au porto* would no longer suit. Instead, perhaps a Southwestern gravlax for the trendy or perhaps a typical French soup, an onion soup, topped with cheese toast, which could still be followed by roast fowl—a roast chicken dressed up with baked garlic—and surely Potatoes Anna, as well as a red pepper salad. The hot soufflé with innards of red ice tempts me. What could the red ice be? Something as mundane as a watermelon? With an omelet soufflé? Or the omelet soufflé, a puffy creation, wrapped around raspberry ice cream? Or, a cake topped with raspberry sherbert, then topped with a meringue and popped in the oven, more like a Baked Alaska, calling for a cake, served with a watermelon basket, perhaps? Rather than the soufflé as a base, I settle for the cake, and maybe a watermelon basket as well! I'd rather not eat it alone at a restaurant, but at home, along with the rest of the meal, with no tears and surrounded by good friends.

☙ M E N U ❧

INFORMAL MENU

Original Buffalo Chicken Wings
Thick Blue-Cheese Dip

SERVES 4 TO 6

WHITE TABLECLOTH MENU

Gravlax or Onion Soup

Roast Chicken

Pepper-stripe Salad

Whole Baked Garlic

Potatoes Anna

Snow Peas (p. 61)

Hot Soufflé with Innards of Red Ice
and/or Watermelon Basket with Fresh Berries

SERVES 4 TO 6

LOGISTICS

Informal Menu: Brown the chicken wings, and make the dip ahead of time, or after turning the wings.

White Tablecloth Menu: The gravlax and soup may be made several days ahead. The Hot Soufflé with Innards of Red Ice may be made ahead and placed in the freezer. The salad may be made the day ahead, ready to toss. The watermelon basket may be made early in the day. Two hours before serving, start the chicken. When it is in the oven, add the garlic (removing when done). Start the Potatoes Anna. Everything should be finished around the same time. The chicken *may* be made ahead and reheated, but truly, there is nothing better than a just-roasted chicken. The same is true for the Potatoes Anna. The snow peas may be made ahead and reheated briefly or cooked at the last minute.

C RECIPES Q

ORIGINAL BUFFALO CHICKEN WINGS
Serves 4 to 6

2 cups oil
4 pounds chicken wings
1/4 cup (1/2 stick)
  butter, melted
Frank's Louisiana
  Sauce
  or Durkee Red Hot
  Cayenne Pepper
  Sauce

Cut the wings in half at the joint, then remove the wing tips and set aside. You will have 32 pieces. Heat the oil in a large skillet. When oil is sizzling hot, add the wings, without crowding the pan, in batches. Brown on one side, turn and brown on second, cooking through, about 8 to 10 minutes. Drain on paper towels. Place the wings in a large bowl. Using a pastry brush, coat the wings with the butter. Coat with the hot sauce.

Tip: The amount of sauce used determines the spiciness. For a mild sauce, use 2 tablespoons; for medium, 1/4 cup; for an incendiary spiciness, 3/4 cup. Serve wings hot, along with Thick Blue-Cheese Dip (p. 228) and celery sticks.

Tip: Although you can't serve the wing tips, I love frying them up for myself, as a cook's treat.

Tip: Chicken wings may be made ahead and served cold, or reheated 10 to 15 minutes in a 350°F oven, but they are best freshly fried.

THICK BLUE-CHEESE DIP

Makes 3 cups

1/4 pound blue cheese
1/4 pound Gorgonzola
  cheese
1/4 pound cream
  cheese
1/4 teaspoon freshly
  ground pepper
1 garlic clove, finely
  chopped or crushed
  with salt
1/4 teaspoon celery salt
1/8 teaspoon
  Worcestershire sauce,
  or to taste
2 cups mayonnaise
celery sticks

Beat together the blue, Gorgonzola, and cream cheeses in a large bowl. Add the pepper, garlic, and celery salt. Mix well. Stir in the Worcestershire sauce. Add the mayonnaise and mix thoroughly. Refrigerate, covered up, for 1 or 2 days. Serve with celery sticks.

Tip: Leftovers will keep several days, refrigerated. Try spreading it on fresh bread and toasting it.

MARY HATAWAY'S GRAVLAX

Makes 3 to 4-1/4 pounds cured salmon

1 (6 to 9-pound) whole
  salmon (see tip below
  for preparation)
1 cup sugar
3/4 cup salt
1 tablespoon ground
  white pepper
1 tablespoon ground
  allspice
4 bunches fresh dill (4
  large handfuls)

Mix together the sugar, salt, white pepper, allspice, and half of the dill. Open the fish on a long piece of plastic wrap, skin side down. Rub the fillets evenly with the seasoning mixture. Spread the remaining dill on top and close the fish. Wrap tightly in plastic wrap, and weigh down and marinate in the refrigerator for 36 hours, turning at least once a day. Liquid will accumulate and become part of the marinade.

When ready, unwrap and rinse off the fish under tepid water. Put it in the freezer for 1 hour to get very cold. With a sharp narrow knife, remove the skin. It will come off easily.

Sauce

1-1/2 cups mayonnaise
1 cup sour cream
1/2 teaspoon lemon
  juice
1/4 teaspoon salt
1 to 2 tablespoons Dijon
  mustard
Garnish:
fresh dill sprigs

To make the sauce, combine the mayonnaise, sour cream, lemon juice, salt, and mustard. Slice salmon thinly on the bias. Serve with brown bread and the sauce. Garnish with fresh dill sprigs.

Tip: Have your fish market remove the head and tail, then debone the salmon by sliding a long sharp knife down either side of the center bone, leaving on the skin to hold the fillets together.

SUSAN PUETT'S SIERRA GRILL GRAVLAX

Makes 3 to 4 pounds cured salmon

5 cups cilantro leaves,
  chopped
6 cups fresh basil leaves,
  chopped
1 cup kosher salt
1-1/4 cups sugar
1-1/2 cups chili powder
3/4 cup ground cumin
  seed
4 tablespoons cayenne
  pepper
1/2 cup tequila
1 (6 to 9-pound) whole
  salmon, skinned and
  boned, divided into
  sides

In a food processor or blender, mix the cilantro, basil, salt, sugar, chili powder, ground cumin seed, cayenne pepper, and tequila to the consistency of a paste. Lay a piece of plastic wrap 3 times as long as the salmon on a tray. Place a side of skinned and boned salmon on the wrap. Spread half the herb mixture evenly over the top of the fish. Repeat with second side. Wrap tightly in the plastic wrap. Weigh down with 2 bricks, or use another pan and some heavy utensils, and refrigerate for 2 to 4 days, turning every day. Remove plastic wrap; rinse well under tepid water, and pat dry. Slice thinly on the bias. May be kept, refrigerated, and tightly wrapped.

Tip: For a smaller salmon, reduce the curing mixture in proportion to the weight.
Tip: Have the fish market skin and bone the salmon.

ONION SOUP
Serves 4 to 6

3 tablespoons butter
1 pound onions, peeled
   and thinly sliced
1/2 tablespoon flour
1 quart beef stock,
   freshly made or
   canned (if canned,
   dilute with an equal
   amount of water)
salt
freshly ground pepper

Melt the butter over moderate heat in a heavy 5 to 6-quart pot. Add the onions and cook slowly over low heat for 20 to 30 minutes (see tip below), letting the onions caramelize, and scraping and stirring regularly to move the brown goodness on the bottom of the pan onto the onions until all are a deep mahogany color. Stir in the flour. Pour in the stock, stirring until the stock comes to the boil. Reduce the heat to a simmer; partially cover the pot and simmer for 20 to 30 minutes. May be frozen or refrigerated for several days at this point. Taste for seasonings. Add salt and freshly ground pepper. Do not oversalt at this point or it may be too salty when reheated, particularly if stock is canned.

Croûtes

3 to 4 slices of French
   bread
oil or butter
1/2 cup mixed Swiss
   and imported
   Parmesan cheese,
   freshly grated

Preheat oven to 325°F. To make *croûtes*, arrange the thick slices of bread side by side on a baking sheet, and place in the upper third of the oven. Toast about 15 minutes. Brush the toasted bread with oil or butter to add more flavor to the soup. May be kept a day or two in the refrigerator.

Preheat oven to 375°F. To serve, reheat soup in a serving pot on top of the stove. Taste for seasoning, adding more salt and pepper if necessary, then transfer to a casserole or individual heatproof bowls. Arrange the *croûtes* side by side on top of the soup, and sprinkle them evenly with the cheese. Bake the soup in the middle of the oven for 10 to 15 minutes, or until the cheese has melted and formed a light brown crust.

Variation
Add 1/4 cup dry sherry or brandy to the soup.

Variation
Use mozzarella cheese and stale French bread.

Variation

Top the *croûtes* with cheese ahead of time, and heat in oven until cheese is melted. Set aside. Heat the soup on top of the stove and add *croûtes*.

Tip: To caramelize onions to a deep brown, without burning, you may have to divide butter and onions into 2 pans, then combine later. The onions should cover the bottom of the pan, but not in too many layers. If the pan is too wide, or the heat too high, they will burn. If the heat is too low or there are too many layers of onions, they won't brown; instead, water will be extruded, so the fat becomes diluted and the onions won't caramelize—they'll simmer.

Tip: The food processor makes the job of slicing onions easier, but the onions are more bitter and watery, perhaps because of the mechanical process. They also measure differently, and as they cook they put out water differently. One pound of onions should be about 3-1/2 cups when not sliced with a food processor—5 cups when sliced with a food processor.

Tip: This doubles easily and freezes well.

ROAST CHICKEN

Serves 4 to 6

1 (5-1/2-pound)
   roasting chicken, at
   room temperature
2 tablespoons olive oil
3 to 4 tablespoons fresh
   herbs or 2 teaspoons
   dried
1 onion, quartered
2 cups chicken stock,
   preferably fresh
Garnish (optional):
fresh sprigs of herbs
3 to 4 tablespoons fresh
   herbs or 1-1/2 to 2
   tablespoons dried
   (crumbled fresh or
   dried rosemary;
chopped fresh or dried tarragon;
chopped fresh or dried thyme,
basil or Herbes de Provence)

Preheat oven to 400°F. Brush the chicken with the oil. Put half the herbs and the onion inside the chicken. Truss the chicken or tie the legs together. Place the chicken, breast side up, in a roasting pan. Add enough stock to come 1 inch up the sides of the chicken, reserving the surplus. Roast about 1-1/2 to 1-3/4 hours, turning breast side down after 20 minutes, then turning again until well browned all over. Check for doneness by inserting an instant thermometer in the breast or thigh; breast meat should register 170°F on a meat thermometer or the juices should run clear when a knife is inserted in the flesh of the thigh. Remove the chicken and let rest for 10 minutes before carving.

Continued

Meanwhile, place the roasting pan on the stove over high heat, add the remaining stock. Bring to the boil, add the rest of the herbs, and deglaze the pan by stirring and scraping the pan to get the goodness, reducing the liquid to a saucelike consistency. Skim the excess fat if desired. Strain the sauce into a small sauceboat and taste for seasoning. Place the chicken on a warm serving dish and coat with some of the sauce. Serve the remaining sauce from the sauceboat. This dish is best served right away, but it may be made earlier in the day and reheated in a 350°F oven for 10 to 15 minutes. Be sure it reaches the internal temperature of 170°F to rid it of any bacteria.

Variation
You may substitute a frying chicken, which is smaller—usually 3-1/2 pounds—and roast for 1 to 1-1/4 hours or until it registers 170°F. Serves 4.

Variation
Use butter rather than olive oil for rubbing the chicken.

Variation
Add heavy whipping cream to the sauce halfway through the reduction.

Variation
Omit the stock entirely and roast the chicken with just olive oil and herbs. It will be a bit drier.

Variation
Serve the chicken cold with Aioli Sauce (p. 25), omitting the natural sauce.

Variation
Serve hot or cold with Red Pepper Sauce (p. 164), omitting the natural sauce.

Variation
Serve roasted chicken with 2 cups Marinara Sauce (p. 182) and serve separately.

Variation
Garlic-stuffed roasted chicken: Microwave or boil 40 to 50 unpeeled garlic cloves (about 4 heads of garlic) in skin until soft. Peel and put in the chicken cavity with rosemary. Surround with onions or shallots. Bake as above. Serve as is or purée the garlic and add to the stock when reducing.

Tip: To carve, cut the skin between the leg and the breast. Turn over and cut around leg joint toward the tail, between the "oyster" and the backbone. Turn chicken over. Bend the leg until the bone breaks away from the carcass. Cut or pull leg off. Remove the other leg in the same way. Cut through the joints to divide into thighs and drumsticks. Cut with a knife or scissors diagonally at a 45-degree angle across the breast, through the bone, to below the wing. Pull the wing and its breast piece away from the backbone. Repeat with the other wing. Slice the remaining breast meat.

PEPPER-STRIPE SALAD

Serves 4 to 6

1 green bell pepper, seeded and thinly sliced

1 red bell pepper, seeded and thinly sliced

1 yellow bell pepper, seeded and thinly sliced (optional)

1 (16-ounce) can artichoke hearts, sliced in quarters
1/4 pound fresh bean sprouts
1 small red onion, thinly sliced (optional)
1 teaspoon grated lemon peel
1-1/2 tablespoons salad oil
1/2 cup red wine vinegar
1 tablespoon fresh basil, finely chopped (optional)
salt
freshly ground pepper

Place the green pepper, red pepper, optional yellow pepper, artichoke hearts, bean sprouts, and red onion in a bowl. Toss with the lemon peel. Pour the salad oil and vinegar over the vegetables, cover tightly, and marinate overnight. Before serving, add the basil. Taste and season with salt and pepper as necessary. May be made two or three days in advance.

Tip: I serve this on a big black platter because the vegetables look dramatic on black, and I let everyone help themselves.

Tip: Yellow bell peppers add to the dish, but at certain times of the year they may be too expensive or not available, so just use more of the green or red.

WHOLE BAKED GARLIC
Serves 4 to 6

4 to 6 whole heads garlic
3 to 4 tablespoons olive
   oil or butter
salt
freshly ground pepper
water or light chicken
   stock

Preheat oven to 350°F. Remove the papery outer skin that covers the whole head of garlic. Either peel it off starting from the root or take a knife and cut around the covering midway up the head, then peel the outer skin. The skin around each clove will stay intact during baking. Place the heads in a small baking dish. Drizzle a little oil or butter over them and sprinkle on salt and pepper. Put a couple of tablespoons of water or stock in the bottom of the dish, surrounding the garlic heads. Cover and bake 1 to 2 hours, depending on size, until tender. Serve one head per person.

Variation
Peel the soft cloves of garlic and add to mashed potatoes.

Variation
Garlic may be "baked" in the microwave. One whole head takes 45 seconds to 1-1/2 minutes in the microwave on full power. Four take 6 to 8 minutes depending on size. I usually wrap individual ones in plastic wrap or place several in a bowl and cover with plastic wrap before microwaving.

Serving tip: Serve baked garlic as an appetizer with olive oil, slices of fresh crusty bread or rolls, and soft goat cheese (such as Montrachet) or herbed cheese. Add a chopped sun-dried tomato or two.

Tip: To eat, squeeze the soft garlic clove out of the clove's skin and spread on bread, toast, potatoes, and so on.

Comment: Baked garlic doesn't leave the same odor that raw garlic does as the baking changes the garlic completely. The flavor becomes almost sweet and the texture is smooth and buttery when popped out of its skin.

Tip: Elephant garlic is not the same as garlic. It will never get the soft, tender consistency of garlic no matter how long it is cooked. Although usually it is milder than garlic it may have a bitter aftertaste.

Tip: Garlic may be purchased in many different sizes. I prefer heads that are 2 inches in diameter.

POTATOES ANNA

Serves 4 to 6

1-1/2 to 1-3/4 pounds
   all-purpose potatoes,
   peeled and sliced 1/8
   inch thick
salt
freshly ground pepper
5 to 8 tablespoons
   butter, cut into pieces

Preheat oven to 450°F. Butter a 6-inch heavy, nonstick, well-seasoned frying pan or cake tin, very thickly. Arrange the potatoes in overlapping circles to cover the base of the pan, making a pretty design. Add a second layer, continuing to overlap, then season with salt and pepper and dot with 4 to 5 pieces of the butter. Continue to fill the pan with overlapping layers of potatoes, seasoning and buttering every other layer. Butter a piece of aluminum foil and cover the potatoes and the pan. Put an ovenproof plate or heavy saucepan on top of the foil to press down on the potatoes and prevent loss of steam during cooking.

Cook the potatoes on the stove over medium heat for 10 to 15 minutes to make the bottom brown and crusty, checking to be sure it is not burning. When medium brown, place the pan in the oven, leaving the ovenproof plate on if it fits. Reduce the temperature to 400°F. Bake about 30 minutes or until the potatoes are soft, depending upon the number of potatoes. May be made ahead to this point and set aside. Reheat 10 minutes in hot oven if necessary. Turn out upside down on a serving dish, crust side up. To serve, cut with knife or scissors.

Variation
Add 1/4 cup ham or cheese to each layer and serve as a lunch dish or starter.

HOT SOUFFLÉ WITH INNARDS OF RED ICE
Serves 4

1 small Pound Cake
  (p. 63)
1 pint raspberry or
  strawberry sherbert,
  slightly softened
4 egg whites
1/2 cup granulated
  sugar
1 cup raspberries or
  sliced strawberries

Split the cake in half horizontally—layers should be 1/2 inch thick. Place the 2 halves side by side and touching on a metal or other freezer-to-oven dish. Spread the ice cream on top. Place in the freezer. Whip the egg whites until stiff peaks form. Fold in the sugar. Spread the meringue mixture thoroughly over the ice cream, swirling, covering the sherbert by at least 3/4 inches. Put back in the freezer. Cover when frozen with foil or plastic wrap if keeping more than a few hours. This may be kept a week or two, depending on the quality of the ice cream. When ready to serve, place the dish straight from the freezer in a preheated 500°F oven or under a broiler until meringue is brown—just a few minutes. Garnish with berries.

WATERMELON BASKET WITH FRESH BERRIES
Serves 8

1 small watermelon
1/2 pint strawberries,
  hulled
1/2 pint blueberries
10 sprigs mint

Draw and cut out a paper design (such as a scalloped edge) to use as a guide for cutting the watermelon into a basket. Draw and cut out another design for the handle, if desired. (I usually use a brown paper bag for this purpose.) Carefully place the design pattern over the watermelon and cut the melon to match it, cutting all the way through. Slowly lift off the top of the basket, then scoop out all the watermelon meat with a melon-ball scoop, leaving about 1/2 inch of the fruit intact to line the basket. Set aside the prettiest sprigs of mint for a garnish. Chop the rest and toss with the watermelon balls, strawberries, and blueberries. Wrap the basket in plastic wrap or foil. Chill until serving time.

Tip: To select a ripe melon, look for a firm, symmetrical melon that is filled out at the blossom end and has a dull (rather than shiny) surface, with a yellow, white, or pale green to yellow underside. A ripe melon will last 4 days in a cool unrefrigerated place, or a week refrigerated.

Tip: *To freeze:* One to 1-1/4 pounds of melon yields 1 pint watermelon balls or cubes; use 1/2 cup sugar and 1-1/2 cups water per pint. Cut melons into balls or cubes. Mix sugar and water. Heat until sugar has dissolved, bring to the boil for 1 minute, then remove from heat. Chill. Pour over melon balls and freeze.

Tip: The number of servings may be increased to 25 by using a large watermelon and increasing the amount of fresh berries used.

⚼24⚼

FOOD TO GO

Take Me Out to the Ball Game

For those of us who love baseball, there is nothing like an early season ball game for sitting in the hot Spring sun and watching your heroes win. Dale Murphy, of the Atlanta Braves, is one of my particular heroes, and never for a moment has my belief in him faltered. Still, for a while in late April, he stumbled a bit and it seemed a good idea one Sunday to get back to the stadium and root from my $8.00 seat on the 1st base line, maybe bringing him a bit of luck.

This particular day, I wanted to add something special to my foray to the game. I wanted to go early and take something good to eat. Mind you, I like hot dogs. A lot. But I can't eat them every game and they are messy. Already my score book has a little mustard on it. I'm a zealot. People hate to go to ball games with me because I spend the time keeping score, drawing little lines and numbers in tiny cubes of space. I don't consider a baseball game the proper time to socialize. Except to say "Was that a fielder's choice?" or, "Was that an error?" Important things.

Hot dogs should contain mustard and my score book didn't need more mustard any more than I needed more hot dogs. I cast around for something to bring to the game to eat. It had to be something I could make from what was around in the house. It had to be something I could make in between all my Sunday projects. It had to honor Dale Murphy. Finally, I made my decision—a bread dough wrapped around garlic herb cheese (like Boursin), olives, ham, cheese, pesto, pimientos, and sun-dried tomatoes. It wouldn't be greasy, could be eaten with two hands, and didn't need any implements or a plate.

Here's how it went. I took my morning walk. I started the dough for my bread right after we finished bagels and cream cheese on the porch. I got all the ingredients ready for the inside of the bread. While it was rising I read the paper. When it was time for Church, I knocked down the dough and put it in the refrigerator. Home at twelve, I rolled out the dough, filled it with the ingredients, shaped it, and let it double. I preheated the oven, and popped the bread in about quarter to one, making two small loaves. I took them out at a little after one, and wrapped them in aluminum foil straight from the oven. Two napkins and some strawberry tarts and a couple of bananas completed the meal, and everything tucked easily into a basket style purse along with my scoring book.

We were in our seats twenty minutes later because there weren't as many fans as on opening night, and we were trying to get there as early as possible. After getting our Cokes, we spread out our napkins on our laps and tore pieces of the bread off, savoring the flavors, grateful there was no mess, relishing the sounds of the warming up players, enjoying the march of the young children around the field. Our baked sandwich was still warm in our hands, the cheese melting just enough.

By the time the line-up was read, our hands were free to write it down. By the time the first home run was hit in the second inning, bringing in two runs, and Dale Murphy's made the third, we were ready for our strawberry tarts. Hardly time—it certainly wouldn't have been time for a ball park ice cream—before Murphy followed up with a home run, and we had to give up all semblance of eating so we could keep standing up and cheering, clutching our score books in our hands. And by the time he made his sixth RBI (the first time he had six RBI's since 1979, I think), well, who cared about food? Still, today, as I reread the scores, and savored the moment, I also remembered eating that delicious bread to the sound of the snapping ball and the cheering crowd. It was a grand day, one of the happiest in my memory, topped only by the day in July when Dale Murphy hit two runs in one inning, batting in six runners. Maybe it was the bread, after all?

Whether traveling to a concert in the park, a church covered dish supper, a lover's picnic, or a simple backyard feast, use several or just one of the recipes that follow, adjusting them to the number of people you are serving as the serving amounts vary.

ᘓ MENU ᘔ
FOOD TO GO

Cold Curried Tomato Soup (p. 58)

Little Baskets or Fried Curried Pasta

Sesame Chicken

Dale Murphy Bread with
Homemade Garlic and Herb Cheese,
Fatima Saada's Palestinian-style Olives,
and Homemade Sun-dried Tomatoes in Oil

Marinated Brussels Sprouts

Marinated Mushrooms

Fresh Grapes (preferably scuppernongs)
or Old-Time Shortcake with Peaches or Strawberries (p. 183)

Strawberry Tarts (p. 132)

LOGISTICS

Adapt recipes to the number of people to be served and the menu of your choice. The little baskets, cheese, and chicken may be made several days ahead or frozen and defrosted. Dale Murphy Bread may be made ahead and frozen as may the tart shells which are to be filled the day of serving. The soup may be made a day or two ahead as may the vegetables. Keep all in a cooler. Fill the little baskets from a separate container if you have that luxury. Otherwise fill and keep in a single layer in a flat, tightly sealed container to avoid crushing through the weight of the filling. The curried pasta may be made ahead and frozen, or kept a week in a tightly sealed container. The shortcake may be made several hours ahead or frozen and defrosted. Put the cream and peaches or strawberries in a separate container, and fill the shortcakes just before eating.

ᏀRECIPES Ꮛ

LITTLE BASKETS
Makes 240 baskets

1 package phyllo dough
3/4 pound (1-1/2 cups)
butter, melted and
clarified (p. 128)

Filling

garlic cheese or Boursin

Preheat oven to 375°F. Defrost dough in refrigerator if frozen, then unroll and place on a clean work surface. To keep the dough moist, cover with foil, then with a slightly damp lightweight kitchen towel. Remove the top sheet of dough over to a clean work surface or baking sheet. Replace the towel. Brush the first sheet of dough with butter. Repeat with 2 more sheets, keeping the original stack covered with the foil and damp towel. Now you should have a stack of 3 buttered sheets of dough. Cut into 24 squares, 6 down and 4 across. Press one square into each muffin tin. Bake 8 to 10 minutes. While baking, prepare the dough for more baskets. Repeat procedures for rest of the dough, reusing the tins and letting the baskets cool at room temperature until ready to fill, or place carefully in an airtight container and store at room temperature a couple of days, or freeze until ready to fill. Fill with Garlic and Herb Cheese (p. 245) or Boursin. Serve at room temperature or reheat quickly in hot oven if desired hot.

Variation
Top garlic and herb cheese with Pico de Gallo (p. 83) just before serving.

Variation
Fill with sautéed crabmeat with green onions and a touch of creole seasoning.

Sweet Variation
Fill with raspberries or strawberries and Crème Fraiche (p. 107).

> *Comment:* Although these appear fragile, if stored unfilled in a container that prevents crushing by a heavy weight, they are very sturdy.

FRIED CURRIED PASTA
Makes 250

1 package wontons (1 pound)
3 cups oil for frying
curry powder

Defrost wontons if frozen. Heat oil in a wok or frying pan to about 350° or 360°F. Slice each of the wontons in 1/2 inch strips or make butterflies and drop in batches into the hot fat. Fry until crisp. Remove and drain. Sprinkle with curry powder to taste. May be kept in a tight container or frozen.

Variation
Try chili powder for appetizers, confectioners' sugar for dessert.

Variation
Sprinkle with coarse salt, if you want something milder than curry or chili powder. Unfortunately, however, this cannot be done much in advance because the salt makes the pasta wilt.

Variation
Cut in thin vermicelli-type strips, season, and top a green salad with them.

Variation
Serve as an accompaniment to soup.

Tip: To make a butterfly, wet your finger and draw a line down the middle of a wonton square. Fold to make a butterfly or cut into quarters and make each quarter into a tiny butterfly.

SESAME CHICKEN
Makes 8 skewers

4 chicken breasts, skinned, boned, and cut into 1-inch chunks

8 tablespoons soy sauce

4 teaspoons dark oriental sesame oil

2 tablespoons honey

2 tablespoons dry sherry

2 teaspoons fresh ginger, grated

2 green onions or scallions, chopped

6 tablespoons sesame seeds, toasted

Mix 4 tablespoons of the soy and 2 teaspoons of the sesame oil together and marinate the chicken chunks briefly. Drain. Put on skewers and grill (over charcoal if possible) until done, basting with rest of marinade, from 5 to 10 minutes, depending on the heat. They are done when all the pink is gone and they are white in the center. Mix the rest of the soy and sesame oil with the honey, sherry, ginger, and green onions, and top the hot chicken with the sauce. Refrigerate, covered, overnight or at least 2 hours. Sprinkle with toasted sesame seeds before serving. Reheat 10 minutes at 350°F or serve cold.

Variation
Serve hot from the grill, over rice.

Tip: It's foolish to buy expensive boned chicken breasts as they are so easy to bone, with a little practice, a sharp knife, and some care. You may have a whole chest (miscalled a whole breast) or a breast (half of the chest). You may start at the keel bone or the ribs. To bone, pull off skin if desired. Insert a sharp knife on the keel bone or the rib bones and slide down, pushing or scraping the flesh away from the bone until removed. There is a little fillet tucked under the bone. Remove. Slide the knife down the tendon to remove the tendon of the little fillet. Cut the fillet into 1-inch pieces and add to the dish. Save the bones for stock.

Serving tip: This recipe may be doubled or tripled. It is very good for picnics as well as large parties.

DALE MURPHY BREAD
Makes 1 large loaf (or 2 or 3 small loaves)

Dough

2-1/2 to 3 cups bread
    flour
1 package rapid-rise
    yeast
1 tablespoon sugar
1 teaspoon salt
2/3 cup water, heated to
    125°F
3 tablespoons butter
1 egg

Filling

1-1/2 tablespoons
    Italian Pesto Sauce
1/4 cup black olives,
    preferably Italian or
    Niçoise, drained,
    pitted, and sliced
3/4 cup grated
    mozzarella cheese
1/2 cup crumbled
    Garlic and Herb
    Cheese (p. 245)
6 ounces smoked ham,
    cut into strips
1/2 cup pimiento or
    roasted red peppers,
    peeled and seeded
1 tablespoon sun-dried tomatoes,
    drained of any oil, and chopped (optional) (p. 247)

Glaze

1 egg, beaten to mix
1 tablespoon water

In a food processor or mixing bowl, combine 1-1/2 cups of the bread flour, the yeast, sugar, and salt. Add the water, butter, and egg to the yeast mixture. Process or knead, adding enough flour in 1/2-cup increments, to make a soft dough. Knead until elastic and smooth as a baby's bottom, 1 minute in a food processor, 10 minutes in a mixer or by hand. Place in a plastic bag or turn in greased bowl, cover with plastic wrap, and let rest 15 minutes or if you have time, let it double.

On a slightly floured board, roll the dough to a 14 × 10-inch rectangle. Place on a greased baking sheet. Spread pesto sauce down the center third of dough, lengthwise. Dot with olives, mozzarella, and garlic and herb cheese. Top with ham strips and sprinkle with peppers and optional sun-dried tomatoes. To encase the filling, cut the unfilled dough diagonally on each side into 1-inch strips down the length of each side of the dough. Criss-cross the strips, bringing one strip over the center, then a strip from the other, until the length of the filling is encased with the overlapping strips. Let double, uncovered, in a warm place for 1/2 hour.

Preheat oven to 400°F. Combine the egg and water and brush the glaze on the loaf. Bake until done, about 25 minutes. Remove from pan and cool on wire rack before slicing. Serve warm or at room temperature.

Variation
Divide dough and ingredients in two and make 2 tiny loaves, half as long but the same width. Reduce baking time 5 minutes.

Variation
Substitute goat cheese or Boursin for the garlic-herb filling.

Variation
Substitute 1-1/2 tablespoons Marco Polo Pesto (p. 87) for the Italian pesto sauce.

Variation
Substitute smoked salmon for the ham.

Tip: To speed up rising, place bowl of covered bread in a pan of water heated to 140°F.

Tip: If rapid-rise yeast is not available, reduce the temperature of the water to 115°F. Add the yeast to the water, dissolve, and add to the dry ingredients in the food processor. Let rise until doubled, then proceed to roll out and fill as directed.

Tip: You can make sun-dried tomatoes (p. 247), or buy them. Sun-dried tomato bits are an acceptable product for this recipe and much less expensive than the imported, packed-in-oil kind. These need to be blanched in boiling water for 1 minute and drained before serving.

Tip: The pesto sauce may also be purchased in the gourmet section of grocery stores or be homemade (p. 87).

HOMEMADE GARLIC AND HERB CHEESE
Makes about 2-1/2 to 3 cups

1 pound cream cheese, at room temperature
1 pound butter, at room temperature
3 to 4 garlic cloves, chopped
3 tablespoons fresh chopped herbs such as basil, chives, marjoram, or thyme
salt
freshly ground pepper

Blend the cream cheese, butter, and garlic in a food processor until smooth. Add the herbs and combine. Salt and pepper to taste. Can be made 1 week ahead, covered tightly, and refrigerated.

Continued

Tip: May be frozen. If using for cooking, use as is. If serving at room temperature, use as is or reblend briefly if a creamier consistency is desired.

Tip: Uses: Use in place of butter with rice or vegetables. Stuff under the skin of Cornish hens or chicken; fills 240 little baskets; use in appetizer bread; place on vegetables and run under the broiler to melt; place on toast points.

Tip: The blends of the butter and cheese reduce the volume somewhat.

FATIMA SAADA'S PALESTINIAN-STYLE OLIVES
Makes 1 quart

1 quart freshly picked
　olives
salt
water

For Green Olives

2 to 3 lemons
5 garlic cloves
olive oil
grape leaves (optional)
salt
water

Cut 2 slits around the circumference of each olive or use a wooden block or hammer to break the skin of the olives and slightly bruise. Make a salt-water solution with enough salt to make an egg begin to stand on edge. Press all the olives under the water with a tea towel covered with a glass plate. Every other day pour off the darkened water from the salt, drawing out the bitterness, rinse, and cover with fresh salt-water solution. Continue for 10 to 14 days and begin tasting after the tenth day. When the taste is as you like it, rinse olives.

For green olives: Pack a 2-inch layer of olives at the bottom of a sterile jar. Squeeze juice from the lemons, then quarter and add quartered lemons, pulp, and skin between every 2 inches of olives. Add peeled garlic cloves. Pour in the lemon juice and a few tablespoons of lightly salted water. Top with enough olive oil to meet all edges of the jar and amply cover the olives to seal. If available, use grape leaves to push olives entirely down under the water and to add a lovely sour taste. Otherwise crumble parchment paper. Seal with lid, store in the refrigerator.

For Black Olives

5 garlic cloves (optional)
rosemary sprigs
  (optional)
1/2 cup vinegar
olive oil
1 tablespoon salt
water to cover

For black olives: Pack a 2-inch layer of olives, then add garlic and 2 sprigs of rosemary, and complete packing the jar. Finish with vinegar and salt water solution. Seal with parchment paper, then oil.

HOMEMADE SUN-DRIED TOMATOES IN OIL
Makes 1 pound

10 pounds ripe Italian
  plum tomatoes,
  halved and seeded
basil, rosemary, or
  thyme, fresh or dried
  (optional)
extra virgin olive oil or
  vegetable oil

Place the tomatoes, cut side up, on a large rack. Put jars at the corners of the rack and drape a cheesecloth cover over the tops of the jars, so it doesn't touch the tomatoes. Secure the cloth. Set the rack in hot sun until the tomatoes are dried out and darkened, from 2 to 3 days, turning 2 or 3 times a day. When partly dried, flatten the tomatoes with a knife or spatula. Continue drying them until they are shriveled and dry like a dried apricot. Place in boiling water for 2 minutes. Drain. Dry thoroughly with paper towels.

Pack in sterile pint jars. Add optional basil, rosemary, or thyme, and pour enough olive oil on to cover. Seal tightly and store in the refrigerator at least 3 to 4 weeks before using. Keeps indefinitely when refrigerated.

Tip: If rain threatens, you may speed up the process in a dehydrator set at 160 degrees.

Tip: To use dried tomatoes packed in oil, simply remove from oil and proceed with recipe.

Tip: If you choose to dry without packing in oil, wipe off and place in airtight container.

Tip: To use dried tomatoes not packed in oil, place in boiling liquid for 2 minutes. Drain if appropriate.

Comment: Dried tomatoes are not a substitute for fresh ones, any more than a raisin is a substitute for a grape.

MARINATED BRUSSELS SPROUTS

Serves 6 to 8

2 pounds Brussels
   sprouts
1/2 cup red wine
   vinegar
1-1/4 cups salad oil
2 garlic cloves, chopped
1 tablespoon sugar
   (optional)
salt
freshly ground pepper
dash of hot sauce
1/4 cup chopped onion

Trim the hard stems off the Brussels sprouts and cut an X in the stem end. Place in a pan of boiling water and cook 3 to 5 minutes. Drain. Whisk together the vinegar, oil, garlic, optional sugar, salt, pepper, and hot sauce. Add the onion and pour over the hot Brussels sprouts while still hot. Marinate up to 3 or 4 days before serving. Drain and serve.

Variation
Substitute lightly cooked cauliflower florets.

MARINATED MUSHROOMS

Makes 4 cups

3 pounds fresh
   mushrooms,
   preferably button
2/3 cup olive oil
juice of 1 lemon
2 onions, chopped
3 garlic cloves, chopped
1 teaspoon thyme
1 teaspoon marjoram
freshly ground pepper
3 bay leaves, crumbled
1 cup red wine vinegar
3 cups Italian tomatoes
1 teaspoon sugar
   (optional)
dash of hot sauce
salt
freshly ground pepper
party rye bread, buttered and sprinkled with chopped parsley

If not using button mushrooms, cut larger ones in bite-sized pieces. Heat 1/3 cup of the oil, add the mushrooms, and sauté briefly. Transfer to a bowl and toss with lemon juice. Pour the remaining 1/3 cup oil into the skillet, heat, add the onions and garlic, and cook them slowly until soft. Add the thyme, marjoram, pepper, bay leaves, and wine vinegar. Drain the tomatoes, saving the juice. Chop, then add to the skillet with 1/2 cup of the reserved juice. Bring to the boil; then simmer for 20 minutes. Add to mushrooms. Season with optional sugar, hot sauce, salt, and pepper to taste. Cool, cover; let marinated mushrooms chill 12 hours. Serve hot or cold with rye bread.

⚓ 25 ⚓

A NON-PRETENTIOUS PARTY FOR FRIENDS

The Key to Success

It was the supreme compliment. "I want you to know," he said, "that party of yours was one of the stars in my memories. I still think about it, laugh about it, talk about it." Jerry, an old friend of mine and of my former husband David, had driven with his wife, Diane, from Toronto and stopped by for a visit with us. We had all been close friends in London nearly twenty years ago. We agreed that that party was the best David and I ever gave. We tried to figure out why.

It wasn't because of a lot of liquor. As a matter of fact, we didn't even drink. Yet our flat was full of rollicking laughter and good times among strangers.

And it wasn't money. We were young, living in a foreign country and didn't have much money. My husband was working for a firm that had hit financial troubles. Still, we were full of optimism about life.

It wasn't the intimacy of the group. The people we knew in London were so diverse we wondered what they would talk about. Some of them, including David, didn't want to talk about work because show-and-tell about what you do for a living is too often standard fare for dinner parties.

We decided to let everyone participate in cooking the meal and gave each person a project that would generate conversation. I devised what now seems to me to be a complicated, pretentious menu, assigning each of the fifteen dinner guests to a team to prepare the meal. We had asparagus cream soup to begin, followed by *poussins farcis au riz,* a complicated salad (with cooked and diced vegetables), and *tonile à pêche.*

Everyone was told to dress casually because they would be doing the cooking. I set up cooking stations around our young-married's flat. I premeasured everything and put cooking equipment by each station. I was, fortunately, well organized. Otherwise, we would have eaten much later than the midnight hour—when we finally did have dinner.

David set up tables around the rooms. One table was set in the living room—boxes on the floor, covered with a paisley shawl as a tablecloth. It worked fine.

When the guests arrived, we gave them each a copy of the menu, their recipe, the alleged time chart, and instructions to find their cooking partners, who had the identical recipe.

Somehow, I had calculated that we could eat the soup by 8:30, the *poussin* by 9:00. The salad, fortunately, could be eaten (and was) earlier if need be, as an hors d'oeuvre. I also had store-bought bread, which turned out to be a saving grace.

The cooks were a little slow to begin with. I think maybe they didn't believe they were really going to make their own meal. When everyone finally realized we were serious, that each person would have to work side by side with strangers in a small space, there was a bit of grumbling, a bit of panic, and nervous laughter. Gales of laughter followed, as people performed impossible tasks in too little space.

The guests boning and stuffing the *poussins* were stationed on the patio outside the kitchen window so they could pass the fowl indoors to the people cooking the stock and fixing the stuffing. This group, of which Jerry was a member, was full of good spirits. "You call that boned?" "Hello, you call that browned?" And laughter.

A *poussin* is a small chicken. The object was to remove all the carcass, which was then browned and used for stock. The wings and legs were left intact, and the cavity filled with bacon, rice, onion, parsley, oregano, saffron, and an egg to bind. The stuffed *poussins* were browned, then surrounded with Madeira, tomato purée, and some well-jellied chicken stock (which, fortunately, I had made ahead). After roasting the *poussins* thirty to forty minutes, the stock from the bones was added to the sauce in the pan, along with more Madeira, boiled up and served around.

According to my time chart, if they each boned a *poussin* (six people were on that team) it would take them only one to one-and-one-half hours to finish, including surrounding the cooked *poussins* with courgettes (the English term for zucchini) sliced and cooked in butter. It took them three. Also, the *poussins* had to share oven space with the *tonile*.

The salad was put together in the guest bedroom, on top of a dresser. It was ready by 9:00 or so, a welcome addition to the bread we had been nibbling on. The asparagus people had to reach over the stock people to get their asparagus soup made and fight for the use of a Cuisinart-type machine to purée the asparagus once it was cooked.

We were able to sit down to a bowl of soup by 9:30 or so. Between courses, the late cooks would rush back to their duties, full of renewed zeal.

Christopher Andreae, then the art critic for the *Christian Science Monitor* and a brilliant artist himself, teamed with Diane to make the *tonile*. This required browning hazelnuts in the oven, rubbing them endlessly in a tea towel to remove their skin, then grating them by hand or in a little hand *mouli* grater before mixing the sugar and butter and then baking. After they cooled, the hazelnut tortes were filled with hand-whipped cream and berries. It took them two hours, maybe three, to finish this process, at the end of which Christopher cried out, "All this for a *biscuit*?" (the British term for cookie). But once he ate one, he was quite happy. And he basked in the raves, as if Diane hadn't rubbed hazelnuts until her fingers were sore. Of course, everyone was *very* hungry.

What then, makes old friends remember a particular moment in their lives? What makes a party stand out in memory as a star? We figured it out—it's laughter, not booze, money, pretentious food, or prestige. Pure and simple. Laughter.

☾ M E N U ☽

A NON-PRETENTIOUS PARTY FOR FRIENDS

Poached Whole Salmon
or *Steamers for a Crowd*

Pasta with Vegetables

Chicken Breasts with Red Pepper Sauce

Mayonnaise or *Béarnaise Mayonnaise* or *White Butter Sauce*

Hazelnut Torte with Fresh Raspberries and Cream
or *Truffle Filled Pastries (p. 62)*

SERVES 12

LOGISTICS

For One Person Cooking

Prepare the hazelnut cookies in advance and keep in container or freeze. Whip cream in advance. The pasta may be made up to a day ahead and the vegetables blanched and kept tightly sealed in the refrigerator. The salmon, mayonnaise, and sauces may be done ahead a day. The chicken may be made earlier in the day and reheated. The steamers and ingredients may be prepared to the point of being ready to turn on 15 minutes before serving.

For a Cooking Party for 12 to 25

Group A: Bake, rub, and chop hazelnuts. Prepare dough, chill. Bake. Whip the cream. Multiply the recipe as necessary.
Group B: Blanch the vegetables, cook the pasta. Toss together 5 minutes before serving. Multiply the recipe as necessary.
Group C: Poach the salmon, make sauces, or clean and cook steamers.
Group D: Prepare the sauce, bone the breasts, cook.

ᚳ RECIPES ᚎ

POACHED WHOLE SALMON

Serves 12 to 16

1 recipe fish-poaching
    stock
1 (3-1/2 to 4-pound)
    whole salmon, with
    head on, gutted, gills
    removed, cleaned and
    scaled
Garnish:
cucumber slices or fresh
    dill

Stock

2 quarts cold water
1 onion, sliced
1 quart fish heads,
    bones and tails
    (optional)
3 parsley stocks
6 peppercorns

Pour the fish-poaching stock in the bottom of a fish poacher or another pan large enough for the salmon. Place the salmon on its belly in the rack of the fish poacher or on a rack that fits the pan. If the fish is too long, turn the tail under to fit. If you have to remove the head of the salmon to fit the fish in a poacher, be sure to place the head on the rack so that it can be reassembled with the fish's body after poaching. Add enough water to the stock to cover at least 3/4 of the fish. Place a damp kitchen towel over the salmon to keep it from sticking to the cover. Place the pan over 2 burners and bring the water up to 180°F; don't let it boil. Cook, covered, for 15 to 20 minutes, or 12 minutes per inch of thickness. Cool in the stock, then serve warm, or refrigerate and serve chilled.

To serve, lift the rack with the salmon on it out of the stock. Carefully move to a platter, placing it belly side down. If you had to remove the head, position it now appropriately. Scrape off the top skin of the salmon. Slide the back fins off with a knife. Scrape off and discard the dark part (mostly fat) from the top center. Garnish with sliced cucumbers and/or dill. Serve warm or chill, covering with plastic wrap.

To make stock, put all ingredients in a stock pot and simmer for 20 minutes. Then strain.

Continued

Variation

To serve cold, serve with Béarnaise Mayonnaise (p. 258) or Pico de Gallo (p. 86).

Variation

To serve hot, serve with lemon Hollandaise (p. 33), Red Pepper Hollandaise (p. 33), or White Butter Sauce (p. 257).

Tip: If no fish bones, etc. are available you may substitute 2 cups of clam juice for 2 cups of the cold water.

Tip: To carve salmon, insert a long thin sharp knife horizontally at the center bone and slide the one side of the meat off the bone. Use the knife to lift the side, then remove the bone.

Tip: This fish is beautiful presented on its belly as if it were still swimming.

Tip: When cooking fish at 400°F or more, the rule of thumb is to cook it 10 minutes to the inch of thickness. Since the water is less than 210°F, use the guide of 12 minutes to the inch.

STEAMERS FOR A CROWD

Serves 10 to 12 for main course (25 for starter)

4 pounds oysters, in the shell
2 pounds clams, in the shell
2 pounds mussels, in the shell
2 pounds large shrimp, in the shell
2 cups dry white wine
2 cups water
8 garlic cloves, chopped
2 onions, chopped
1 cup parsley sprigs
1 lemon, sliced
1 cup chopped parsley or thyme
lemon slices or wedges for serving
salt
freshly ground pepper

Scrub the oysters, clams, mussels, and rinse the shrimp. To make the broth, put the wine, water, garlic, onions, parsley sprigs, and lemon slices in a large, 8 to 10-quart pot and bring to the boil. Reduce heat and simmer 20 minutes to allow the flavors to blend. Bring back to the boil and add the oysters. Cover and cook 2 to 3 minutes until they barely begin to open. Add the clams and mussels to the pot, cover, and cook 2 to 3 minutes until they are hot to the touch and are beginning to open. Stir, then add the shrimp. Cook just until the shellfish open about 1/2 inch and the shrimp are pink. Remove the shellfish to a large, deep-serving platter. Taste the broth for seasoning, adding salt and pepper if necessary, and spoon some over the shellfish. Top with the chopped parsley. Pass the lemon wedges and serve immediately.

Variation
Cook onions, garlic, 2 cups chopped fennel, and 2 tablespoons chopped, fresh hot pepper, in 4 tablespoons of olive oil. Add the broth ingredients and proceed as above.

Variation
Add hot sauce or Tabasco to taste.

Variation
Use 10 pounds of oysters, clams, or mussels to serve 8 to 10.

Variation
Use 10 pounds shrimp to serve 20 to 25.

Tip: Oysters, clams, and mussels are cooked when they open.

PASTA WITH VEGETABLES

Serves 12

1-1/2 pounds fettucini, vermicelli, or spaghetti
9 cups vegetables (broccoli florets, zucchini sticks, carrot sticks, shelled green peas, snow peas or sugar snap peas, snap green beans, or asparagus)
2 cups cherry tomatoes
3/4 cup olive oil or butter
salt
freshly ground pepper
1/2 cup chopped fresh parsley; or 1/2 cup chopped fresh basil, parsley, and thyme, mixed

Bring a large quantity of water to the boil and boil pasta as directed. (For fresh pasta, see p. 21; for packaged, follow package directions.) Drain and set aside if using immediately. If not, place back in water to cover, or in a plastic bag to prevent drying out. Meanwhile, boil the florets, zucchini, carrots, peas, beans, or asparagus separately, cooking until just tender. Drain and set aside. May be done ahead to this point. Heat the oil or butter in a pan large enough to accommodate pasta and vegetables. When sizzling hot, add the cooked vegetables. Toss carefully over heat, coating with the oil, then add the tomatoes, pasta, salt, freshly ground pepper and herbs to taste, and continue to toss until heated through.

Variation
Add 1-1/2 cups freshly grated imported Parmesan.

Variation
Use 1/2 cup butter, add 1-1/2 cups freshly grated imported Parmesan and 1-1/2 to 2-1/2 cups heavy whipping cream, and reheat together, tossing. Very decadent. Very delicious.

Tip: To make batons, cut carrots and zucchini into strips 2-1/2 inches long and 1/2 inch wide.

CHICKEN BREASTS WITH RED PEPPER SAUCE
Serves 12

3 tablespoons butter
3 tablespoons olive oil
10 to 12 chicken
  breasts, boned and
  skinned
1-1/2 cups chicken
  stock
3 red bell peppers,
  seeded and chopped
3 to 4 tablespoons red
  wine vinegar (can be
  balsamic) or sherry
3 tablespoons sugar
2 green bell peppers,
  seeded, julienned,
  and blanched
salt
freshly ground pepper

Preheat oven to 400°F. Heat the butter and oil in a large casserole until singing. Add the chicken breasts, skin side down, and brown, quickly. Turn the chicken and cover the pan. Place the pan in the oven to finish cooking, about 6 to 8 minutes.

Simmer the stock and chopped peppers in a saucepan over medium heat for 10 minutes. Remove the solids and purée until smooth. Add the vinegar and sugar and stock.

Remove the cooked chicken from the oven. Skim most of the fat from the pan. Pour in the pepper purée and the wine vinegar, and bring to the boil, stirring. Boil until thick and glossy. Pour over the chicken and garnish with the blanched green pepper. Salt and pepper to taste.

Tip: To blanch the bell peppers, bring a small pan of water to the boil, add the julienned peppers, and simmer 2 minutes. Drain. Run under cold water, drain again.

Tip: To remove a lot of fat, slip the pan about halfway off the burner to collect the fat and tip into a measuring cup or one of those wonderful gadgets that separates fat. Pour off the fat and return the juices to the pan.

WHITE BUTTER SAUCE

Makes 1-1/2 cups

2/3 cup lemon juice or
    white wine vinegar
2 shallots, chopped
3/4 pound butter, cut
    into 1 to 2-inch pieces
salt
freshly ground pepper

Place the lemon juice or vinegar and shallots in a saucepan and bring to the boil. Boil down until only 2 tablespoons remain. Whisk the butter, piece by piece, into the sauce over low heat. If the butter gets too hot and separates, remove pan from the heat and place in the refrigerator briefly, then return it to heat and whisk the sauce until it is milky-white again and creamy, whisking all the while. Taste for seasoning and add salt and pepper if necessary. May be made ahead and refrigerated or set aside at room temperature. To reheat, whisk over low heat. Strain or serve as is.

Variation
Use mint and thyme to taste, chopped hot, or hot red peppers.

Variation
Substitute a favorite white wine, red wine, or lime juice for the vinegar.

Variation
Add a little garlic, or try some ginger. Add chopped tarragon or basil.

MAYONNAISE

Makes 2 cups

3 egg yolks or 1 whole
    egg and 1 yolk
1-1/3 to 1-1/2 cups
    olive oil
3 tablespoons lemon
    juice
salt
freshly ground pepper
boiling water (optional)

In a small bowl, blender, or food processor, beat the egg yolks with a pinch of salt, pepper, and 1 tablespoon of the lemon juice until thick. Gradually whisk or beat in the oil, drop by drop at first, until the mixture thickens. Continue whisking, adding the oil in a slow, thin stream until the mayonnaise is thick. Season with remaining 2 tablespoons lemon juice, salt and pepper to taste. Thin with the water if too thick.

Continued

Variation

If you are cholesterol-conscious, try making mayonnaise without egg yolks, just using 3 egg whites to about 1 cup oil. It will look better if you use a blender or food processor.

Variation

Use 3 to 4 tablespoons herbs (tarragon, dill, thyme, etc.).

Variation

Add 1 peeled and chopped red pepper, fresh or roasted, before serving.

Tip: When making mayonnaise by hand, whisk, or mixer, the egg yolks need to be thick and the oil added slowly. The food processor thickens more easily, and the oil may be added more quickly in a steady stream.

BÉARNAISE MAYONNAISE
Makes 2-1/4 cups

2 shallots, peeled and finely chopped
1/3 cup white wine vinegar plus 1 teaspoon
5 tablespoons chopped dried or fresh tarragon
2 egg yolks
1/2 teaspoon Dijon mustard
1-1/3 cups vegetable oil
salt
freshly ground white pepper

In a small saucepan, bring the shallots, the 1/3 cup vinegar, and tarragon to the boil. Boil to reduce mixture by half. Set aside.

Place yolks, mustard, the 1 teaspoon vinegar, and 2 tablespoons of the oil in a bowl or food processor. Whisk until ingredients are well combined. Gradually whisk in the oil, drop by drop at first, until the mixture thickens. Continue whisking, adding the remaining oil in a slow thin stream until the mayonnaise is thick. Add the reduced tarragon mixture to the mayonnaise. Season to taste with salt and pepper.

Variation

Try other fresh herbs. Basil is particularly nice.

HAZELNUT TORTE WITH FRESH RASPBERRIES AND CREAM
Makes one 3-layer 9-inch torte or 15 sandwiched cookies

10 tablespoons unsalted
  butter
1/2 cup sugar
1-1/2 cups all-purpose
  flour
1/3 teaspoon salt
1-1/4 cups toasted and
  finely chopped
  hazelnuts

Filling

1 to 2 cups fresh
  raspberries, or other
  berries in season,
  sliced
1 cup heavy cream,
  whipped with 1
  teaspoon peach
  brandy or
  schnapps and 3
  teaspoons sugar
additional whipped
  cream (optional)
confectioners' sugar
  (optional)

Preheat the oven to 375°F. Beat the butter and sugar together until light. Sift the flour with the salt, add the hazelnuts, and stir into the creamed mixture to make an even dough. Divide into 3 pieces, placing each between 2 sheets of wax paper. Roll each piece out 1/8 inch thick. Chill 30 minutes or until firm. Remove the top sheet of wax paper, and cut the dough into matching rounds, using a 9-inch pie plate as a guide. Tidy up any rough edges with the unused dough. Carefully flip circle of dough over to an ungreased baking sheet. Peel off wax paper. Bake 8 to 10 minutes, in a 375°F oven.

Remove from oven. Torte will be soft but will harden as it cools. While still warm, carefully press an indention dividing the torte into 10 equal-size wedges. This will later aid in slicing the assembled torte. When the torte hardens, remove from pan to baking rack to cool completely. Repeat with other two circles.

When assembling the torte, line up serving indentions evenly. Fill torte with whipped cream and fresh fruit. Decorate each wedge with a swirl of whipped cream and a slice of the fresh fruit used.

Variation

For cookies, remove the top sheet of wax paper and cut the dough into 3-inch rounds with a cookie cutter. Remove to a cookie sheet. Bake 10 minutes or until the edges begin to brown. The rounds will be soft even though done and will harden as they cool. When they are nearly hard, remove to racks to cool.

When cool, place in an airtight container or cookie jar at room temperature, or freeze. Thirty minutes before serving, sandwich the whipped cream and raspberries between the cookie rounds. Immediately before serving, decorate the top with additional whipped cream or sprinkle with confectioners' sugar.

✄26✑

LOVER'S MENU

The Way to a Man's Heart Is His Stomach

She never saw a harvest moon without thinking of him and the duck that flew for them the night of a full moon. From shrimp to duck, the story of a love affair.

When he first told her he loved her, it was while eating shrimp from the Georgia coast. "You're wonderful," he said. The way to a man's heart is his stomach.

He said he loved her food. She woke up planning what she wanted to feed him for dinner. She became more desperately in love as time went on, even as the relationship began to deteriorate. He was frequently late for dinner and too busy to call. Her grocery menus were frantically made, obsessive lists of things she wanted to cook for him—asparagus, roast duck, chocolate mousse. The way to a man's heart is his stomach.

One night they made plans for dinner out. She would rather have cooked for him—to have exercised her culinary prowess. He wanted control, to be free of her food, and made reservations at a country restaurant an hour's drive away. She decided she had to have her hair done for him so he would tell her again she was beautiful. Her hairdresser was running late and she sat in the beauty shop, trapped and full of foreboding. She arrived home and he was sitting on the doorstep, silently, angrily waiting, his control thwarted.

There was a full harvest moon, their dominant companion as

they drove, with the smell of her harshly permanented, now frizzy and ugly, hair filling the car. They squabbled about her being late, at the distance he was choosing to drive rather than eat her cooking. He didn't say she was beautiful. She had to force herself to breathe through the pain in her chest.

They arrived at the allegedly romantic restaurant only to find it nearly closed, wearily patient waiters holding the dinners he had preordered. They sat alone in the empty dining room. When she cut into her duck, it was so tough it flew off the plate and slid down his starched white shirt front. Distressed, she still couldn't suppress a grin. He said she had done it on purpose. She hadn't, but might have if she'd thought of it. He stormed out and waited in the car. Picking the duck off the floor, she told the stunned waiter to bring the check. Her rage at her love's rejection of all she was rippled through her physically. They had a violent fight in the light of the moon. When her hysterics abated, they drove the long way home in silence, and separated for a long time.

Ten years later, after he had married and divorced another, she wanted him to eat a duck she had cooked herself. She took it on a trip to the mountains. They remembered that night with uneasy laughter, recalling what they might have lost. She had cooked many ducks since then with crisp tender skins. And she always removed the backbone and ribs. One had never shot off her plate again. The way to a man's heart is his stomach.

ꙅ M E N U ꙅ

LOVER'S MENU

Boiled Shrimp (p. 95) or **Marco Polo Shrimp**
Roast Duck with Orange Rhubarb Sauce
Duchesse Potatoes
Kay's Zucchini-stuffed Tomatoes or **Fiddlehead Ferns**
Caesar Salad
Pecan Lacy Wafers with Chocolate Mousse

LOGISTICS

To serve 2 look for "variation for 2" on individual recipes.

The potatoes, rhubarb sauce, mousse, and cookies may be made several days ahead or even frozen. The shrimp and duck may be cooked earlier in the day and reheated when ready to serve. The tomatoes may be assembled several hours in advance, ready for heating, as may the fiddlehead ferns. The salad may be washed and dried, the dressing made and refrigerated, all ready for tossing. The shrimp may be assembled for last-minute reheating.

If you wish, this menu can also be easily multiplied to serve 4 to 6.

☾ R E C I P E S ☾

MARCO POLO SHRIMP
Serves 6 to 8

2 pounds large shrimp
   in the shell

Marco Polo Pesto

3 tablespoons oil
1 to 3 tablespoons hot
   peppers, seeded and
   chopped (preferably
   fresh)
2 cups fresh basil leaves,
   chopped
2 garlic cloves, chopped
1 to 3 tablespoons fresh
   ginger, chopped
1 teaspoon dark oriental
   sesame oil
1 tablespoon lemon juice or dry white wine
salt
freshly ground pepper
Garnish:
3 to 4 fresh basil leaves

Cut each shrimp shell along the back, keeping the shell on. If the vein that runs along the back is full and black, remove by scraping it out with the tip of your knife. Purée the oil, hot peppers, basil, garlic, ginger, sesame oil, and lemon juice in a food processor. Season with salt and pepper to taste. Spoon a little purée under each shrimp shell. Cover and refrigerate until needed, up to 4 hours.

To broil, place the shrimp on a broiler pan and broil under high heat about 3 minutes per side. To grill, heat up the grill and place the shrimp on a narrow wire rack, then grill until just pink, about 3 minutes per side. Peel, if you like, before serving. Top with fresh basil leaves.

Variation for 2

Use 1/2 pound shrimp, in the shell; 2 teaspoons oil; 1/2 to 1 tablespoon hot peppers, seeded and chopped; 1/2 cup fresh basil leaves, chopped; 1 clove garlic; 1/2 tablespoon fresh ginger; 1 teaspoon lemon juice; and 1/2 teaspoon dark oriental sesame oil. Top with 1 to 2 basil leaves, chopped.

Variation

Mix the sauce with shelled shrimps and bake, rather than stuffing it under the shells, for 20 minutes at 350°F.

Variation

Add 1/4 pound butter, the oil, and sesame oil to a frying pan with the sauce, add the shrimp, and heat until shrimp turn color, then bake at 350°F for 15 to 20 minutes.

Variation

Try serving the shrimp on thin pasta or oriental egg noodles lightly coated with sesame oil.

Variation

Add 2 tablespoons chopped green onions or scallions to the sauce.

Tip: This serves 6 to 8 as a starter, 4 to 6 as a main course.

Tip: 2 cups fresh basil leaves, chopped, makes only 4 to 5 tablespoons chopped basil!

ORANGE RHUBARB SAUCE

Makes 2 to 3 cups

1 pound rhubarb, sliced in 1-inch pieces, fresh or frozen
1 cup orange juice
1/4 cup sugar
zest of 1 orange, all white removed and shredded

Place the rhubarb in a heavy saucepan, with its juices, along with the orange juice and half the zest. Bring to the boil, reduce the heat to a slow simmer, and simmer uncovered for 10 to 15 minutes, until the rhubarb is soft and there is some thick sauce surrounding the remaining slices. Add the sugar and cook 15 minutes more on low heat, until thick. Be careful not to scorch or let the liquid boil out. Will keep several days in the refrigerator or may be frozen. Garnish with remainder of the orange zest.

Continued

Variation for 2:
Use 1/2 pound rhubarb, 1/2 cup orange juice, 1/8 cup sugar, and half the zest of an orange when serving duck for 2 people.

Variation
Add 1/2 tablespoon freshly chopped ginger.

Variation
Serve cold, with cream, for breakfast.

Variation
Add more sugar and you have a sweet sauce.

Tip: Serve with duck, lamb, pork, turkey, and game.

ROAST DUCK WITH ORANGE RHUBARB SAUCE
Serves 2

1 (5-pound) duck,
    defrosted if necessary
zest of 1 orange, with all
    white removed,
    shredded finely
1 recipe Orange
    Rhubarb Sauce
    (p. 263)

Preheat oven to 400°F. Remove the neck, liver, giblets, and so on from inside the duck's cavity; also remove excess fat around the opening inside thigh area. Prick the duck's skin all over, about 1/8 inch deep, to release the fat, taking care not to puncture the duck's breast meat. Place the orange peel inside the duck. Truss or tie together the legs. Place on a rack in a roasting pan with at least 2-inch sides and put the pan in the middle of the hot oven for 1 to 1-1/2 hours. Keep thick hot pads next to the oven, and prepare a work surface that will accommodate the roasting pan and a metal pan or bowl to receive the fat. Periodically remove the duck from the oven, move to the work surface, and use a metal spoon or baster (avoid a rubber or plastic baster; it may melt) to remove the fat. Put the duck back in the oven until it reaches 170°F on an instant meat thermometer inserted in its thigh. Cook the duck ahead of time and cool. Split or cut down either side of the backbone from neck to tail and divide the duck in 2 pieces. Pull out the breast and rib bones. When ready to serve, place the halves under broiler to crisp the skin and warm through. Serve with orange rhubarb sauce. May be served hot or cold.

Variation

Substitute grated ginger for the orange zest. Brush with hoisin sauce, fresh chopped ginger, and soy sauce, mixed. Garnish with green onion brushes.

Tip: One duck serves 2 people well, 4 people skimpily. For 6 people, roast 2 or 3 ducks.

Tip: Make a Brown Duck Stock (see p. 218) with the giblets and neckbone. Chop up the backbone and breastbone and add to the stock for further flavor.

Tip: The fat can be rendered and used to sauté croutons for Caesar salad.

Tip: Tie legs together to insure even roasting.

DUCHESSE POTATOES

Serves 8 to 10

7 to 8 medium potatoes, peeled and quartered
1 cup milk, heated to 180°F
5 to 6 tablespoons butter
salt
freshly ground pepper
2 to 3 egg yolks
1/2 cup imported Parmesan cheese, grated

Glaze

1 egg, beaten with 1/2 teaspoon salt

Put the potatoes in a pan with enough cold water to cover, bring to the boil, reduce heat, cover, and simmer approximately 1 hour until completely tender. Drain. Place the pan over low heat and add the potatoes. Beat over low heat with electric mixer or mash until soft. Beat in the hot milk and butter. Add salt and pepper to taste. Beat the egg yolks into the mashed potatoes and add the cheese.

Preheat oven to 400°F. While the potatoes are still warm, spoon them into a pastry bag fitted with the large star tube. Pipe rosettes, figure eights, or tablespoon-sized mounds of potato onto a buttered baking sheet or oven-to-table dish. Brush with the egg glaze. Bake 8 to 10 minutes or until browned, or do up to a day ahead, warm in a low oven, then brown quickly under the broiler. Remove from baking sheet.

Continued

Variation for 2:
Combine 2 medium-cooked, peeled, and quartered potatoes, 1/4 cup hot milk, 1 to 2 tablespoons butter, salt, pepper, and 1/4 cup grated Parmesan, and 1/2 an egg yolk. Pipe. Brush with the remainder of the yolk beaten with a dash of salt.

Variation
Substitute sweet potatoes! Sounds funny, but they are very pretty and very tasty.

Variation
Use as a garnish around meat dishes.

KAY'S ZUCCHINI-STUFFED TOMATOES
Serves 8

2 tablespoons butter
1 tablespoon chopped
  shallots or onions
1/2 pound zucchini,
  grated
1/4 teaspoon fresh
  chopped thyme
1 tablespoon finely
  chopped parsley
pinch of ground cloves
salt
freshly ground pepper
2 tablespoons pine nuts
  (optional)
8 small or 4 large
  tomatoes

Preheat oven to 400°F. Melt the butter in a skillet, add the shallots, and sauté until soft. Add the grated zucchini, thyme, parsley, cloves, salt, pepper, and optional pine nuts. Toss for 1 or 2 minutes over medium heat. Remove the tops and insides of the tomatoes, leaving about 1/2-inch pulp against the skin so the tomatoes will not collapse while baking. Slice a small portion of the bottom of the tomato to level. Put the tomatoes on a baking sheet. Spoon the zucchini stuffing into the tomatoes. Bake 6 minutes or until done.

To do ahead: Let the tomatoes drain upside down on a rack in the refrigerator. Make and refrigerate the filling. Assemble several hours in advance. Place room-temperature tomatoes in oven 6 minutes before serving.

Variation for 2:
Use 1 teaspoon butter, 1 teaspoon chopped shallots or onions, 1 small zucchini, 1 teaspoon chopped parsley and thyme, dash of ground cloves, salt, freshly ground pepper, 1 teaspoon pine nuts (optional), and 2 small tomatoes.

Variation
Use cooked, drained spinach or grated summer squash for the zucchini.

FIDDLEHEAD FERNS

Serves 6 to 8

1 pound ostrich-fern
   fiddleheads, washed
4 to 5 tablespoons
   butter or olive oil
salt
freshly ground pepper

Dry ferns. Heat the butter or olive oil in a large frying pan. Add the ferns and toss over low heat for 2 to 3 minutes or longer if you desire softer ferns. Season with salt and pepper.

Variation

Sauté 1 pound button mushrooms, chanterelles, shiitake mushrooms, or morels in butter. Add the cooked ferns and heat all together.

Variation for 2:

Use 1/3 pound fiddleheads and 2 teaspoons butter or oil.

Tip: Fiddleheads come frozen as well as fresh. Frozen ones need only be defrosted.

CAESAR SALAD

Serves 6 to 8

4 to 5 garlic cloves,
   peeled
8 anchovies
6 tablespoons Dijon
   mustard
3 egg yolks
6 tablespoons red wine
   vinegar
1-1/2 tablespoons
   Worcestershire
1 cup oil
1 large head romaine lettuce (1-1/2 pounds)
1/2 cup fresh imported Parmesan, grated or sliced
2 cups croutons
salt
freshly ground pepper

Crush the garlic and anchovies together in a food processor or blender. Add the mustard and egg yolks, blend, and then add vinegar and Worcestershire. Beat or whisk in the oil. Wash and tear the romaine lettuce.

At the table toss the romaine with the dressing, Parmesan, croutons, and salt and freshly ground pepper to taste.

Continued

Variation for 2:
Use 1 garlic clove, 1 anchovy, 2 teaspoons Dijon mustard, 1 egg yolk, 1 teaspoon red wine vinegar, dash of Worcestershire, 1 tablespoon oil, 1/2 head of romaine lettuce, 1 ounce Parmesan, 1/3 cup croutons, salt and pepper.

Variation
Southwestern Caesar: Toss croutons in 1/2 cup melted butter and 2 tablespoons chili powder. Shave the Parmesan off with a peeler in long strips and serve on top.

Tip: 1 large head = 1-1/2 pounds = 8 to 9 cups = 2 small heads.

PECAN LACY WAFERS
Makes 50 cookies

4 ounces whole pecans, toasted
2 ounces whole almonds, toasted
1/2 cup unsalted butter, softened
3 tablespoons sugar
1/2 cup brown sugar, packed
1 egg
1 teaspoon vanilla
1/2 cup currants or raisins
peel of 1 orange, grated
1/4 cup flour, sifted
salt
1/8 teaspoon baking soda
1/2 teaspoon ground cinnamon
1/2 teaspoon ground allspice

Preheat oven to 350°F. Chop half the nuts finely and leave the other half chopped roughly. Beat the butter until light. Gradually add the sugars, beating well. Beat in the egg and vanilla. Add the currants and orange peel. Sift the flour with the salt, baking soda, cinnamon, and allspice onto a piece of waxed paper. Add the flour mixture and nuts to the butter mixture. Stir well.

Line 2 baking sheets with aluminum foil. Grease well with butter. Drop teaspoonfuls of batter onto the aluminum foil at least 2 inches apart. Bake each sheet 11 to 13 minutes, until batter is spread and golden at the edges. Move the cookies with a spatula to a wire rack to cool. Repeat until all cookies are baked. If cookies lose crispness, they may be recrisped in oven for about 2 minutes. They freeze well.

SIMPLE CHOCOLATE MOUSSE
Serves 6

8 ounces semisweet
  chocolate bits
4 tablespoons water
1/2 teaspoon rum or
  vanilla flavoring
1-1/2 tablespoons
  butter
4 egg yolks
4 egg whites
Garnish:
1/2 cup heavy whipping
  cream, whipped

Melt the chocolate and water together in a small pan or the microwave. Stir in the rum flavoring and butter, then the egg yolks, one by one. Beat the egg whites until stiff. Fold the chocolate mixture into the egg whites using a rubber spatula or a metal spoon. When thoroughly mixed, pour into small pots or a glass bowl. Cover and chill overnight. Serve with a rosette of whipped cream piped on top. May be made several days in advance or frozen.

Variation for 2:
Use 4 ounces semisweet bits, 2 tablespoons water, dash of flavoring, 2 teaspoons butter, 2 egg yolks, and 2 egg whites. Garnish with 1/4 cup whipping cream, whipped. Or make whole recipe, spoon into individual pots, serve 2, and freeze the rest for another time.

✝ 27 ✝

A THANKSGIVING MENU FOR EIGHT TO TEN

Giving Thanks

Thanksgiving is a holiday in which food takes on the leading role. There is perhaps no other day in America when the entire activity rests on feeding and eating. Yet it is also fraught with hidden agendas and mixed feelings. In addition to the joy of being with family and friends, tensions can develop that stretch the full length of the table. The pressure on the cook, as well as the diner, is enormous, and the power exchanges mighty. Let's assume that there is great love and affection at the meal. But as relationships change, there are issues in a family that need to be negotiated and understood. Sometimes these are unspoken, but they are still there.

Learning how to negotiate and to be flexible in feeding others on this day brings food into its seat of power. Who, for instance, when agendas are mixed, determines the time of eating? Will the meal interfere with a football game, a date, or perhaps a commitment to another set of family, such as in-laws? Why, on this one day of all days should people who normally eat at twelve or one and then again at seven or eight be hungry at three or five? A wise cook focuses the fete as close to a normal eating time as possible, and makes provisions for her guests clear when making arrangements. Tummies and tempers will be better for it. Providing a snack if the meal is to be delayed will help.

The cook is subject to a set of skewed feelings. Will she or he feel obligated to rise early, give up the greater portion of a day (or days) to work the serving time around people who would rather be elsewhere? Does the cook feel that if the meal isn't eaten with gusto at a certain time it is evidence of lack of appreciation? And will she or he have time to clean up, alone, while everyone flees to another activity?

I can rarely be gracious about delayed meals (in my home or others') when others don't want to give up another activity to come to the table, or because they think the time of eating is not crucial.

The guest list is important—to everyone. Fantasies on one person's part of inviting the homeless or great aunt, but counting on others to entertain them, can cause family upheaval. At the same time, omitting a favorite aunt or girl friend of a teenager, or not figuring out a way to include in-laws or the needy may make someone feel a real sense of loss at an otherwise happy time.

Some people like strangers, others don't. I'll never forget the time I spontaneously invited a stranger in town to an in-law's table, thinking I had checked and understood. I didn't.

Expectations of the diners become a force as well. Do they expect someone who never cooks for more than four all year long to all of a sudden be able to prepare dinner for fifteen with no help? Is their idea of the holiday to just show up and be fed? Has the cook prepared a way for them to help?

Hopefully, we are beyond the days of one person feeling that she or he has to do it all. It's not realistic. But there are still people who sense a loss of control if others help, and there are still eaters who feel they have no responsibility to others or themselves for their pleasure at table.

Some of them don't even think they should express thanks. They are the greatest losers, for by not expressing their gratitude, they give up the acknowledgment of the good in their lives. What a good holiday meal for everyone means is finding a way to understand each other's needs and to give a little—time, companionship, help—to make everyone feel loved. This is the way we will learn to feed the world.

Comments on How Much to Make

In the realm of unanswerable cooking questions, the most difficult when making a recipe is, "How many does it serve?"

My Chicken and Asparagus recipe (p. 119) taken to a picnic, with a cold soup to start, sesame noodles, a salad, and a big dessert, will serve 6 to 8. On the other hand, for Chinese food, the rule of thumb is to plan on having a dish for each person, and one extra, such as rice, to make a complete meal. So when a recipe from a Chinese cookbook says "serves 4," by and large it would feed 4 when serving four other dishes from the same book.

Recently I asked a friend who runs a private club how she planned for a party. She said that her rule of thumb is 5 ounces of fish, meat, or poultry per person, and 3 to 4 ounces of vegetables, in addition to potatoes, rice, or pasta.

But then there is Thanksgiving—a nightmare all its own. A casserole of sweet potatoes for 4, for instance, would yield everyone at the table about 2 tablespoons, which is plenty for people also eating mashed potatoes with gravy, stuffing, butter beans, two kinds of peas, and two kinds of pies. But if it is particularly delicious, then there will be a run on the dish, and guests will load up, not leaving enough for everyone. So at Thanksgiving, 3 ounces of vegetables is not enough—figure 6 ounces.

There are other considerations. When the weather is hot, we eat less. When it is cold, we eat more. People who work outdoors or do physical labor eat more than those who sit at a desk all day. And of course teenage boys have notorious appetites. Those training for football season may especially want an enormous amount of food. Teenage girls may binge, or they may pass up the sweet potatoes for a double helping of chicken and asparagus; or they may pass up the food altogether, simply pushing a piece of asparagus around in circles on their plates.

Which leads us back to another guideline—whenever possible, know your guests. That is always one of the greatest aids in planning a menu. When unsure, always make more than you need. After all, you can almost always use any leftovers later on.

ᘓ M E N U ᘒ

A THANKSGIVING MENU FOR EIGHT TO TEN*

Smoky Moist Turkey Breast
or Quick Unstuffed Turkey with Gravy

Stuart Woods's Rich Herbed Dressing

Cranberry Sauce

Decadent Mashed Potatoes or Orange Sweet Potatoes
or Low-Cal Buttermilk Mashed Potatoes (p. 279: Variation)

Make-Ahead Green Beans with Mushrooms (p. 72)

Cucumber and Carrot Salad

Cranberry Nut Bread or Food Processor Rolls

Famous Pumpkin Pie
and/or Ginger-Rhubarb Pie (p. 174: Variation)

SERVES 8 TO 10

LOGISTICS

Organization:

A good cook and Thanksgiving hostess should have an organizational chart posted. (I use my refrigerator door.) It should list the time of reheating, the pot to be used, and the serving dish. This enables the cook and the guests to know that heating a casserole in the oven is impossible if it is full of dressing and turkey. So the casserole must be reheated in the microwave or served at room temperature. The only large platter in the house, for instance, may need to be reserved for the turkey, not used for something else. A plan for the table, showing where each dish is to go, is very helpful. Another trick is to place a piece of paper in each dish on the table with the name of the recipe to be placed in it.

A clean and empty sink, counter, and dishwasher before guests enter is important. After dinner, plates can then be easily cleaned off and put directly into these places. Large pots and pans should be temporarily set

with Enough Leftovers for a Small Late-night Supper

aside and washed at the end. (I've known cooks who placed pots in plastic washing containers in the bathtub or under the sink to soak before cleaning, getting them out of the way!)

There is nothing that should be uncooked when the first guest walks in the house. The cranberry sauce may be made earlier in the week. The turkey may be made early in the day, or the night before, covered, and refrigerated. (It will be every bit as good as any caterer's!) The dressing (which may be doubled if necessary) is a real time-saver over a stuffing. It may be made ahead a day or even frozen, but the sausages need to be cooked that day, ready for reheating with the turkey. The green beans and mushrooms may be made earlier in the day, as can the cucumber salad. The potatoes may be made an hour before serving and reheated. The pies may be made a day ahead or even frozen.

I like to carve up the turkey before reheating, unless there is someone who takes great pleasure in carving *who has volunteered.* It's a pretty mean thing to force someone into the uncomfortable role of wielding the knife in front of family and friends. And pity the poor turkey. A great flurry can be made, showing everyone the turkey before it goes to the kitchen to be sliced and plattered.

A turkey breast is a good alternative to a whole turkey. I like the flavor of a smoked or grilled turkey, which also means the oven is free. I cook it in a pan to keep it moist and to have enough juice for gravy.

Reheating:

Forty-five minutes before serving, preheat oven to 325°F and place turkey in oven. Half an hour before serving, put the dressing with the sausages in the oven (or reheat in the microwave somewhat later). About 15 minutes before serving, reheat sweet potatoes, then 10 minutes before serving, heat green beans and mashed potatoes in the oven, on the stove top, or in the microwave. Place the rest of the food on the table.

Cleanup:

The cook who insists on using fine china and silver that can't go in the dishwasher faces the possibility of tears at being left alone over soapy water long into the night. I don't use anything that can't go into the dishwasher. People are more important to me than treasures. If washing by hand is mutually agreed upon, a proper space should be cleared for washing and drying (and it can be used as a wonderful catch-up time for news and concerns). Guests are usually very helpful in the post-meal stage, provided the cook has arranged an easy way to join in the cleanup.

ꙮ R E C I P E S ꙮ

SMOKY MOIST TURKEY BREAST
Serves 8

1 (5-pound) turkey
  breast
1/3 cup Garlic-Pepper
  Oil (p. 6)
3 tablespoons rosemary,
  chopped
juice of 2 lemons
2 cups Basic Poultry
  Stock (p. 218)
salt
freshly ground pepper
1 cup heavy whipping
  cream (optional)

If turkey breast is frozen, defrost. Mix 1/4 cup of the oil, 2 tablespoons of the rosemary, and the lemon juice. Pour over turkey breast and marinate 1 hour, covered and refrigerated. Prepare the grill. Place the turkey with its marinade in a pan over the center of the grill. Add 1 cup of the chicken stock. Cook until the turkey skin is brown and crisp and turkey registers 180°F on a thermometer, about 4 hours. (Keep the heat in the grill around 300°F.) Brush with marinade as needed. Add more stock if it boils out. When ready to serve, add the rest of the stock to the pan and boil down until thick. Skim juices. Season with salt and pepper. Add lemon juice as needed. Add optional cream and boil until thick. Slice turkey and serve with sauce.

To cook whole meats by indirect heat, position the charcoal rails as far as possible to the outside edge of the lower grill. This will allow a large area in the center for a drip pan. Stand in front of the kettle and place an equal number of briquettes on the left and right sides of the lower grill. For meats that require more than 1 hour to cook, additional briquettes must be added to keep the fire going. (Refer to manufacturer's instructions for your grill.) Ignite charcoal. Leave the cover off the grill until coals have a light coating of gray ash (about 30 minutes). Place a drip pan in the center of the lower grill. If you want gravy, meat may be placed in a roaster holder inside the drip pan and centered on the cooking grill.

Continued

Position the cooking grill in the kettle with handles directly over coals. Add charcoal through openings by grill handles. Place the meat on the cooking grill directly above the drip pan. Cover the kettle. Consult the recipe for recommended cooking times.

QUICK UNSTUFFED TURKEY WITH GRAVY
Serves 10

1 (12 to 14-pound)
  turkey, fresh or
  thawed
1/2 cup olive oil or
  melted butter
1 onion, quartered
1 carrot, quartered
4 to 6 cups chicken or
  turkey stock
salt
freshly ground pepper
1/2 to 1 cup heavy
  whipping cream
  (optional)

Preheat oven to 500°F. Butter a piece of aluminum foil and place in the bottom of a roasting pan. Place the onion and carrot inside the turkey, for flavor. Truss the turkey or tie its legs. Place in the foil-lined pan. Brush with oil. Add enough stock to come 1 to 2 inches up the sides of the turkey. Turn the turkey breast side down. Place in the oven and roast for 1 hour. Carefully, remove the turkey from the oven, watching out for steam. If the stock has boiled down to less than 1 inch up the sides, add enough to bring it up to 2 inches. Turn the turkey breast up and return it to the oven. When the oven has returned to a temperature of 500°F, reduce the heat to 450°F, and roast for 1 hour more. Cover with foil if browning too much.

Remove the turkey; check for doneness with a meat thermometer—it should read 170°F inserted in the thigh—or when juices run clear when a knife is inserted in the flesh of the thigh. Let sit 30 minutes before carving. You should have some wonderful pan juices. If the juices seem fatty, skim off the fat with a paper towel. Add any remaining stock to the pan. Place the pan over high heat, and bring the juices to the boil, stirring constantly, and reduce until rich and flavorful. Taste. Season with salt and pepper and use as gravy. If you want a richer sauce, add the cream and boil until thick.

Tip: A good "instant read" thermometer is a must for judging accurately when a turkey is done.

STUART WOODS'S RICH HERBED DRESSING
Serves 8

1 pound butter
4 large onions, finely
  chopped to make 2 to
  3 cups
15 cups bread crumbs or
  biscuit crumbs
2 cups whole pine nuts,
  or 2 cups pecans or
  walnuts, chopped
1 cup chopped parsley
about 2 tablespoons
  chopped tarragon
2 teaspoons chopped fresh thyme or 1 teaspoon dried
salt
freshly ground pepper
2 cups turkey or chicken stock
Garnish:
10 to 20 thin link pork sausages, pricked
(optional)

Preheat oven to 350°F. Heat 1/2 cup of the butter in a heavy skillet, add the onions and cook until soft. Mix with the bread crumbs and nuts of your choice. Melt the remaining butter and add to the bread crumb mixture along with the parsley, tarragon, and thyme. Toss well and add salt and pepper to taste. Meanwhile, brown the sausages in a frying pan. Drain and set aside. Place the dressing in a casserole dish, cover, and bake 1 hour. Add stock as needed. Garnish turkey with optional sausages.

Variation
Substitute 2 dozen shallots, peeled and chopped, to make 2 to 3 cups, for the onions. Add 3 garlic cloves, chopped.

CRANBERRY SAUCE
Makes 3 to 4 cups

4 cups raw cranberries
2 cups sugar
1 cup water
1/2 teaspoon cinnamon
1 teaspoon grated
  orange peel

Place the cranberries, sugar, and water in a heavy saucepan. Bring to the boil, stirring until the sugar is dissolved. Reduce heat and simmer until the berries break open and the liquid is reduced a bit. Remove from heat; add cinnamon and orange peel. The sauce will thicken as it cools. It will last, refrigerated, up to a month.

ORANGE SWEET POTATOES
Serves 4 to 6

4 large sweet potatoes,
    peeled
6 tablespoons butter
1/4 cup brown sugar
1 to 2 tablespoons
    orange peel, grated
1/2 cup orange juice
salt
freshly ground pepper
Garnish:
2 tablespoons orange
    peel, blanched and
    julienned

Preheat oven to 375°F. Cut the sweet potatoes in wedges. Bring a large pot of water to the boil, add the potatoes, and cook 15 minutes or until tender. Drain the potatoes well and place in a buttered baking dish. Put the butter, sugar, orange peel, and orange juice in a pan and cook over low heat until the butter melts. Spoon the mixture over the potatoes. Season with salt and pepper. Bake about 15 minutes, basting and turning until glazed and brown. Garnish with orange peel. Reheats easily in oven or microwave.

Tip: If serving mashed potatoes as well, this may be a sufficiency for 8. If no other starch is being served, use 6 large sweet potatoes, 8 tablespoons butter, 1/3 cup brown sugar, 2 to 3 tablespoons orange peel, and 3/4 cup orange juice. Garnish is the same.

DECADENT MASHED POTATOES
Serves 4 to 6

2 pounds potatoes,
    peeled and cut into
    quarters or chunks
4 tablespoons butter
1/2 to 3/4 cup heavy
    cream or milk
salt
freshly ground pepper

Put the potatoes in a heavy pan with enough cold water to cover. Place a lid on the pan and bring to the boil. Boil until very soft and tender when pierced with a fork and there are no uncooked hard dots of potatoes left. Drain the potatoes and set aside. Return the empty pan to the heat, add the butter, and melt. Meanwhile, bring the cream or milk to the boil in a separate pan. Put the potatoes through a food mill, or mash with a potato masher, or beat with an electric mixer over the heat. Beat in the butter and hot cream or milk to desired texture. Season with salt and pepper to taste. To keep, cover with a thin layer of hot cream or milk. Preheat gently and stir when ready to serve, or reheat in the microwave.

Variation
Add 4 garlic cloves, peeled, to the potatoes when boiling. Mash with the potatoes. Delicious!

Variation
Low-cal buttermilk mashed potatoes: For 8, use 4 pounds potatoes. Substitute 3/4 to 1-1/4 cups hot buttermilk for the cream and wait until potatoes are mashed before adding only 1 tablespoon butter.

Tip: It's very important to mash the potatoes over heat. The steam fluffs and lightens the potatoes and keeps them from seizing into starchy lumps.

CUCUMBER AND CARROT SALAD
Serves 8

4 cucumbers, thinly sliced, peeled if skins are waxed
salt
8 tablespoons sugar
3/4 cup cider vinegar
1 medium carrot, grated or finely julienned
2 green onions or scallions, chopped
3 tablespoons sesame seeds

Sprinkle the cucumbers with salt, and let stand in a colander for 15 minutes to 1/2 hour. Rinse and drain. Squeeze water out with your hands or a paper towel. Dissolve the sugar in the vinegar and pour over cucumbers. Sprinkle the carrot, green onion, and sesame seeds on top.

Variation
Add 1 or 2 slices hard-cooked eggs.

Variation
Serve in lettuce cups garnished with green-onion fans.

Comment: Forsythia is the wonderful cook in charge of the food preparation for my television series. This salad recipe of hers appears in many countries in slightly different dress; the Japanese call it *namasu* and serve it as a relish or side dish; the Chinese make it as a kind of pickle or hors d'oeuvre. Forsythia's partner Gary says his Jewish mother made a salad like this, except that her version included sliced hard-cooked eggs. For me, minus the sesame seeds and green onion, it's a typical Southern side dish!

FOOD PROCESSOR ROLLS
Makes 12 rolls

1 package active dry
   yeast
1 tablespoon sugar
1-1/4 cups warm milk
   (105°F)
8 tablespoons (1/4
   pound) butter
1/2 teaspoon salt
2-1/2 to 3-1/2 cups
   bread flour

In a bowl or food processor, dissolve the yeast and sugar in the warm milk. Turn on the processor or electric beater and add 4 tablespoons of the butter, the salt, and enough of the flour, 1/2 cup at a time, to make a soft dough. Knead until dough is elastic and smooth as a baby's bottom. Shape into a ball. Put the dough in an oiled bowl and turn to coat and cover with plastic wrap, or place in an oiled plastic bag and let rise until doubled, approximately 1 to 1-1/2 hours.

Pull off dough in egg-sized pieces and roll into balls. Place on a greased baking sheet leaving an egg-sized space in between and let rise until doubled, about 1/2 hour.

Preheat oven to 425°F. Brush dough pieces with water to give them a crisp crust. Cut a cross on the top of each piece with a sharp knife. Bake for 20 minutes, until nicely browned. Remove to a rack and brush with the remainder of the butter, melted.

Variation
For refrigerator rolls: Place the bowl of kneaded dough in the refrigerator, covered, and use over a period of 4 or 5 days, removing however many pieces of dough you need. Shape, then place on greased baking sheet and let double on the sheet about 45 minutes before baking.

CRANBERRY NUT BREAD
1 loaf or 18 muffins

1-1/3 cups flour
1 teaspoon baking soda
1-1/4 teaspoons salt
3/4 cup sugar
peel of 1 orange, grated

Preheat oven to 350°F. Grease a 9 × 5 × 3-inch loaf pan and line with a strip of wax paper, greased; or place 18 paper muffin cups in muffin tins. Mix together the flour, baking soda, and salt. Put the sugar and orange peel

6 tablespoons butter,
   cut into 1-inch pieces
2 large eggs
juice of 1 orange
1-1/4 cups fresh
   cranberries, chopped
1 cup walnuts or pecans,
   chopped

in a bowl, food processor, or mixer, along with the butter, eggs, and 1/2 cup of the orange juice. Beat or process until smooth. Add the cranberries, nuts, and the flour mixture, beating until just combined. Pour into the pan or cups. Bake 1 hour for the loaf and 30 minutes for the muffins. Remove from pan and cool on a wire rack.

Tip: May use self-rising flour and omit baking soda and salt called for in recipe.

FAMOUS PUMPKIN PIE

Makes 1 pie

2 eggs, slightly beaten
2 cups canned or cooked
   and puréed pumpkin
3/4 cup sugar
1/2 teaspoon salt
1 teaspoon cinnamon
1/2 teaspoon ginger,
   preferably fresh,
   chopped, or ground
1/4 teaspoon ground
   cloves
1-2/3 cups evaporated
   milk or light cream
1 (9-inch) unbaked pie
   crust, chilled and
   shaped (p. 142)
Garnish:
1/2 cup heavy whipping
   cream, whipped

Preheat oven to 425°F. Mix together the eggs, pumpkin, sugar, salt, cinnamon, ginger, cloves, and evaporated milk. Pour the mixture into the chilled and shaped pie crust. Bake in the hot oven for 15 minutes, then reduce temperature to 350°F, and continue baking for 40 to 45 minutes or until knife inserted in center of pie filling comes out clean. Cool on a rack. Garnish with whipped cream.

Tip: Many frozen pie shells are shallower than pies made in pie plates. Filling ingredients will frequently fill 1 homemade pie crust or 2 frozen. This is one of those recipes.

Appendix

MISCELLANEOUS RECIPES

The following recipes have been demonstrated on my television
show, "New Southern Cooking,"
but were not included in the book based on the series.

FORSYTHIA'S CRAB CAKES

Makes 8 crab cakes

1 pound lump crabmeat
2 eggs
3 tablespoons heavy
   cream
1 small onion, finely
   chopped
1 green onion,
   including stem,
   chopped
3/4 cup fresh bread
   crumbs
1 teaspoon dry mustard
1/8 cup cayenne pepper
salt
freshly ground pepper
1 cup fresh bread crumbs to coat
2 tablespoons butter
2 tablespoons vegetable oil

Pick over crabmeat and remove any
pieces of shell and cartilage. Beat eggs with
cream; mix in onion, 3/4 cup bread crumbs,
mustard, cayenne pepper, and salt and pepper
to taste. Gently fold in crabmeat. Shape into 8
cakes approximately 3 inches in diameter.
Coat the cakes lightly in bread crumbs. Heat
the butter with the vegetable oil in a skillet
until sizzling, add the crab cakes, and sauté
until golden brown on both sides.

18-MINUTE CHICKEN

Serves 4

1 medium onion, sliced
4 boneless chicken
   breast halves, skin
   removed
salt and pepper
Dijon mustard
   (optional)
2 medium zucchini or
   yellow squash, sliced
   1/4 inch thick
1/2 pound mushrooms,
   sliced
3 tablespoons butter
3/4 teaspoon basil
   leaves, chopped
1 clove garlic, chopped
1/8 teaspoon paprika
1/2 cup grated
   Parmesan cheese

Preheat oven to 400°F. Tear off four 12 × 18-inch squares of heavy-duty aluminum foil. Divide ingredients into 4 parts on the foil as follows: Place onion slices in center of lower half of each sheet of foil. Place chicken over onions; season with salt and pepper and spread lightly with mustard. Top with squash and mushrooms. Season vegetables with salt and pepper. Dot with butter; sprinkle with basil, garlic, and paprika. Fold top half of foil over food, meeting bottom edges of foil. Seal edges together making a tight 1/2-inch fold. Fold again, allowing space for heat circulation and expansion. Repeat to seal each side. Place foil packet on cookie sheet. Bake 18 minutes in preheated 400°F oven. Foil packet will puff while cooking. To serve, transfer foil packet to dinner plate using pot holder or oven mitts. Cut an X in top of packet; fold foil back. Top each serving with cheese.

OKRA WITH TOMATO SAUCE

Serves 6

2 pounds okra
1/2 recipe Tomato
   Sauce (p. 284)
salt
freshly ground pepper

Stem the okra. Bring a large pan of water to the boil. Add the okra. Boil 45 seconds; drain. Rinse under cold water. Arrange in an ovenproof dish. Heat oven to 350°F. When ready to serve, place in oven for 8 to 10 minutes. Top with tomato sauce, salt and pepper to taste.

Variation
Top with White Butter Sauce (p. 257).

TOMATO SAUCE

Makes 5 cups

1/4 cup peanut oil
2 small onions, chopped
2 cloves garlic, crushed
  with salt or chopped
2 (1-pound) cans plum
  tomatoes, seeded and
  chopped, with juice
1/4 cup tomato paste
1/2 teaspoon oregano
1/2 teaspoon basil
1/2 teaspoon thyme
1 tablespoon sugar
salt
freshly ground pepper

Heat the oil in a heavy saucepan. Add onions and cook until soft. Add garlic, cook briefly, and add tomatoes with their juice, tomato paste, oregano, basil, thyme, sugar, and salt and pepper to taste. Bring to the boil; reduce to a simmer, and cook, partially covered, 30 to 45 minutes, stirring occasionally. If the sauce gets too thick, it may be thinned down with water or tomato juice. If too watery, simmer to reduce liquid, then purée in a food processor or blender, or work through a sieve.

JERUSALEM ARTICHOKES

Serves 4

1 pound Jerusalem
  artichokes
butter
salt
freshly ground pepper

Wash artichokes thoroughly and peel them. Place in a pot of water and bring to the boil. Boil steadily until the consistency of cooked potatoes, soft but not mushy; drain. Toss with butter, and salt and pepper to taste.

ENGLISH PEAS

Serves 4

3 cups shelled fresh
  English peas
5 tablespoons butter
1/2 cup chicken stock,
  canned or fresh
  (p. 218)
salt
freshly ground pepper

Put stock in a pan and bring to the boil. Add butter and peas; bring back to the boil and continue cooking for 6 to 8 minutes. Taste for seasoning and add salt and pepper as desired.

GLOBE ARTICHOKES WITH BUTTER
Serves 4

4 artichokes
1 sliced lemon
water
1 cup butter
juice of 1 lemon
hot sauce (optional)
salt to taste

Clip or cut the top and side points of the artichokes. Trim the stem. Rub cut surfaces with lemon. To boil, bring a large pot of water to the boil with the lemon. Place the artichokes in the boiling water, place a clean tea towel over the artichokes and a wire rack or heat proof plate over the towel. This will weigh down the artichokes (otherwise they will bob up and down and not get done). Boil 1/2 hour or until the outside leaves pull off easily. Remove from water and refresh with cold water to cool to the point where you can handle. Open up the center and scoop out the choke with a spoon. Discard the choke and the stem. Serve with butter seasoned with lemon juice and hot sauce.

To microwave: Wrap in plastic wrap and cook as directed by the microwave manufacturer, usually about 5 minutes per choke.

Comment: Artichokes may be served hot or cold, stuffed or unstuffed, but they should always have the "choke" removed. There are varieties of artichokes; in Europe the violet artichokes (smaller and more tender than the globe variety) are seen more frequently. Bottled or canned "artichoke hearts" are not hearts at all, but whole baby artichokes, and do not need to have the choke removed.

YORKSHIRE PUDDING POPOVERS

Makes 6 popovers

1 cup bread flour
1/2 teaspoon salt
2 eggs
1 cup water mixed with
   1/2 cup milk
2 tablespoons drippings
   or oil

Preheat oven to 450°F. Sift the flour with the salt into a bowl. Mix together the eggs with 3/4 cup of the milk and water. Whisk the egg mixture into the flour carefully until you have a smooth batter. Add half the remaining liquid and beat again for several minutes. Add the rest of the liquid, cover, and let rest in a cool place, preferably not the refrigerator, for at least 1 hour before cooking. Pour 1 teaspoon of the fat in each of the cups of a 6-cup popover pan. Place pan in the oven to heat the fat. When hot, remove and half fill each popover cup with batter. Bake in a very hot oven until puffed and brown, about 20 minutes.

Tip: The purpose of "resting" the batter is to soften the starch so the popovers aren't rubbery.

QUICK PECAN ROLLS

Makes 24 rolls

3-1/2 to 5 cups all-
   purpose flour
2 packages rapid-rise
   yeast
1 teaspoon salt
1/2 cup water
3/4 cup milk
2 tablespoons honey
2 tablespoons butter
1 large egg
1/3 cup sugar
1 tablespoon cinnamon

Preheat oven to 375°F. In food-processor bowl, mix together 2 cups flour, yeast, and salt. In saucepan or microwave, heat water, milk, honey, and 2 tablespoons butter together until 130°F. Add to flour mixture, then add egg. Process in food processor or beat with mixer until well combined. Gradually add enough remaining flour to make a soft dough. Knead until smooth and elastic, about 5 minutes. Place in oiled bowl, turning to oil all over, and cover with plastic wrap or place in an oiled plastic bag. Let rise in warm but not hot place for 20 minutes.

To prepare filling, mix together the 1/3 cup sugar and cinnamon; set aside.

Continued

Topping

1/2 cup packed brown
  sugar
1/4 cup butter
3 tablespoons honey
1/2 cup pecans
To finish:
2 tablespoons butter,
  softened

To prepare topping, grease two 13 × 9-inch cake pans. Divide all topping ingredients between the two pans. Sprinkle each pan with the brown sugar. Divide the 1/4 cup butter into small pieces and sprinkle evenly over brown sugar. Slather with honey, then add nuts on top.

Punch down dough. Divide in half. On lightly floured surface, roll half of dough to a 15 × 12-inch rectangle. Spread with softened butter and then spread filling over dough. Starting with the shorter sides, roll up tightly. Pinch edges to seal. Cut into 12 slices; repeat. Place on topping in pan. Cover; let rise in warm place about 20 minutes. Bake at 375°F for 25 to 30 minutes until golden brown. Cool.

MUSCADINE MUFFINS

Makes 3 dozen muffins

1 cup butter
1 cup sugar
1 teaspoon baking soda
1 cup buttermilk
3 cups sifted all-purpose
  flour
1/2 teaspoon cinnamon
1/2 teaspoon ground
  cloves
1/2 teaspoon nutmeg
1/2 teaspoon salt
3 egg yolks, slightly
  beaten with 1
  tablespoon water
1 (12-ounce) jar
  muscadine preserves
1 cup pecans, chopped
3 egg whites, stiffly
  beaten

In a large mixing bowl, cream together butter and sugar. Dissolve baking soda in buttermilk. Combine flour, cinnamon, cloves, nutmeg, and salt; add alternately with buttermilk to creamed mixture, blending well. Add egg yolks, preserves, and pecans; blend well. Fold in egg whites. Fill greased muffin pans half full. Bake at 400°F for 15 minutes.

FOOD PROCESSOR ZUCCHINI PECAN BREAD
Makes 1 loaf

10 ounces (2 small)
  zucchini, ends
  removed
3/4 cup sugar (optional)
2 tablespoons grated
  lemon peel, with no
  white
1/2 cup unsalted butter
2 large eggs
1/2 cup shelled pecans
1-3/4 cups self-rising
  flour

Preheat oven to 350°F. Butter and flour the shorter sides of an 8-1/2 × 4-1/2-inch loaf pan. Place a sheet of wax paper in the pan to line the longer sides and bottom. Butter and flour the paper.

Shred zucchini in a food processor or by hand. Dry with paper towels. Place sugar, lemon peel, butter, and eggs in a food processor or mixer bowl. Process or mix only until blended. Add 1/3 of the pecans and 1/3 of the shredded zucchini. Process or mix, and repeat for remaining 2/3 of ingredients only until shreds disappear. Add flour and mix or process, turning on and off only until dry ingredients are incorporated.

Pour batter into prepared pan. Bake on center rack of the preheated oven for 55 to 60 minutes or until bread shrinks slightly from the sides of the pan and a toothpick inserted in the center comes out clean. Cool in the pan on a wire rack for 10 minutes. Remove bread from pan; peel off wax paper and cool completely on wire rack.

Tip: For self-rising flour substitution, see p. 37.

WHITE LILY'S DAFFODIL CAKE

This cake recipe was given to me by White Lily's testkitchen. If you love lemon meringue pie or angel food cake, you'll love this high, airy lemony flavored confection!

1-1/4 cups soft wheat
  flour
1-3/4 cups sugar
1-3/4 cups egg whites
  (12–14 large eggs)
1-1/2 teaspoons cream
  of tartar
1/4 teaspoon salt
1-1/2 teaspoons vanilla
5 egg yolks
2 tablespoons soft
  wheat flour
2 tablespoons sugar
1 tablespoon grated
  fresh lemon peel (no
  white)

Preheat oven to 375 degrees. Sift the flour and 3/4 cup of the sugar together three times. Reserve. In a large mixing bowl, whisk the egg whites, cream of tartar, and salt until soft peaks form. Gradually beat in 1 cup sugar and continue to beat until very stiff peaks form. Sift about 1/4 of the flour mixture over the egg whites; gently fold. Repeat with remaining flour mixture, 1/4 at a time. Fold in vanilla. Remove one-third of the batter and set aside.

In a separate bowl, beat the egg yolks, 2 tablespoons flour and 2 tablespoons sugar until thick and pale yellow. Stir in the lemon peel. Pour egg yolk mixture over reserved one-third batter and fold until blended.

Spoon white and yellow batters alternately into an ungreased tube pan. Run knife gently through batter to eliminate air pockets and to swirl the two batters. Bake in lower third of preheated 375-degree oven for 35–40 minutes. Invert in pan to cool. When completely cool, remove from pan. To remove, run a thin knife up and down between cake and pan to loosen. Serve with warm Jeweled Lemon Sauce.

JEWELED LEMON SAUCE
Makes 1-1/2 cups

1/2 cup sugar
2 tablespoons
  cornstarch
1 cup water
2 teaspoons grated fresh
  lemon peel (no white)
2 tablespoons lemon
  juice
1 tablespoon butter

Cook sugar, cornstarch and water over medium heat until smooth and thickened. Add lemon peel, lemon juice and butter and heat until warm.

OUR FAVORITE ANGEL FOOD CAKE
Makes one 10-inch cake

1-3/4 cups egg whites
  (about 14 large eggs)
1 teaspoon cream of
  tartar
1/4 teaspoon salt
1-3/4 cups sugar, sifted
1-1/4 cups soft wheat
  all-purpose flour,
  sifted twice
1-1/2 teaspoons vanilla
  extract
3/4 teaspoon almond
  extract
3/4 teaspoon lemon
  juice
1 cup heavy cream,
  whipped
1 cup berries, such as
  strawberries,
  raspberries,
  blueberries,
  and/or blackberries

Preheat oven to 300°F. Place a round of wax paper in the bottom of a tube pan. Put egg whites in a large mixing bowl. Sift cream of tartar over whites, add salt, and beat egg whites to very soft peaks, using the whisk attachment. With the mixer on lowest speed, gradually whisk in sugar; then gradually whisk in flour. Sprinkle vanilla, almond extract, and lemon juice over batter and fold in. Pour batter into an ungreased 10-inch tube pan with a removable bottom and smooth the top with a rubber spatula. Run spatula gently through the batter to remove air pockets. Bake in preheated oven until pale brown and springy to the touch, about 1 hour and 10 minutes.

Remove from the oven, turn the pan upside down, and cool in the pan 1 hour. If the pan has no feet, invert over neck of a bottle. Turn cake right side up and loosen around edges and around central tube. Remove cake gently from the pan. Remove the wax paper. Serve with whipped cream and berries.

Selected Bibliography

Berenbaum, Rose Levy. *The Cake Bible*. New York: William Morrow, 1988.

Braker, Flo. *The Simple Art of Perfect Baking*. New York: William Morrow, 1985.

Butel, Jane. *Jane Butel's TEX-MEX Cookbook*. New York: Harmony Books, 1980.

Byrn, Anne. *Cooking in the New South*. Atlanta: Peachtree Publishers, 1984.

Carpenter, Hugh. *Pacific Flavors*. New York: Stewart, Tabori, & Chang, 1988.

Child, Julia. *From Julia Child's Kitchen*. New York: Alfred A. Knopf, 1975.

Childs, Karen. *White Lily Cookie Recipes*. Knoxville, Tenn.: White Lily Test Kitchens, 1988.

Clayton, Bernard. *Bernard Clayton's New Complete Book of Breads*. New York: Simon and Schuster, 1983.

Dupree, Nathalie. *New Southern Cooking*. New York: Alfred A. Knopf, 1988.

Field, Michael. *All Manner of Food*. New York: Alfred A. Knopf, 1970.

Greene, Bert. *Greene on Greens*. New York: Workman Publishing, 1984.

Greene, Bert, and Denis Vaughan. *The Store Cookbook*. Chicago: Contemporary Books, 1974.

Greer, Anne Lindsay. *Foods of the Sun*. New York: Harper & Row, 1987.

Harvey, Ann H., ed. *The Southern Heritage: Plain and Fancy Poultry Cookbook*. Birmingham, Ala.: Oxmoor House, 1983.

Hazan, Marcella. *More Classic Italian Cooking*. New York: Alfred A. Knopf, 1978.

Hom, Ken, and Harvey Steiman. *Chinese Technique*. New York: Simon and Schuster, 1981.

Jones, Judith, and Evan Jones. *The L. L. Bean Book of New New England Cookery.* New York: Random House, 1987.

Junior League of Jackson, Mississippi. *Southern Sideboards.* Jackson, Miss.: Junior League of Jackson, 1977.

Kafka, Barbara. *Food for Friends.* New York: Harper & Row, 1984.

_____. *Microwave Gourmet.* New York: William Morrow, 1987.

Lang, Jenifer Harvey, ed. *Larousse Gastronomique.* New York: Crown Publishers, 1988.

Lee, Karen, and Alexandra Branyon. *Nouvelle Chinese Cooking.* New York: Macmillan Publishing Co., 1987.

Lewis, Edna. *The Taste of Country Cooking.* New York: Alfred A. Knopf, 1976.

Montague, Prosper. *Larousse Gastronomique.* New York: Crown Publishers, 1961.

Montant, Jane, ed. *The Best of Gourmet.* New York: Condé Nast Books, 1986, 1987, and 1988.

Morgan, Jinx, and Jeff Morgan. *The Sugar Mill Hotel Cookbook.* Tortola, British Virgin Islands: The Morgan Corporation, Ltd., 1987.

Nathan, Joan. *The Jewish Holiday Kitchen.* New York: Schocken Books, 1988.

Prudhomme, Paul. *Chef Paul Prudhomme's Louisiana Kitchen.* New York: William Morrow, 1984.

Puck, Wolfgang. *Modern French Cooking for the American Kitchen.* Boston: Houghton Mifflin, 1981.

Rice, William. *Feasts of Wine and Food.* New York: William Morrow, 1987.

Rombauer, Irma S., and Marion Rombauer Becker. *Joy of Cooking.* New York: New American Library, 1964.

Rosbottom, Betty. *Betty Rosbottom's Cooking School Cookbook.* New York: Workman Publishing, 1987.

Sax, Richard. *Cooking Great Meals Every Day.* New York: Random House, 1982.

Schultz, Phillip Stephen. *Cooking with Fire and Smoke.* New York: Simon and Schuster, 1986.

Willan, Anne, ed. *Grand Diplome Cooking Course.* Danbury, Conn.: The Danbury Press, 1971.

INDEX

295

D

A Note About the Author

Nathalie Dupree has been one of the South's leading cooking authorities for more than a decade. She received an advanced certificate from the Cordon Bleu in London, cooked at a restaurant in Spain, and was then chef at her own restaurant in Social Circle, Georgia. She founded Rich's Cooking School in Atlanta, where she now lives, served as food editor of *Atlanta* magazine, and has written a weekly column on food for *The Atlanta Journal and Constitution*. Her first book, *Cooking of the South*, earned a Tastemaker Award, and her second, *New Southern Cooking*, received an International Association of Cooking Professionals award. Her public television series "New Southern Cooking with Nathalie Dupree" has been aired throughout the United States and has made her nationally known.

A Note on the Type

The text of this book was set in Elante, a Compugraphic version of a face designed by W. A. Dwiggins (1880–1956). This face cannot be classified as either modern or old style. It is not based on any historical model; nor does it echo any particular period or style. It avoids the extreme contrasts between thick and thin elements that mark most modern faces and attempts to give a feeling of fluidity, power, and speed.

Designed and composed by G&H Soho, Inc.
New York, New York

Printed and bound by
R. R. Donnelley & Sons,
Harrisonburg, Virginia